O9-BTI-835

Other books by B. Kliban

CAT

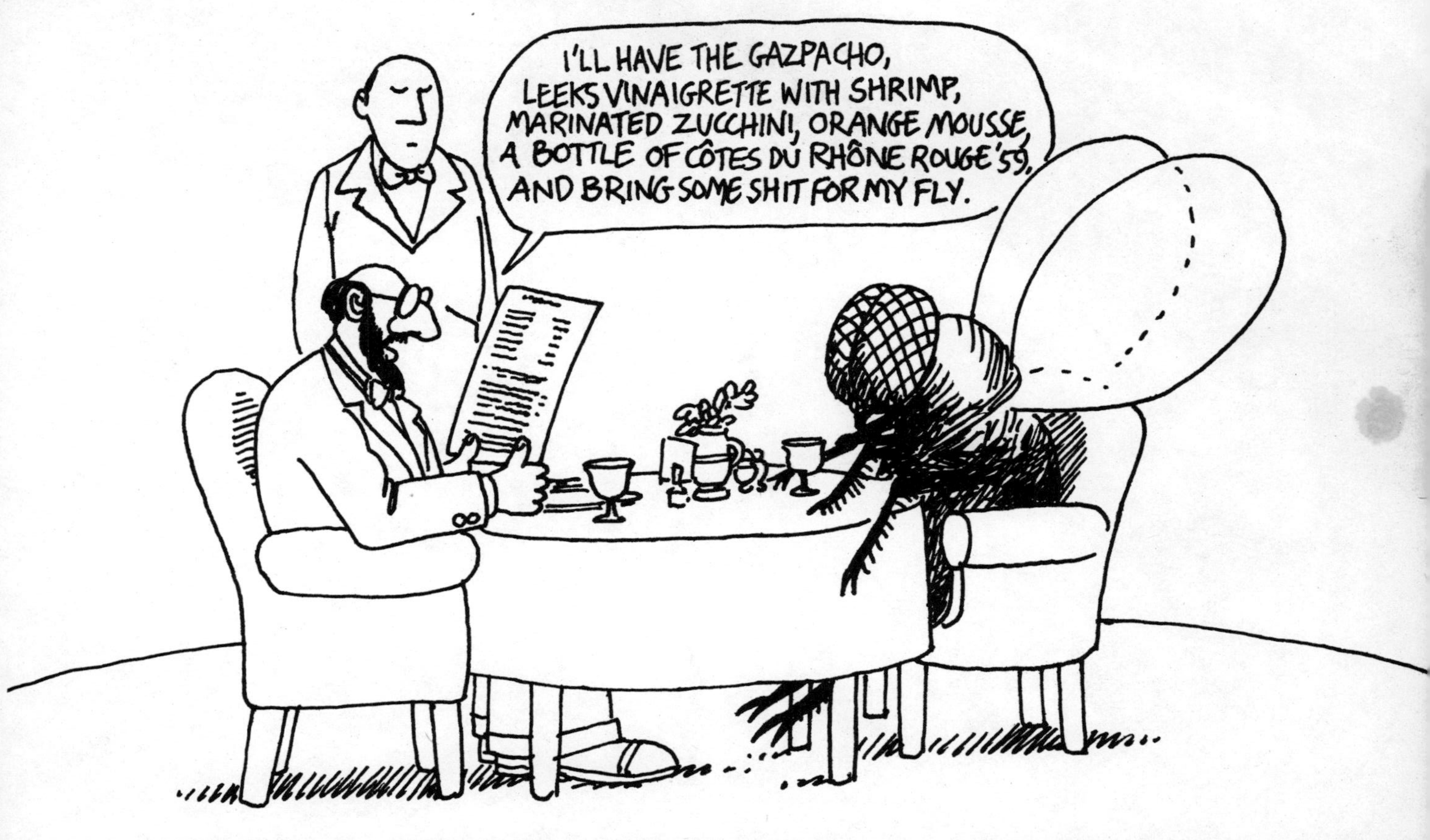
I'LL HAVE THE GAZPACHO, LEEKS VINAIGRETTE WITH SHRIMP, MARINATED ZUCCHINI, ORANGE MOUSSE, A BOTTLE OF CÔTES DU RHÔNE ROUGE '59, AND BRING SOME SHIT FOR MY FLY.

NEVER EAT ANYTHING BIGGER THAN YOUR HEAD & OTHER DRAWINGS

by B. Kliban

wp Workman Publishing Company, Inc. New York

Copyright © 1976 by B. Kliban

All rights reserved. This book may not be
reproduced in whole or in part, by mimeograph
or any other means, without permission in writing
from the publisher.

Library of Congress Cataloging in Publication Data

Kliban, B.
Never eat anything bigger than your head and other drawings.
 1. American wit and humor, Pictorial.   I.   Title.
NC1429.K58A53   1976   741.5'973   75-43837
       ISBN 0-911104-67-4 pbk.

Design by Paul Hanson

Workman Publishing Company, Inc.
231 East 51 Street
New York, New York 10022

Manufactured in the United States of America

First printing April 1976
1 3 5 7 9 9 8 6 4 2

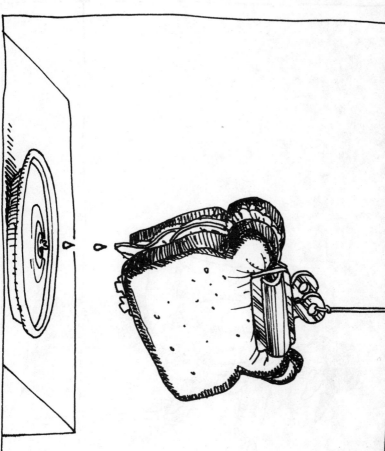

ETERNALLY LEAKING SANDWICH

Los Angeles Museum of Science

"IT WAS HELL", RECALLS FORMER CHILD.

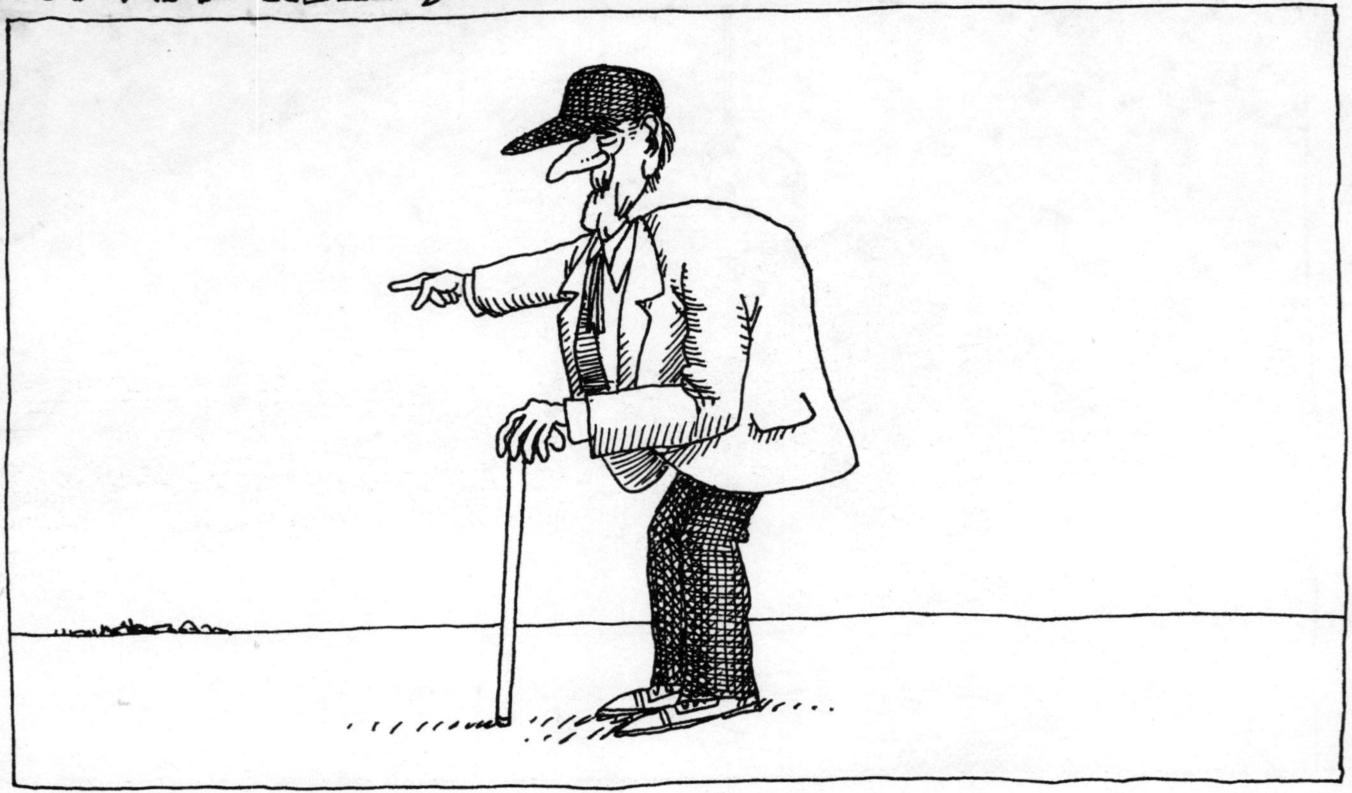

HOUDINI ESCAPING FROM NEW JERSEY

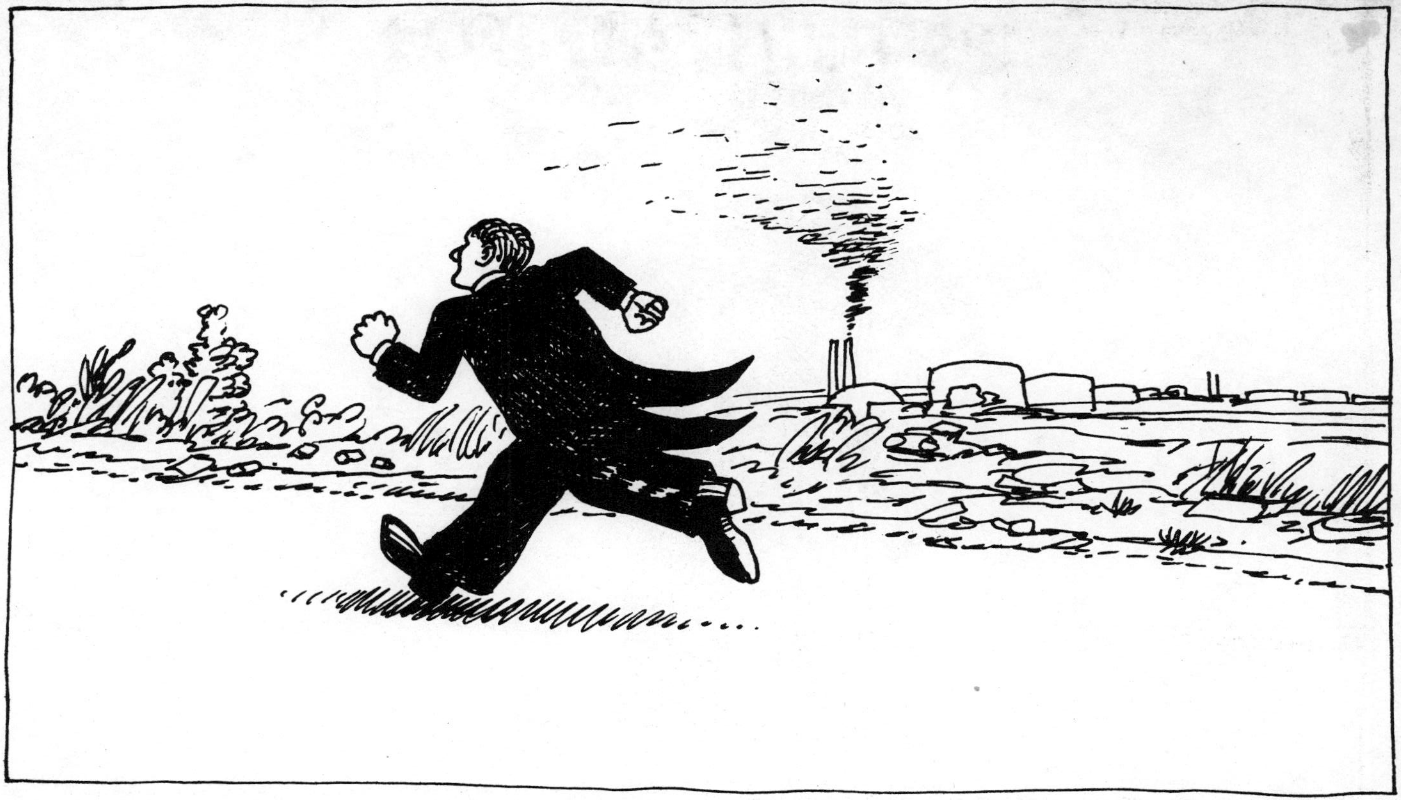

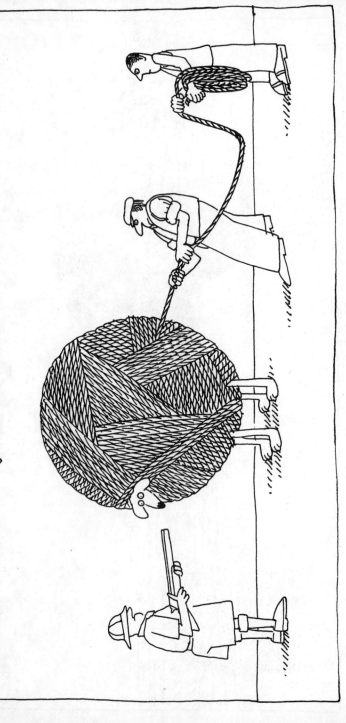

HOW THEY GET ROPE
(NUMBER 12 OF A SERIES)

THE BIRTH OF ADVERTISING

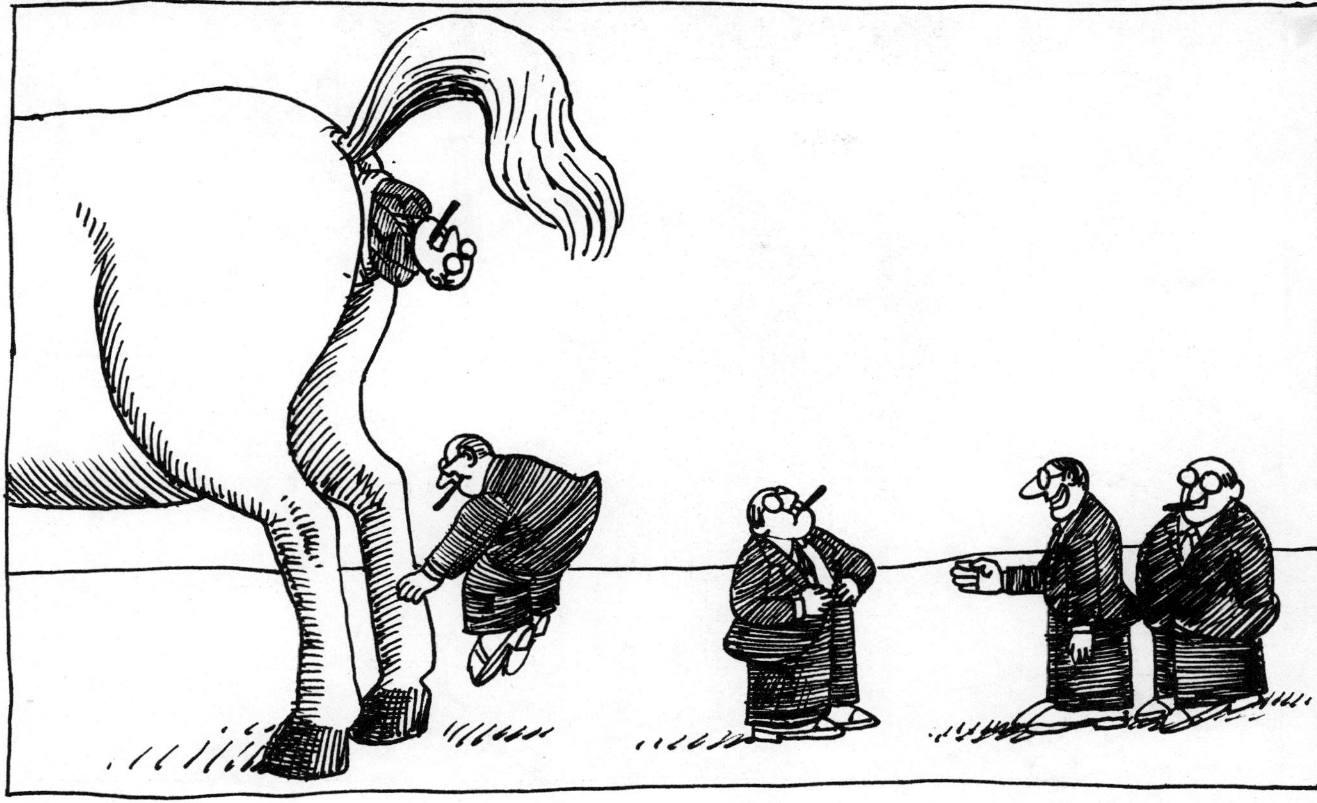

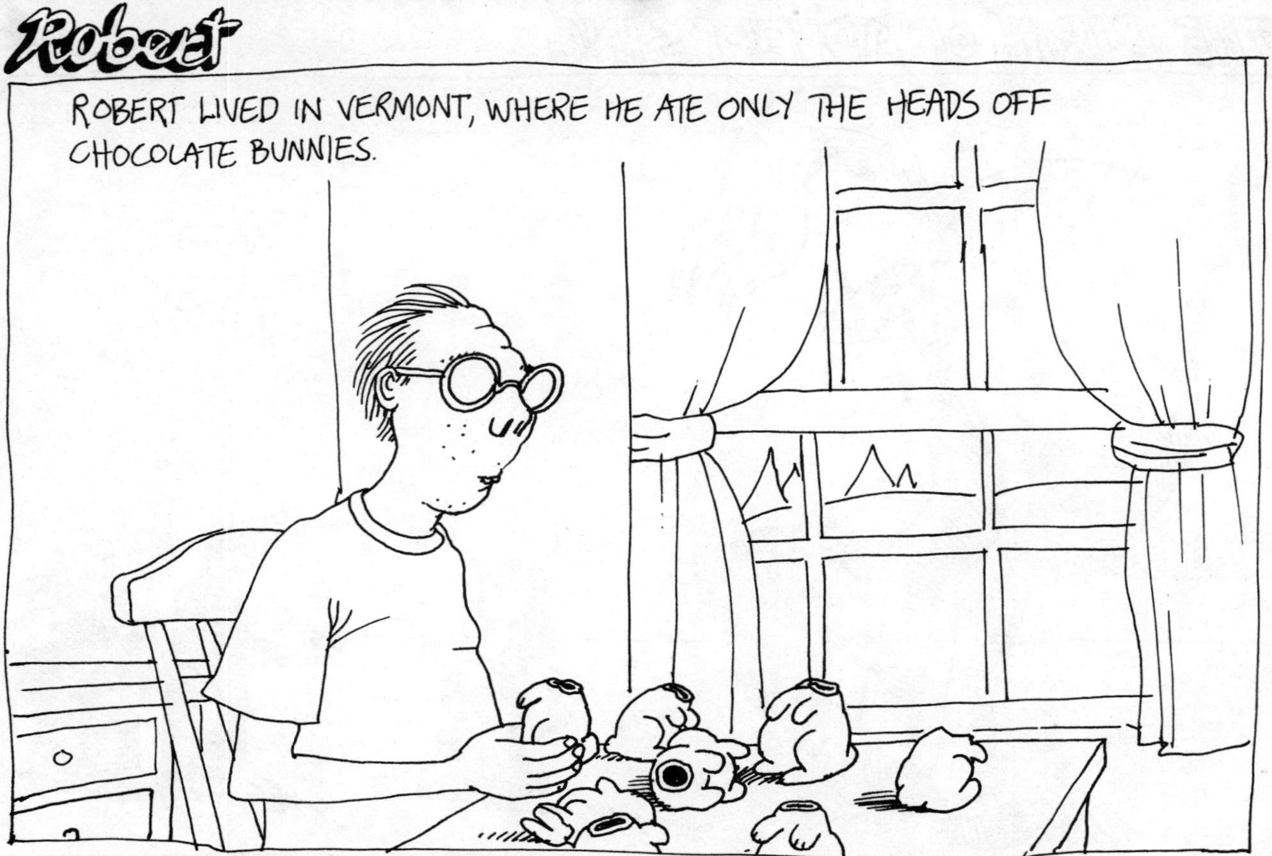
Robert
ROBERT LIVED IN VERMONT, WHERE HE ATE ONLY THE HEADS OFF CHOCOLATE BUNNIES.

Music. Beethoven Composing Himself

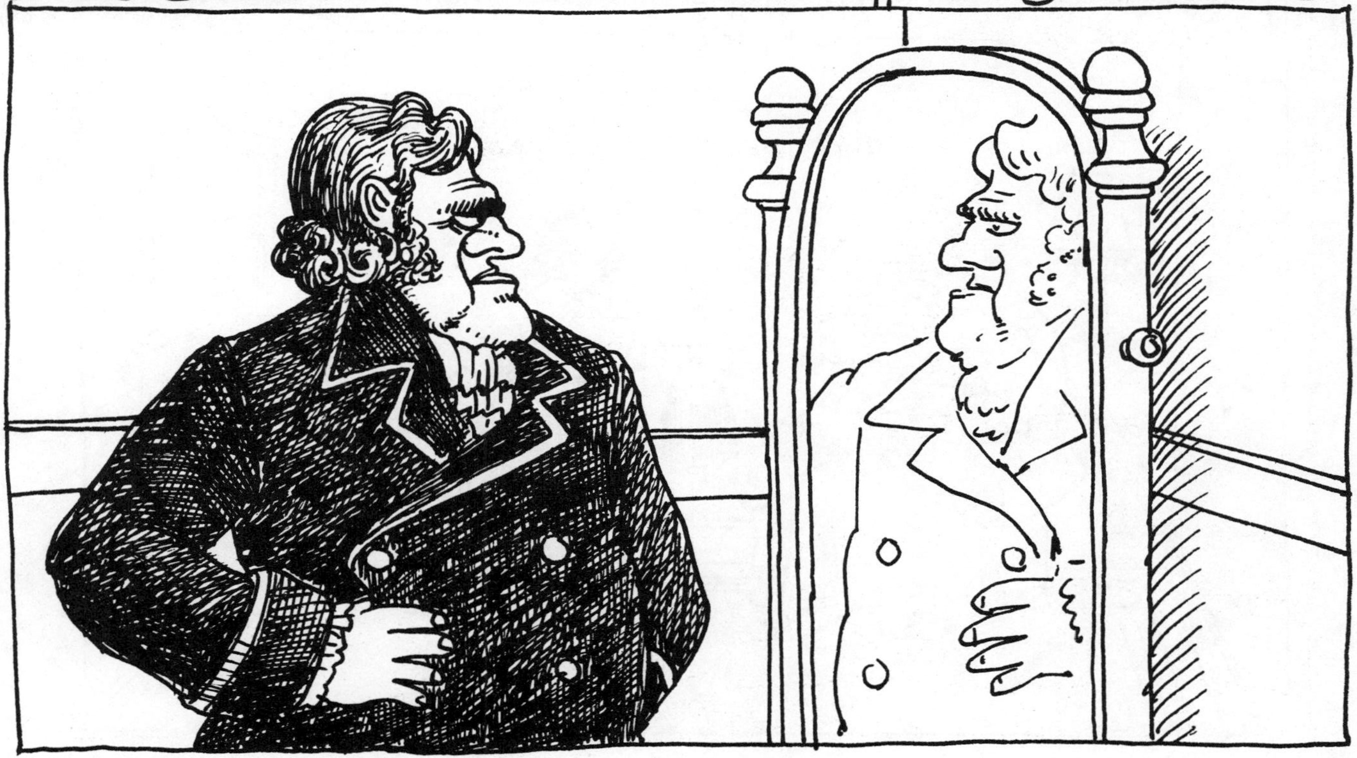

Downstairs at the Mormon Tabernacle

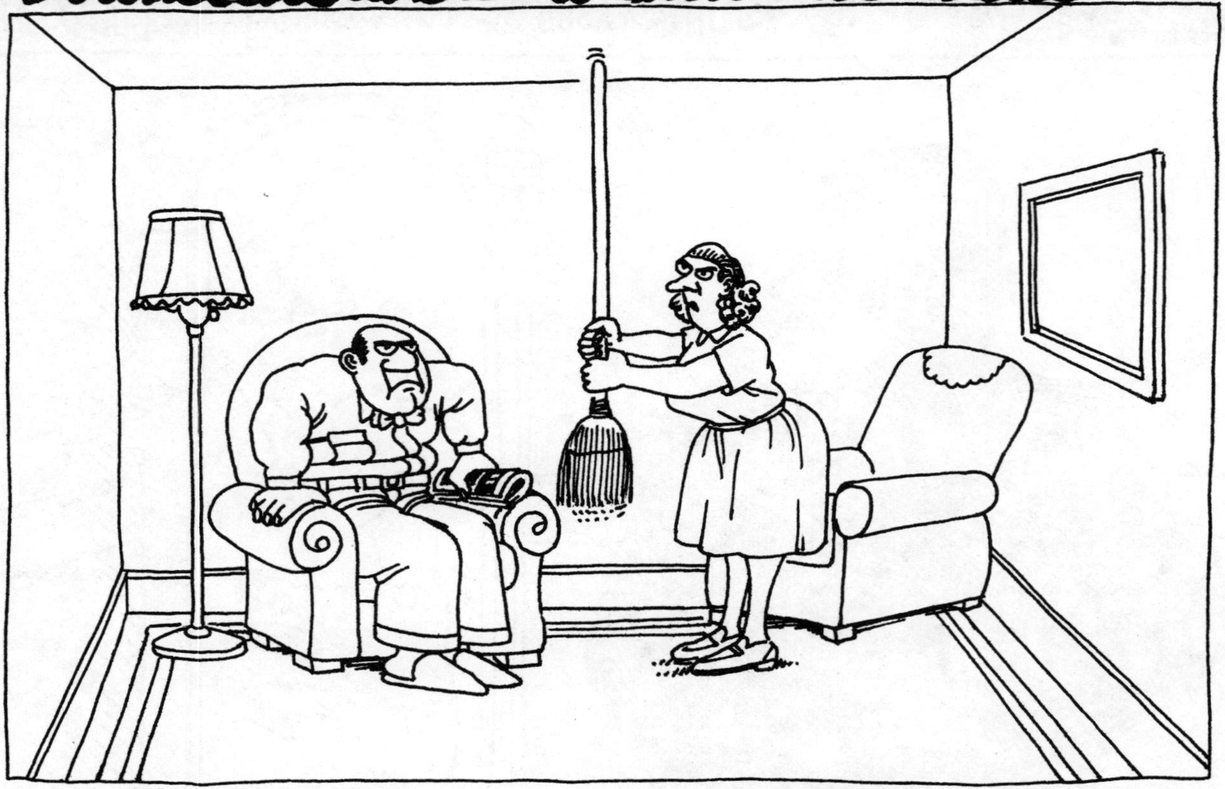

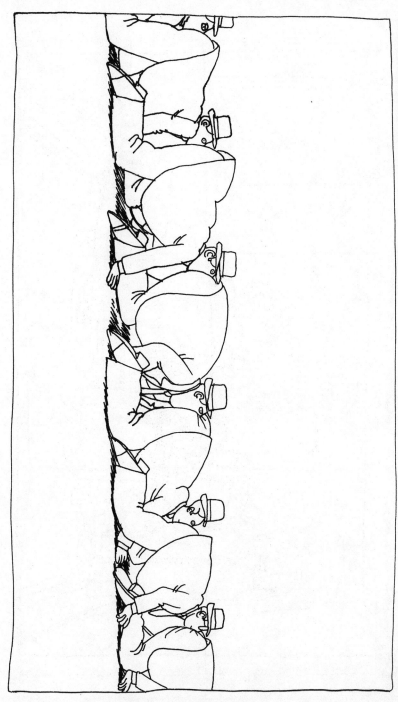

Business on Parade

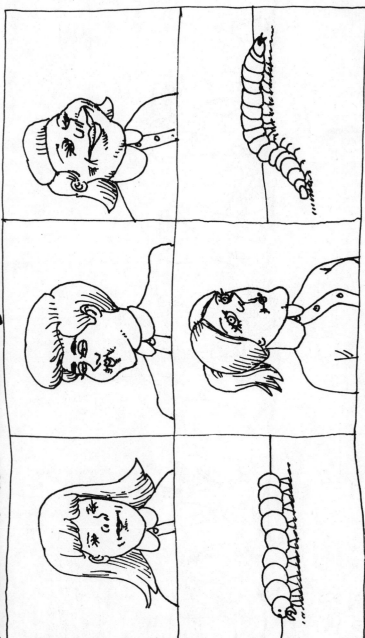

Debutantes & Centipedes

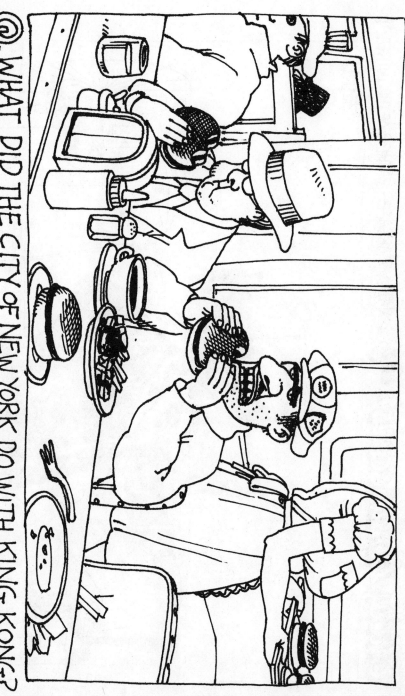

Q. WHAT DID THE CITY OF NEW YORK DO WITH KING KONG?

Early Americans • #3 • NANCY CABBAGE - FATHER OF THE WIRETAP

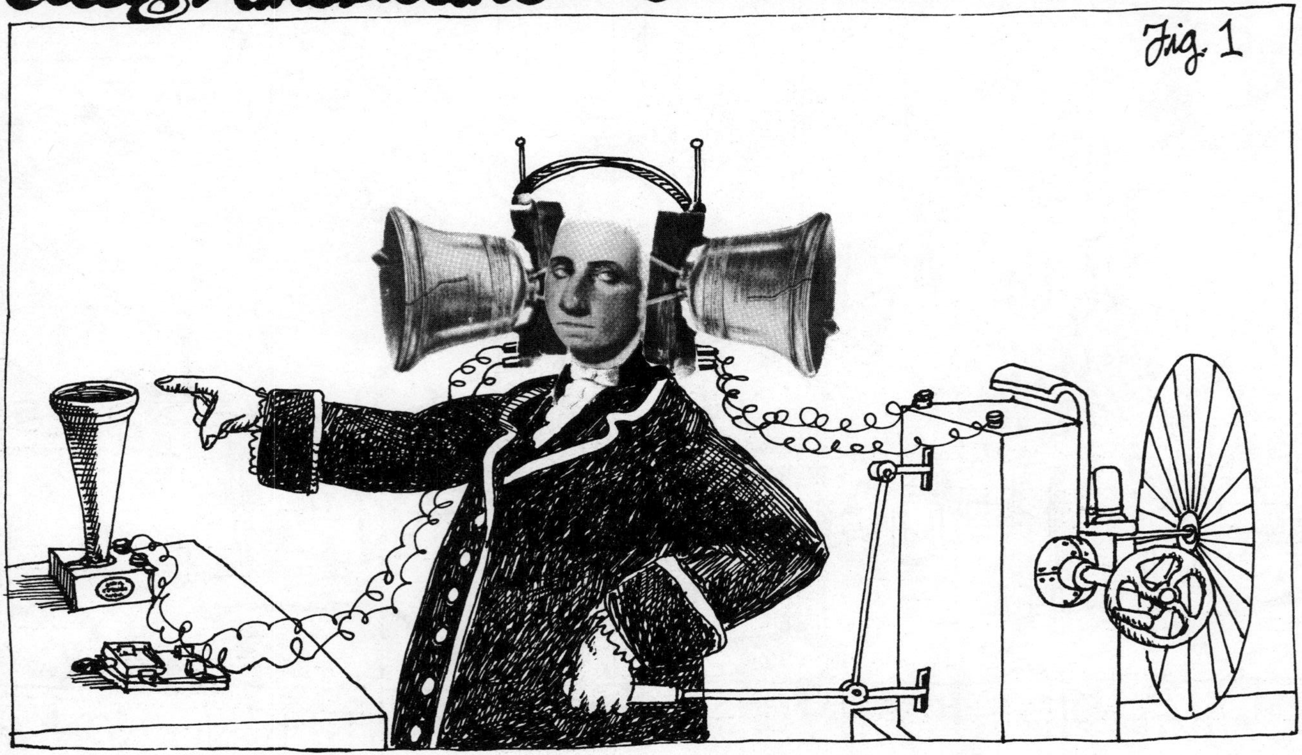
Fig. 1

Cracker Salter

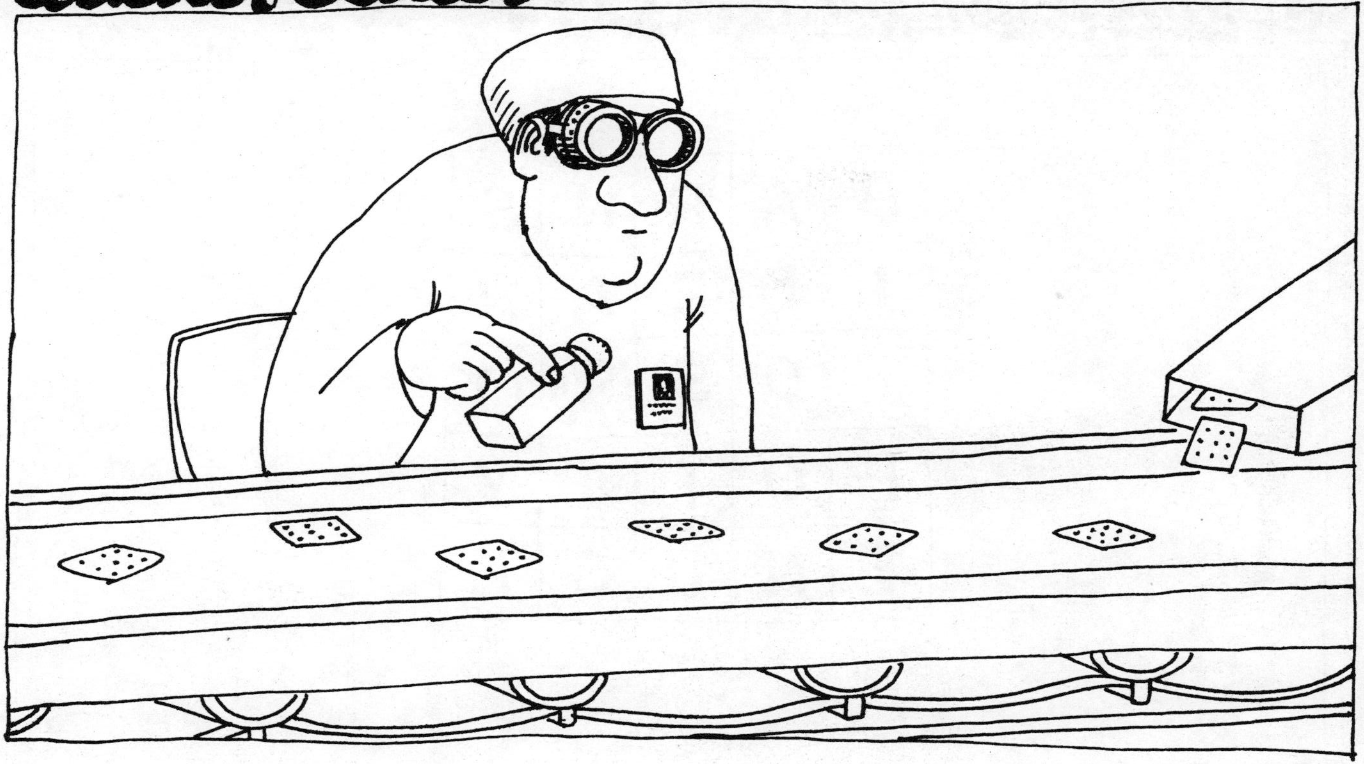

Solution to Last Week's Puzzle

B	A	R	N	S
I	D	E	A	N
F	O	S	~~X~~ Q	O
P	O	T	J	Y
E	N	U	G	L

Polar Puns #129

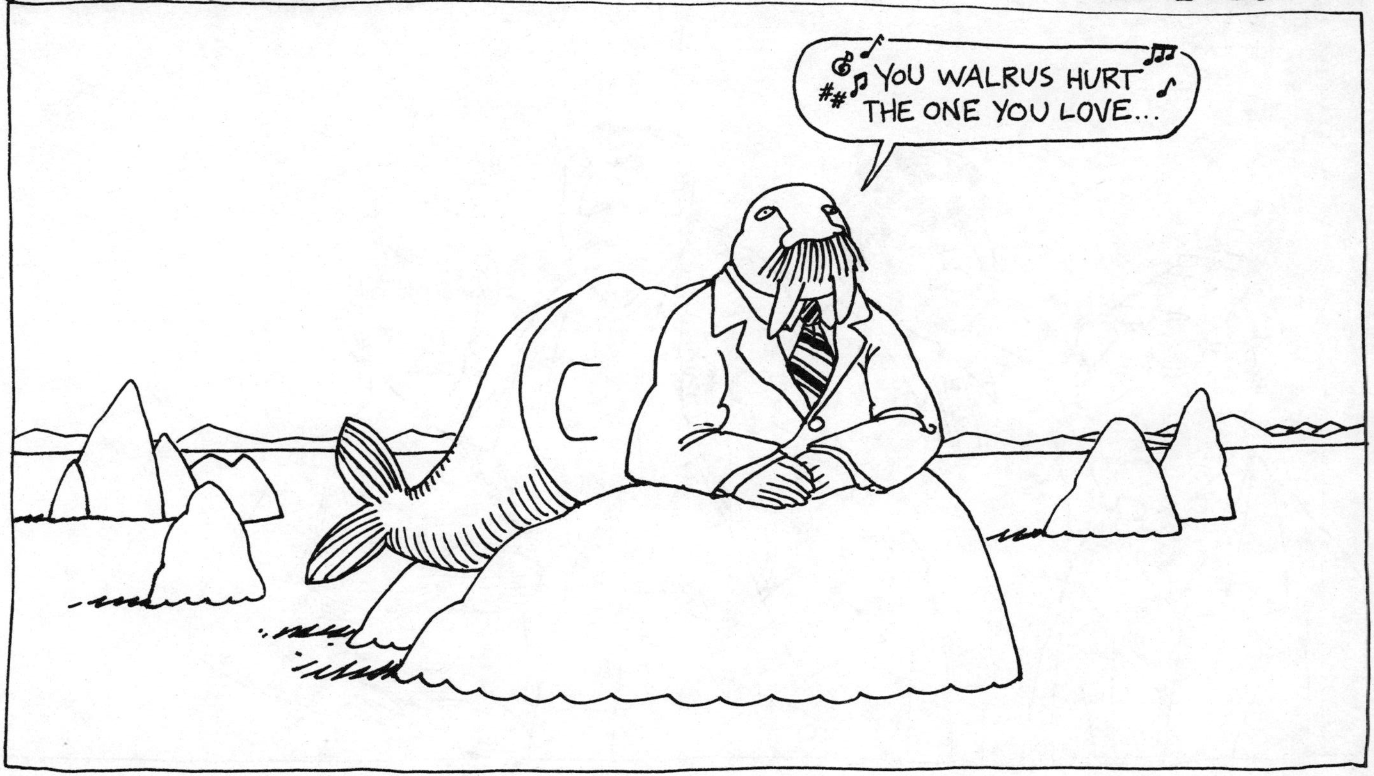

ODD BIRD, BLACK SHEEP, FAT CAT, ROTTEN APPLE, TOUGH COOKIE

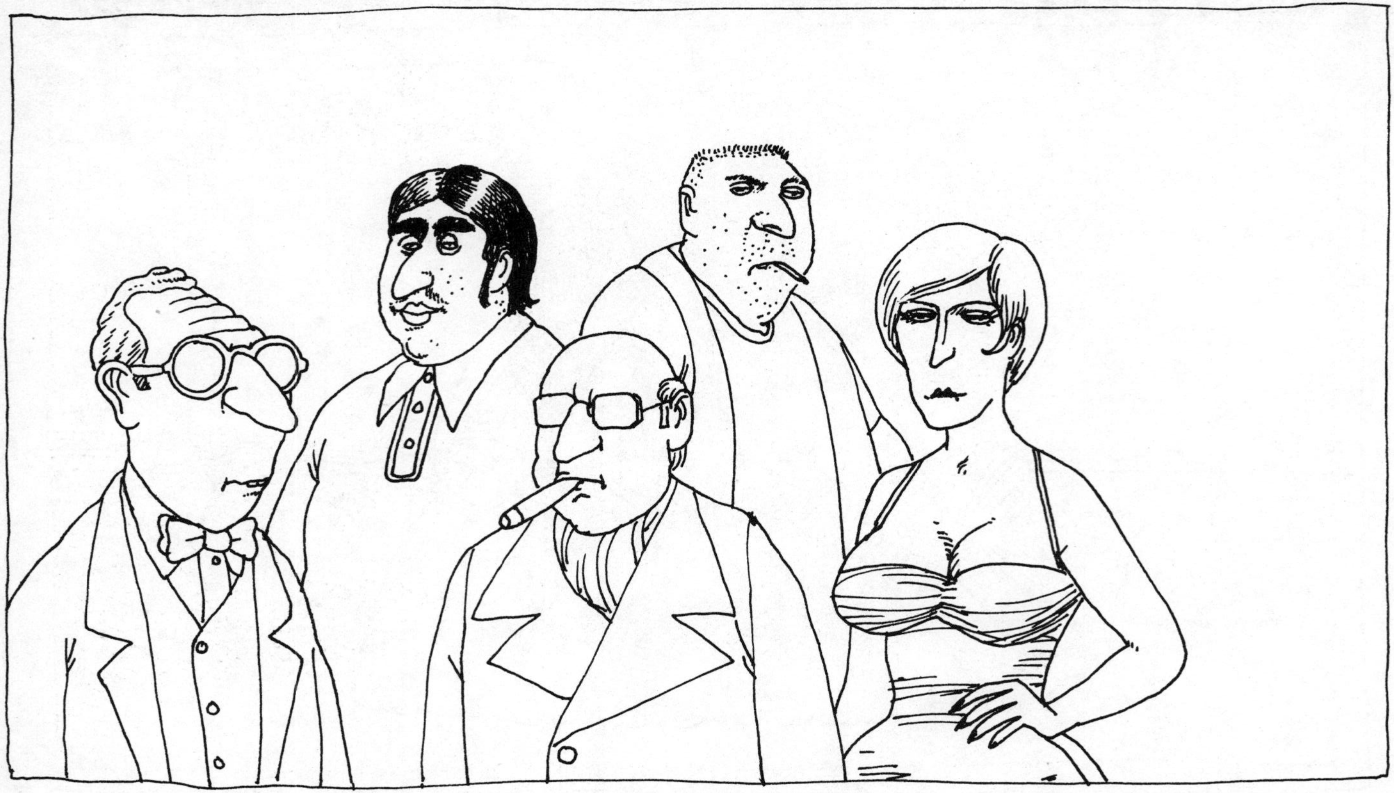

Wanda Among the Bushmen

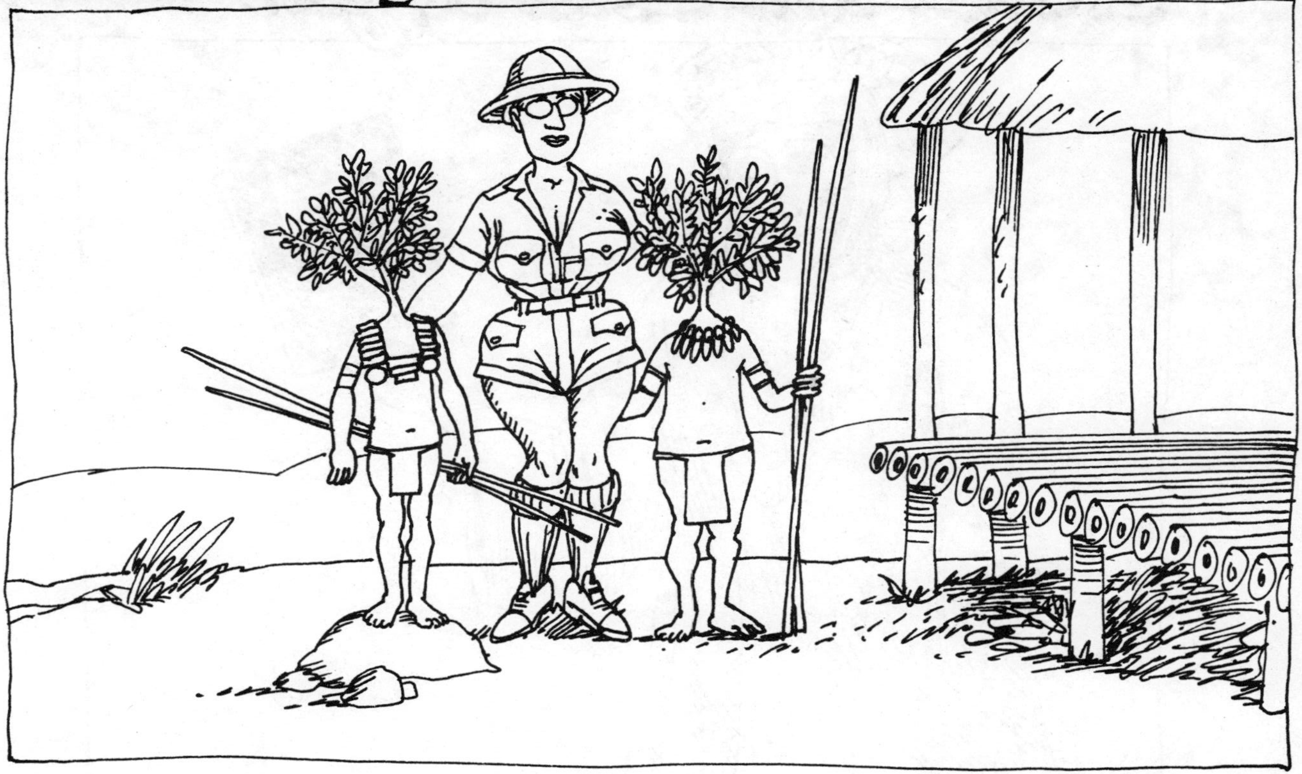

El Cuaderno de la Virgen

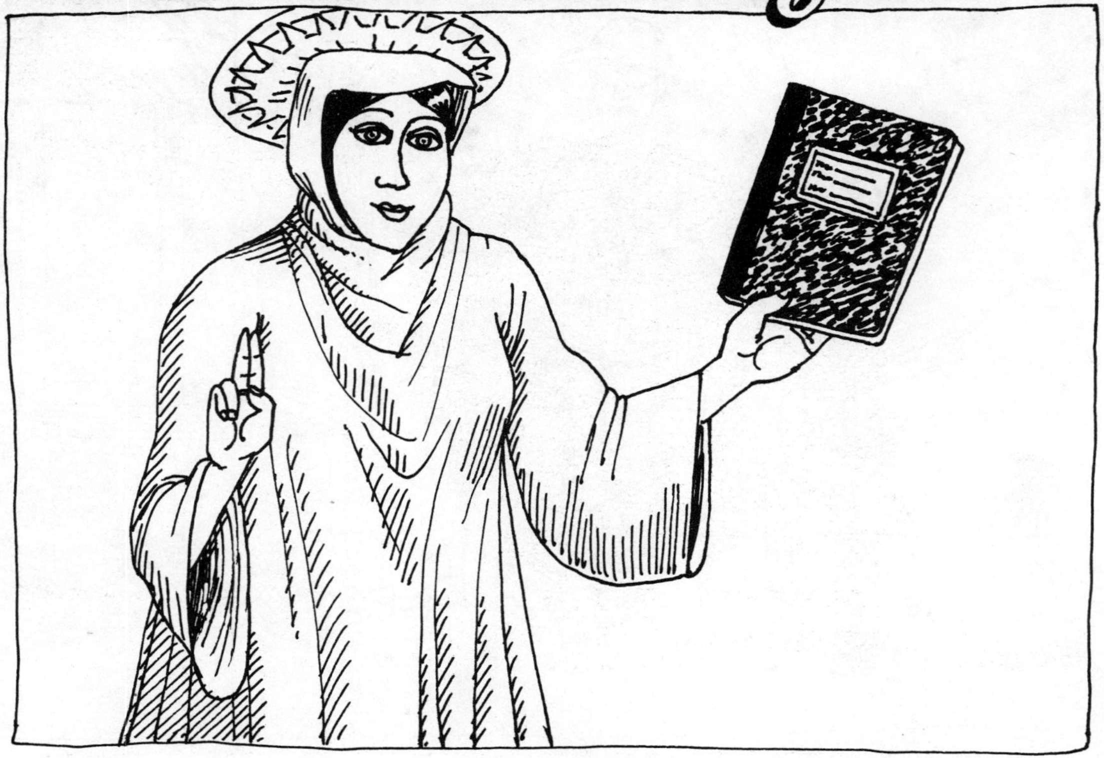

Our Animal Pals #32

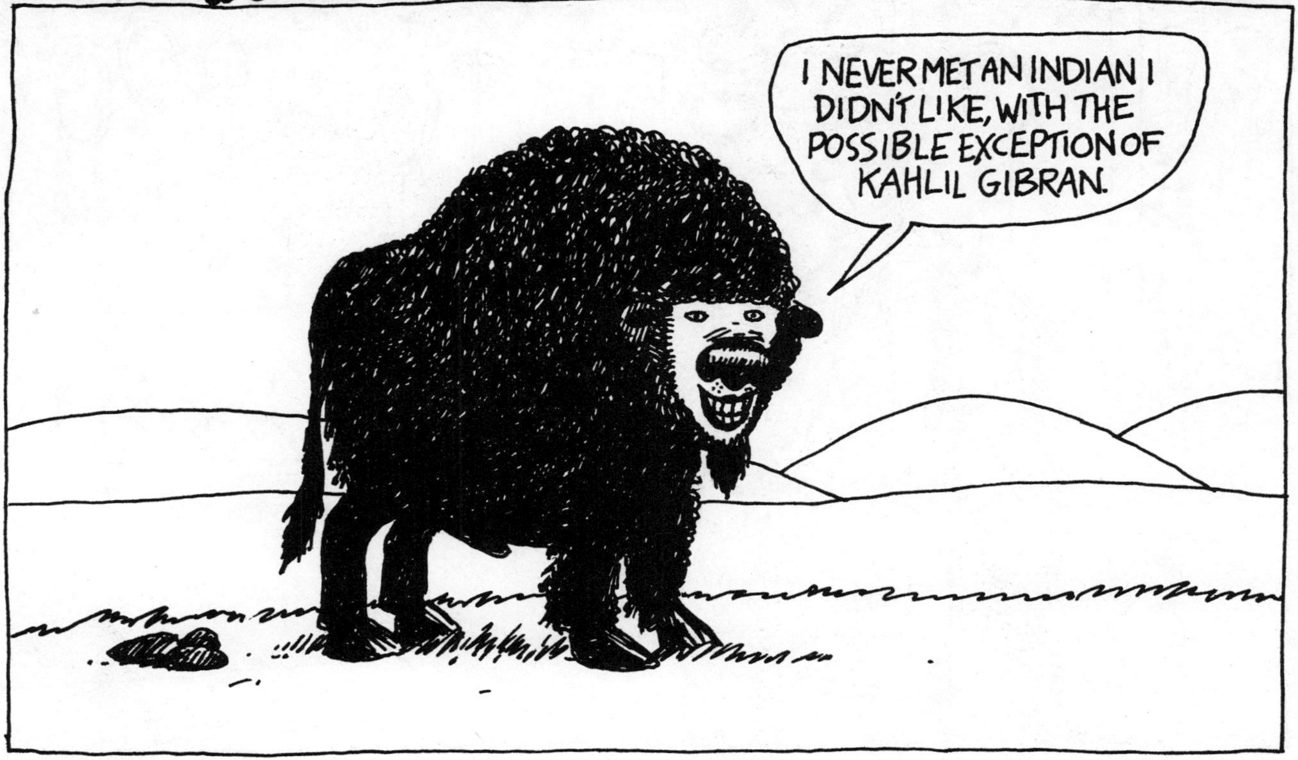
I NEVER MET AN INDIAN I DIDN'T LIKE, WITH THE POSSIBLE EXCEPTION OF KAHLIL GIBRAN.

A Visit to the Spoon Museum

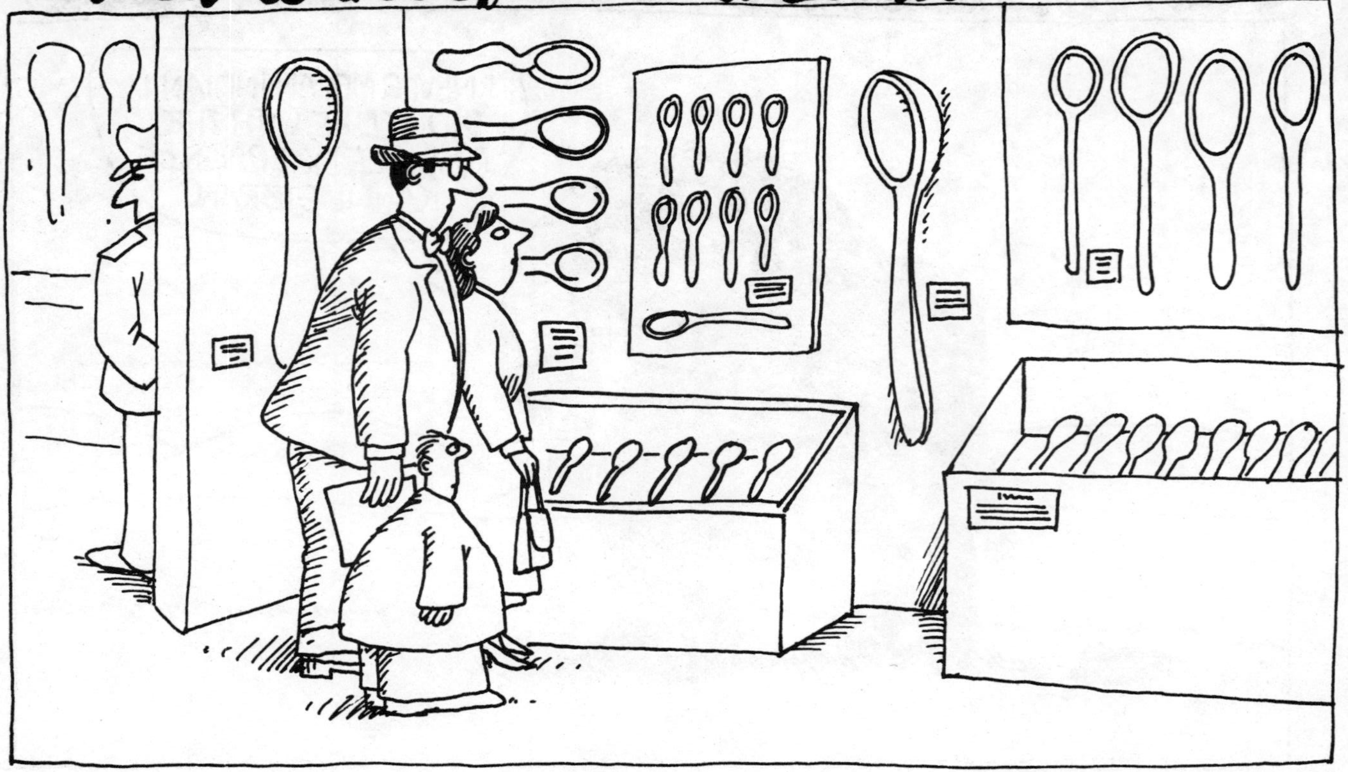

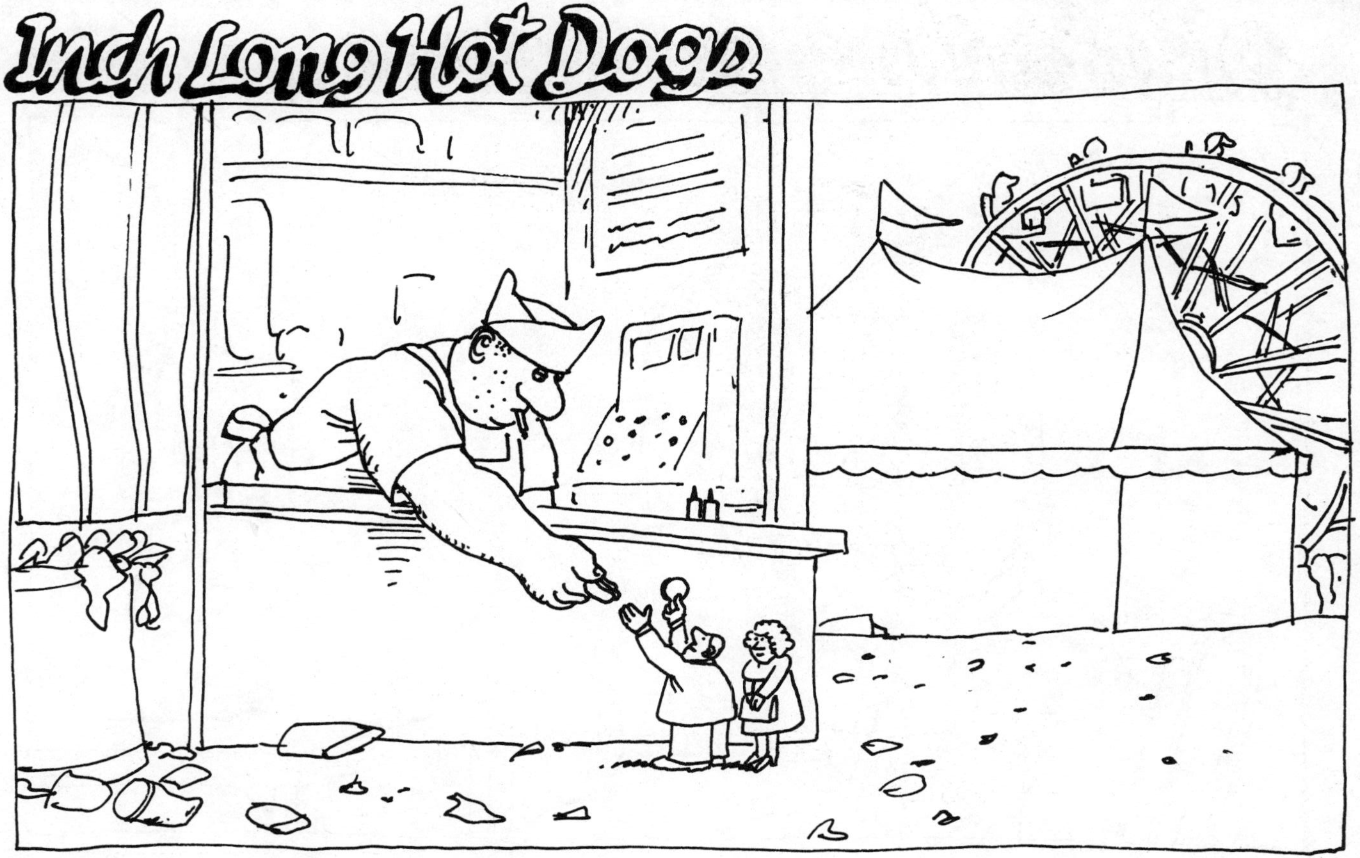
Inch Long Hot Dogs

Poignant Device

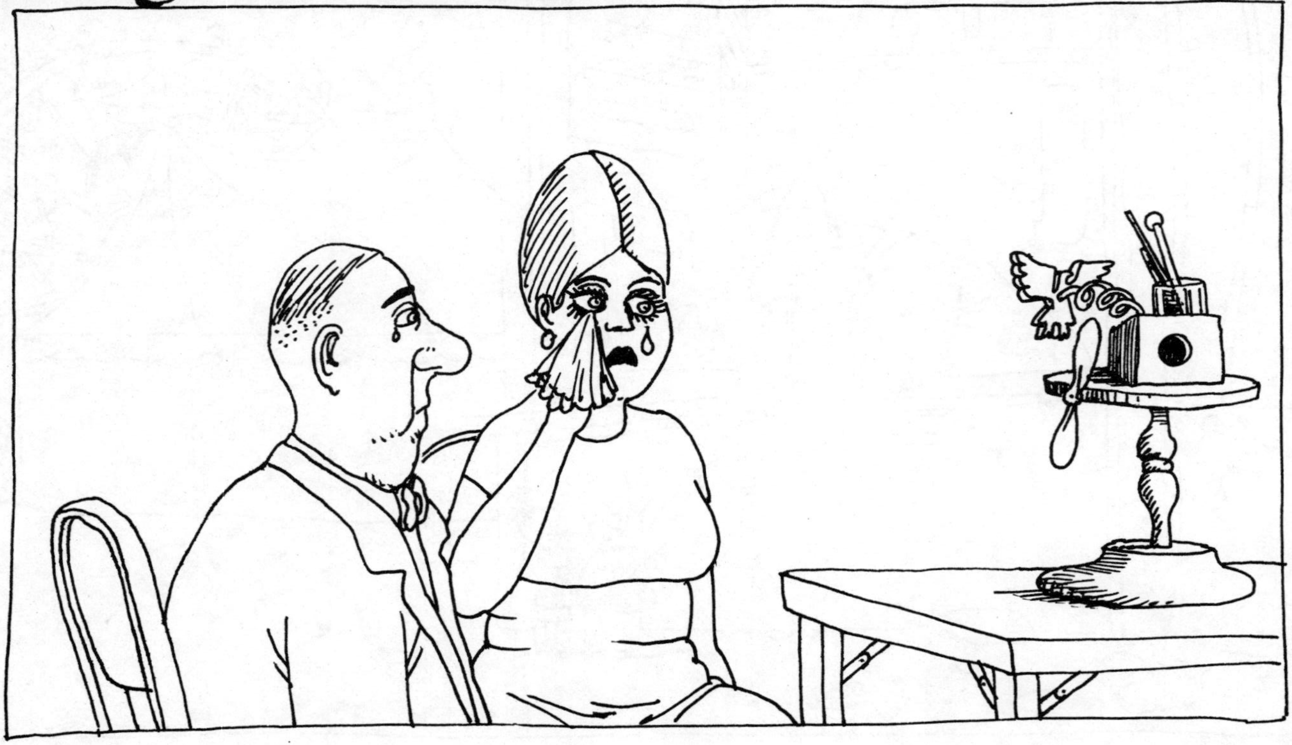

The Holy Filament

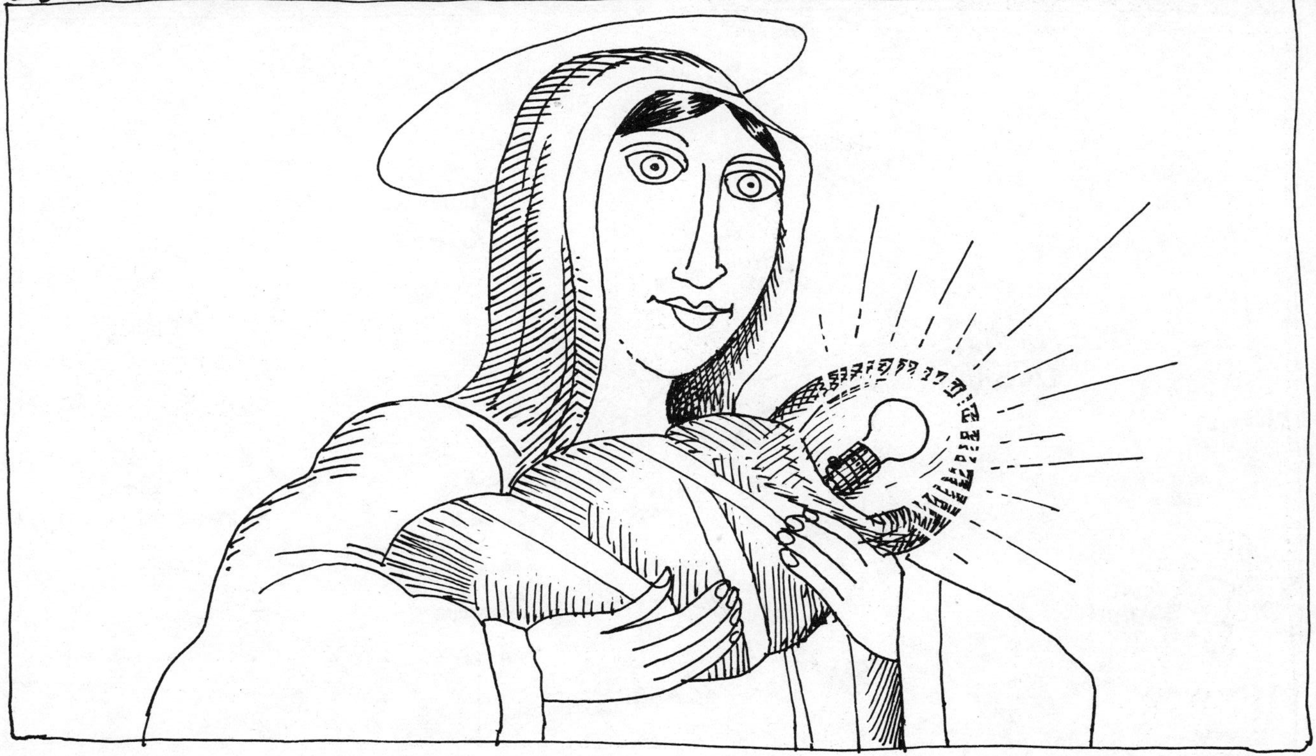

Map

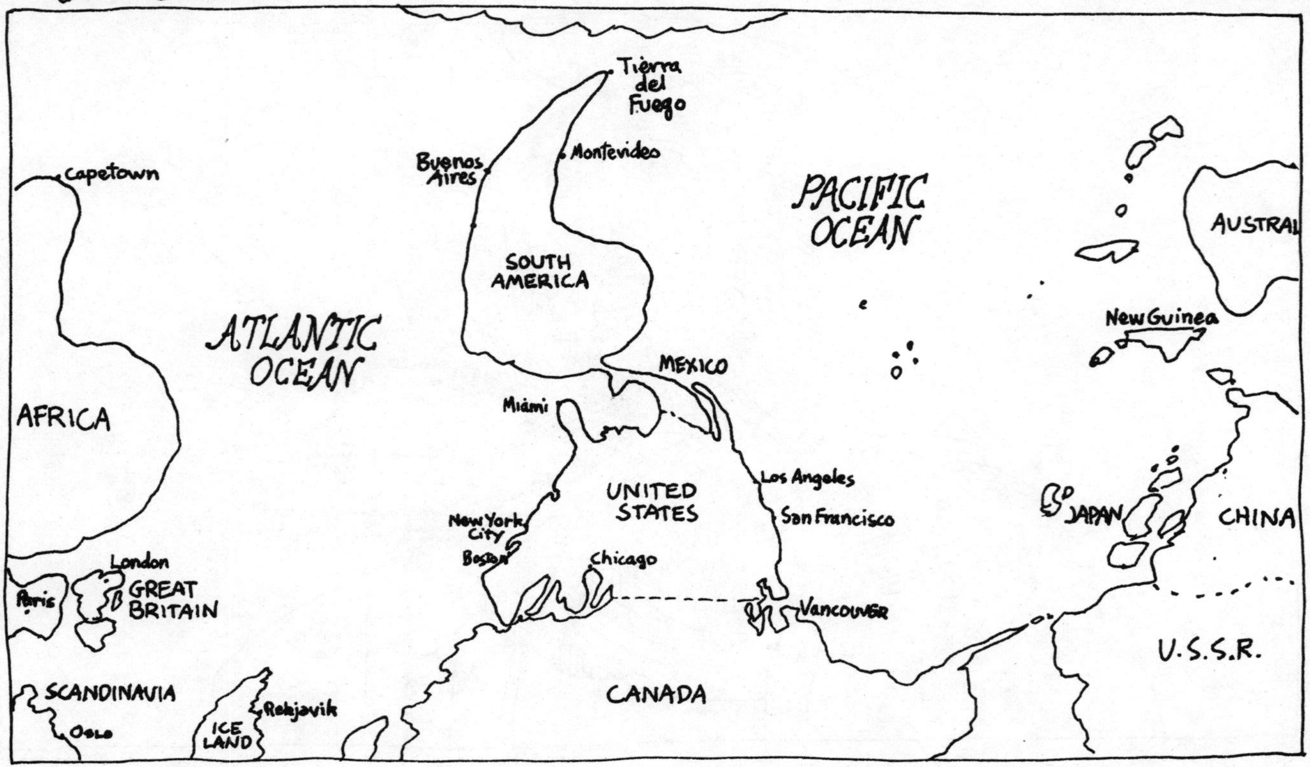

Tierra del Fuego
Montevideo
Buenos Aires
Capetown
PACIFIC OCEAN
AUSTRAL
SOUTH AMERICA
ATLANTIC OCEAN
New Guinea
MEXICO
AFRICA
Miami
Los Angeles
UNITED STATES
New York City
San Francisco
JAPAN
CHINA
Boston
Chicago
London
GREAT BRITAIN
Paris
Vancouver
U.S.S.R.
SCANDINAVIA
CANADA
Rekjavik
ICE LAND
Oslo

Fred's House

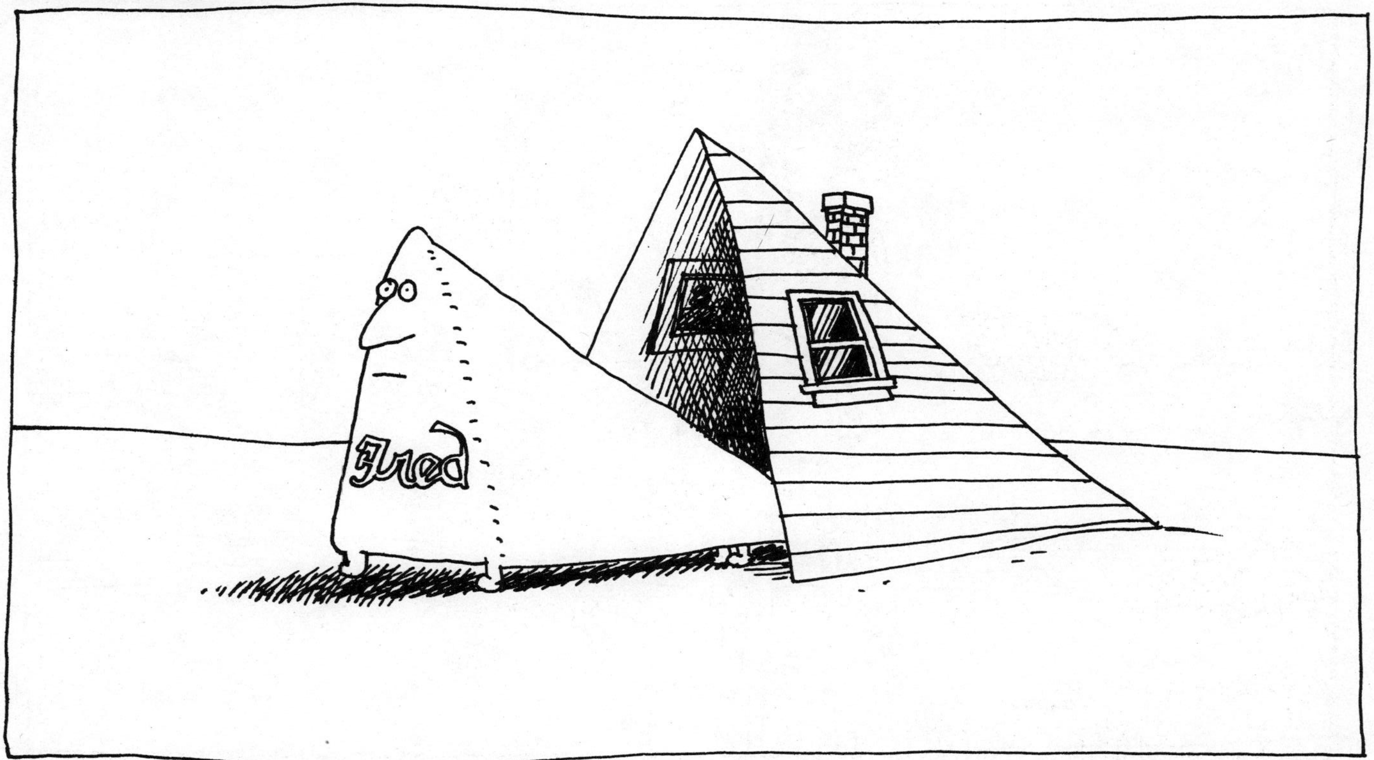
Fred

Aphid, B-girl, C Serpent

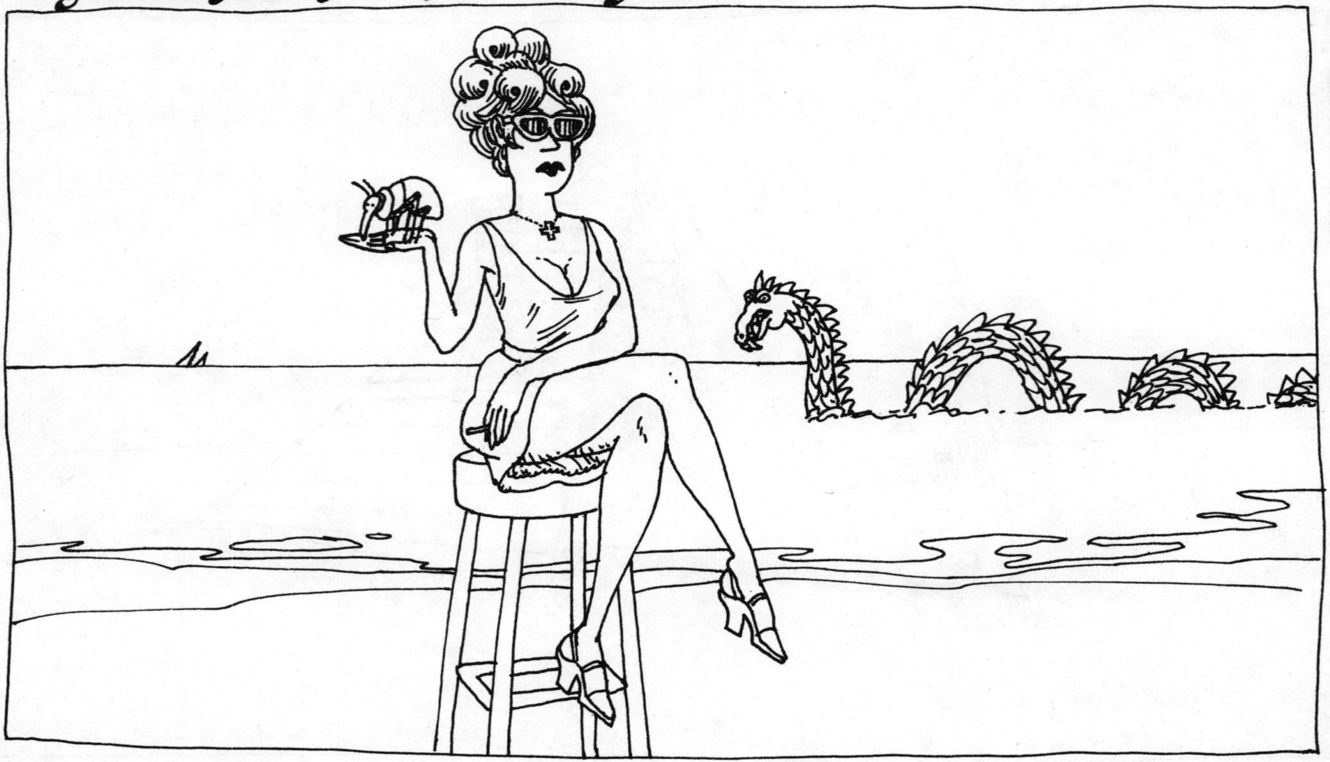

THE CALLOUS SOPHISTICATES LAUGHED AT JUDY'S TINY HEAD.

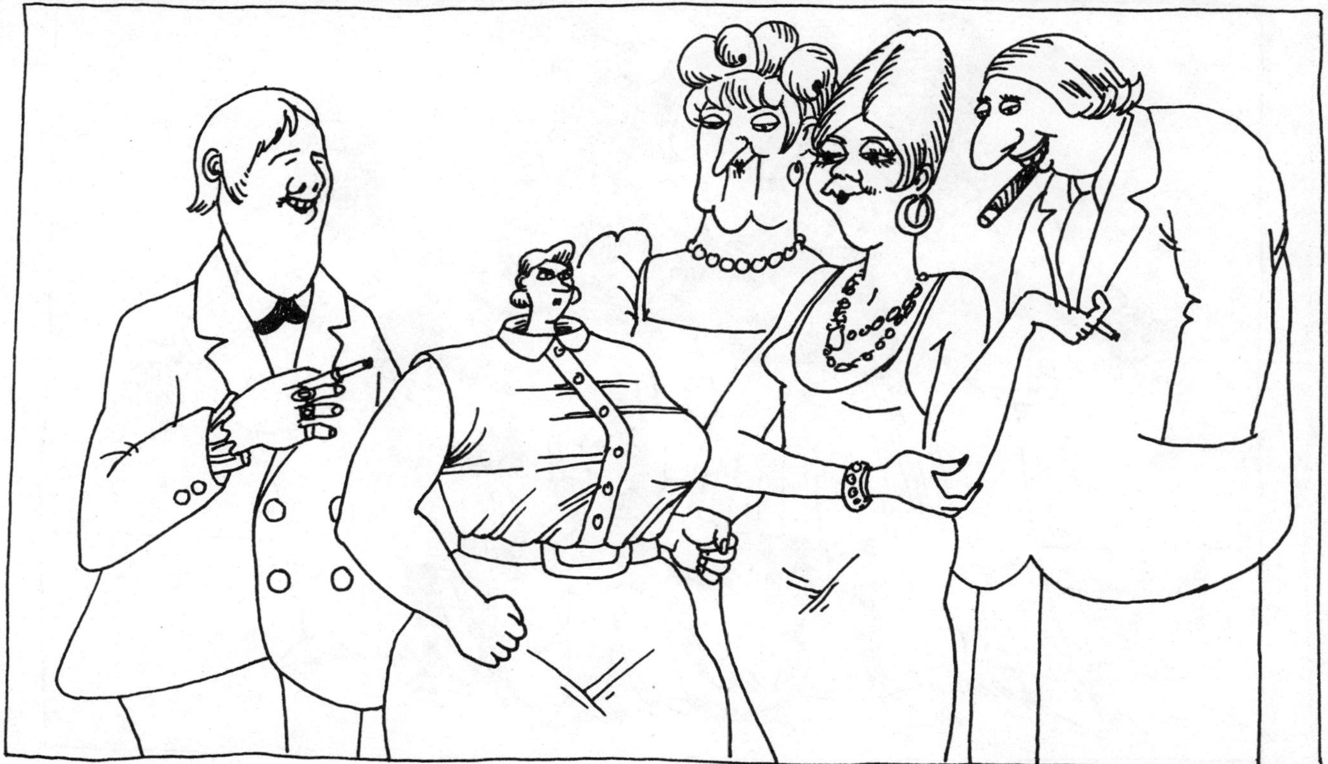

The Hairy Family Singers

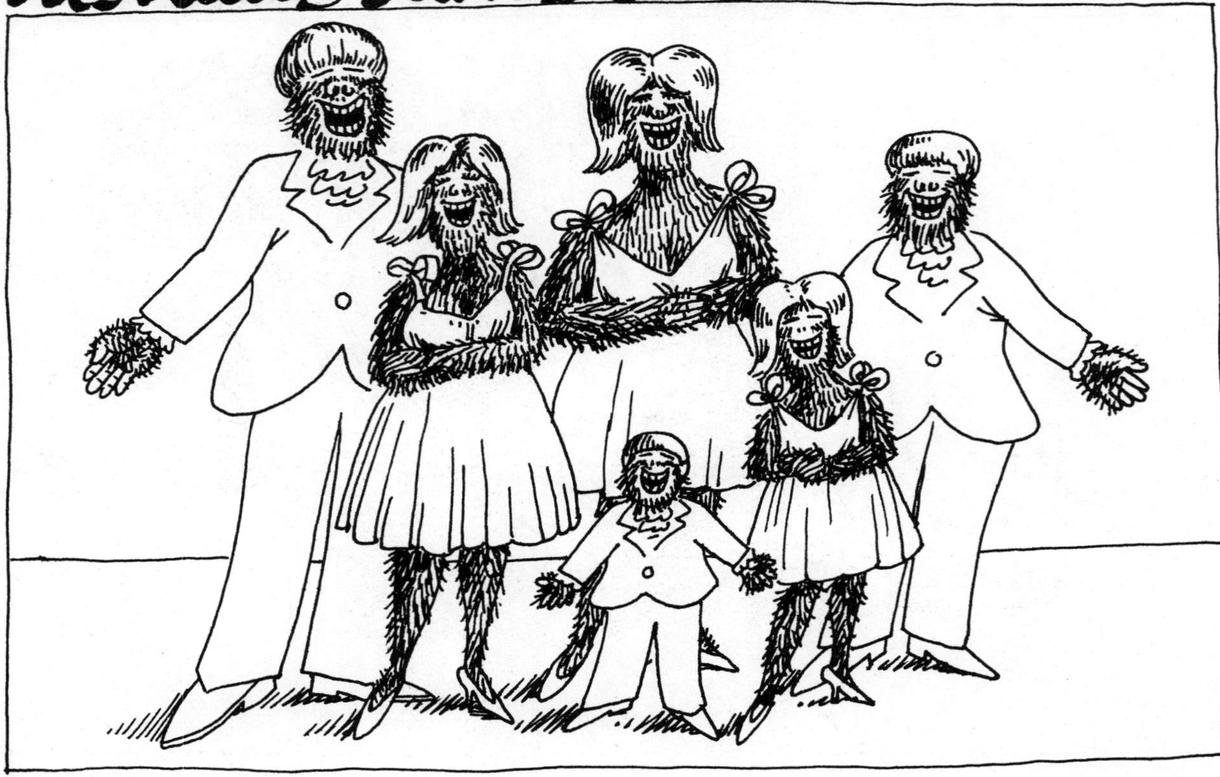

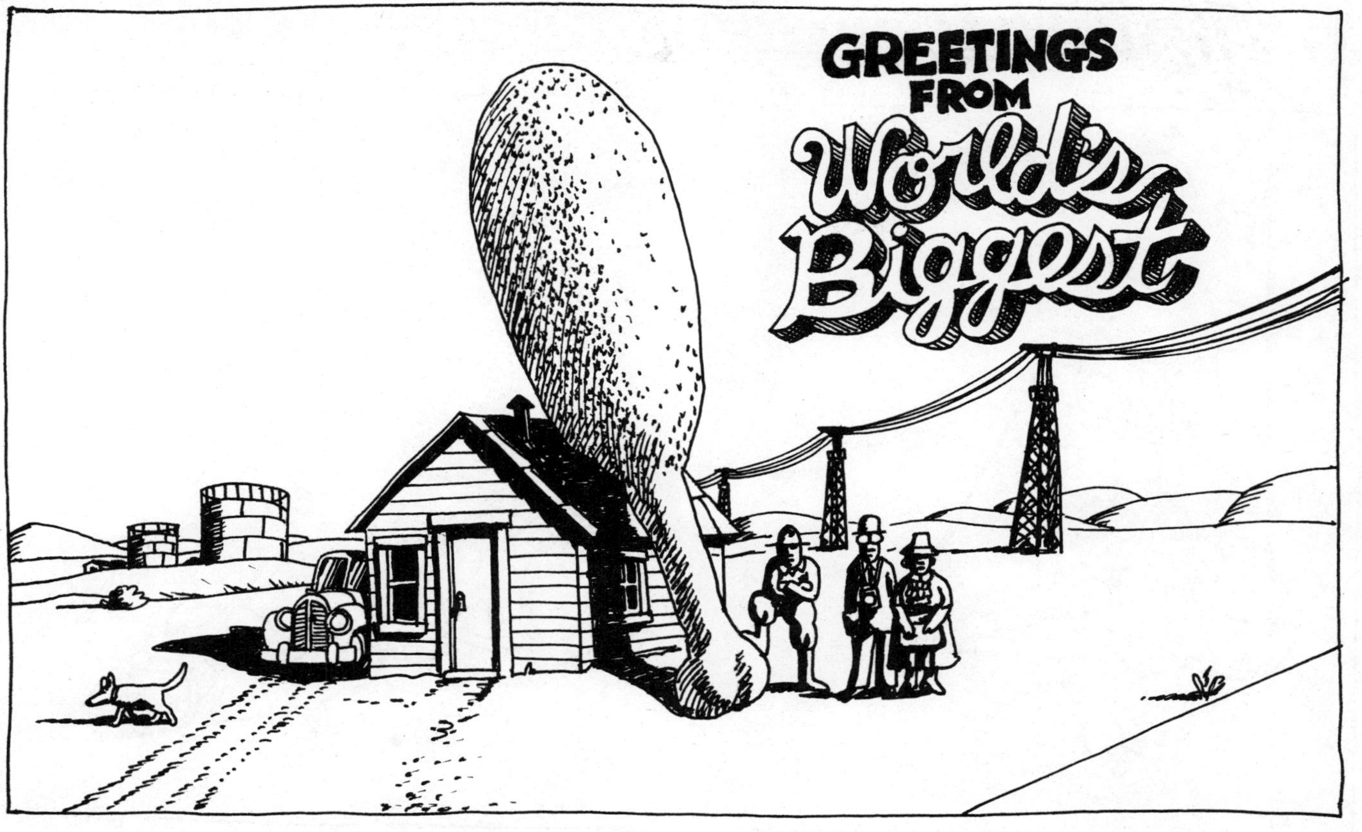
GREETINGS
FROM
World's
Biggest

Gymnastics

B

Fig. 1

B

Fig. 2

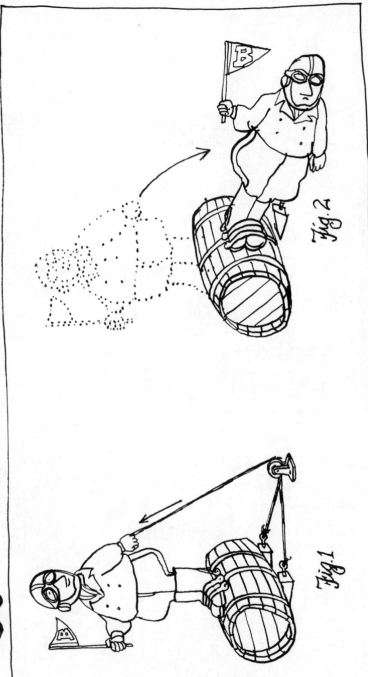

ALWAYS HIDE IN A PLACE WHERE THERE ARE A LOT OF THE SAME THINGS.

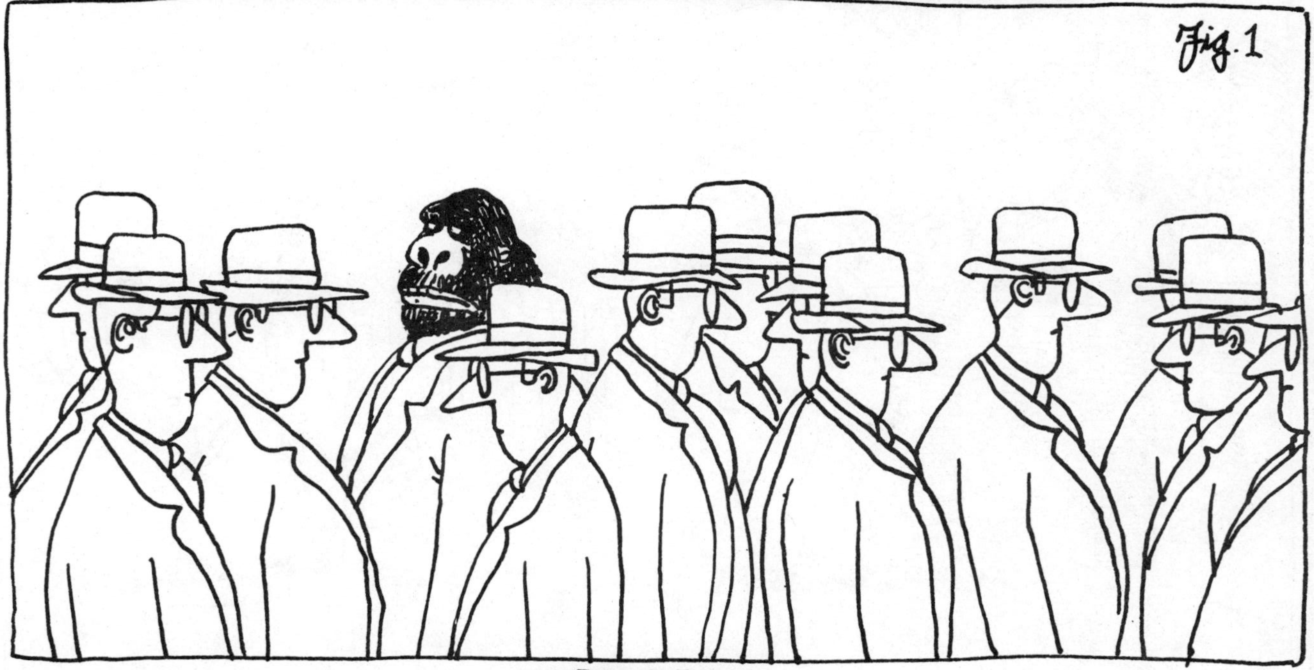
Fig. 1

WRONG

Hall of Imbeciles

WASHINGTON, D.C.

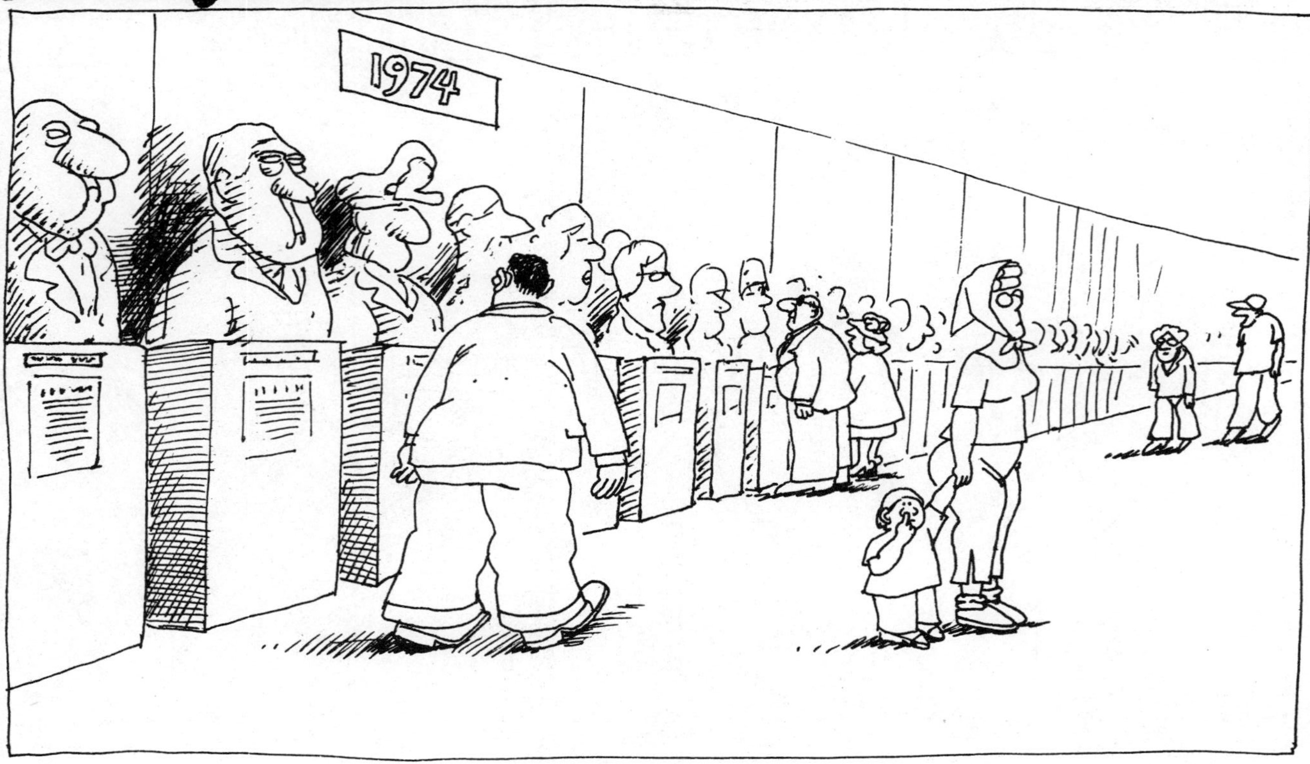
1974

The Victim's Family

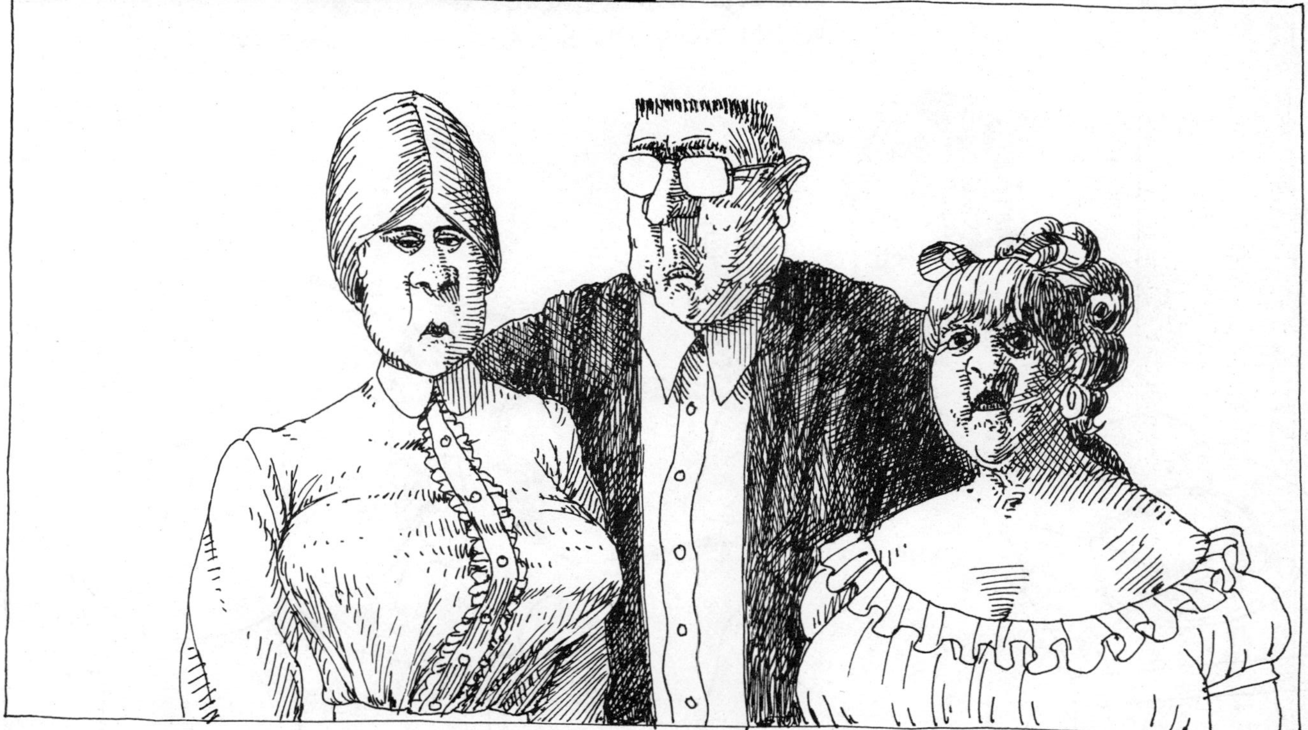

Chapter XI

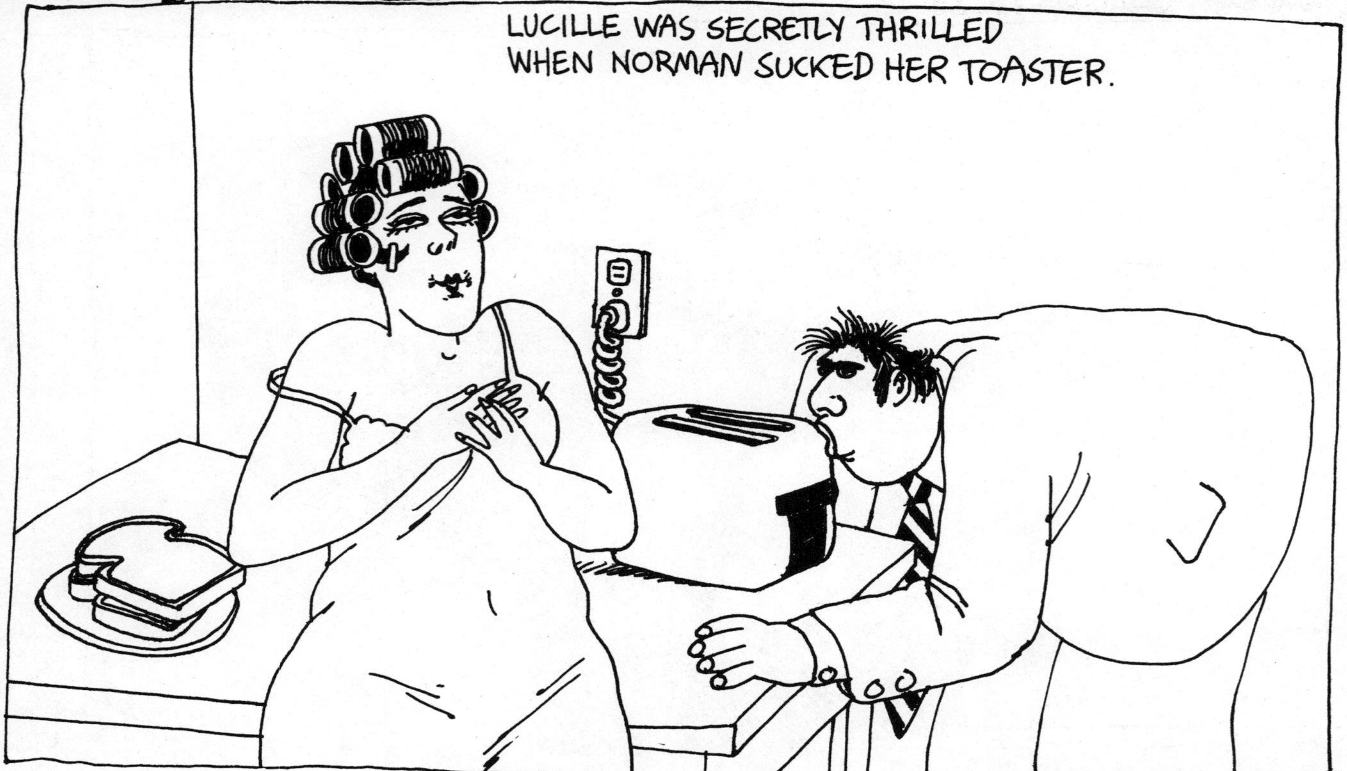
LUCILLE WAS SECRETLY THRILLED
WHEN NORMAN SUCKED HER TOASTER.

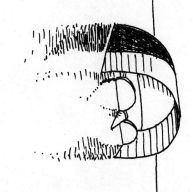

Sunken Nun

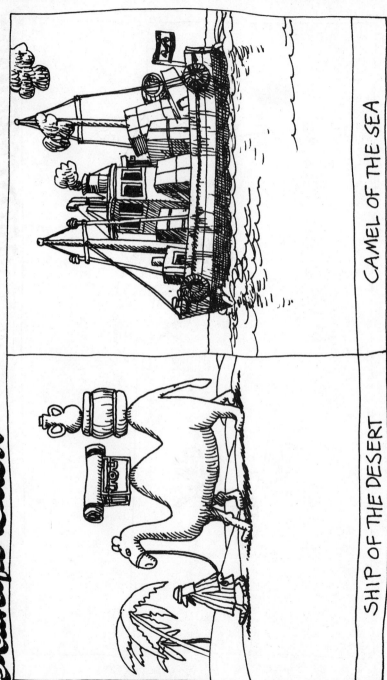

Transportation

SHIP OF THE DESERT

CAMEL OF THE SEA

CYNTHIA IS MISTAKENLY CROWNED KING OF NORWAY

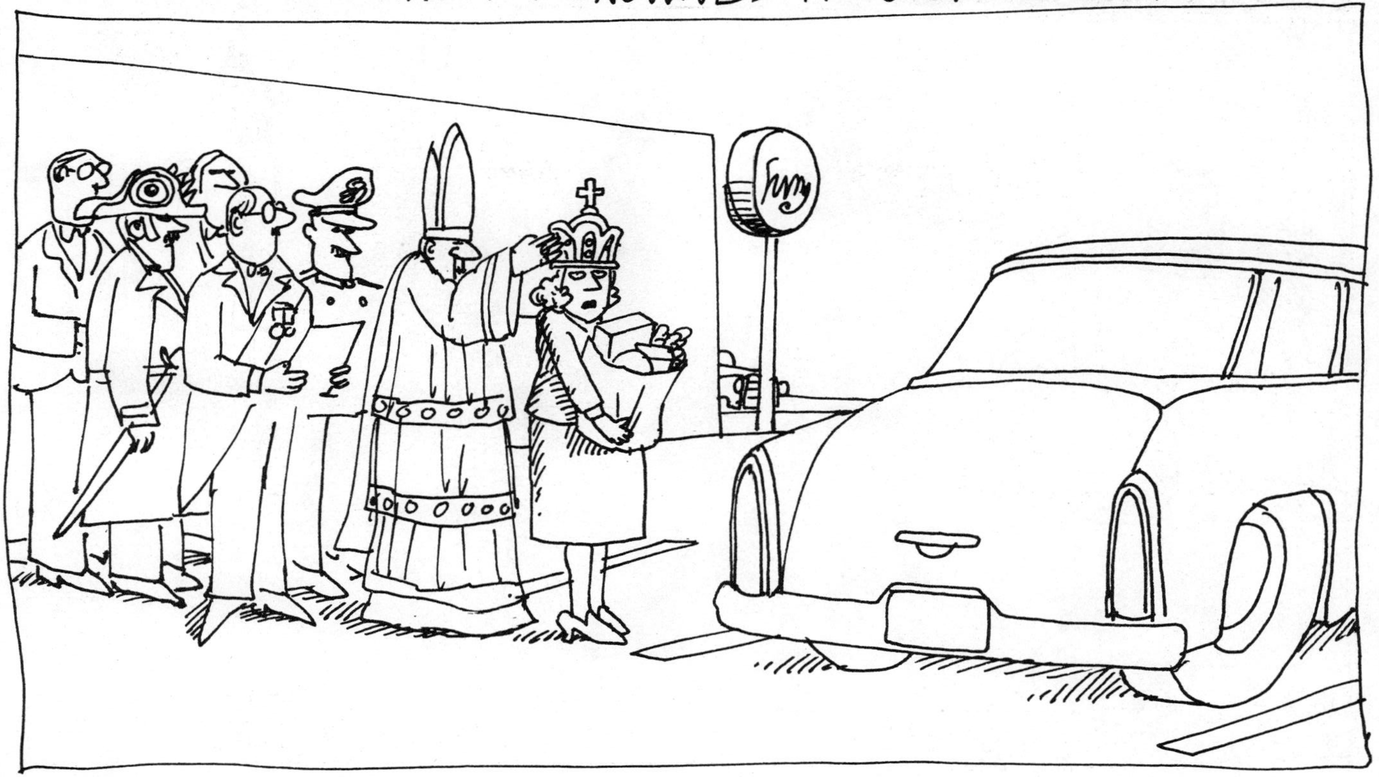
Lyyny

Clown Building

TULSA, OKLAHOMA

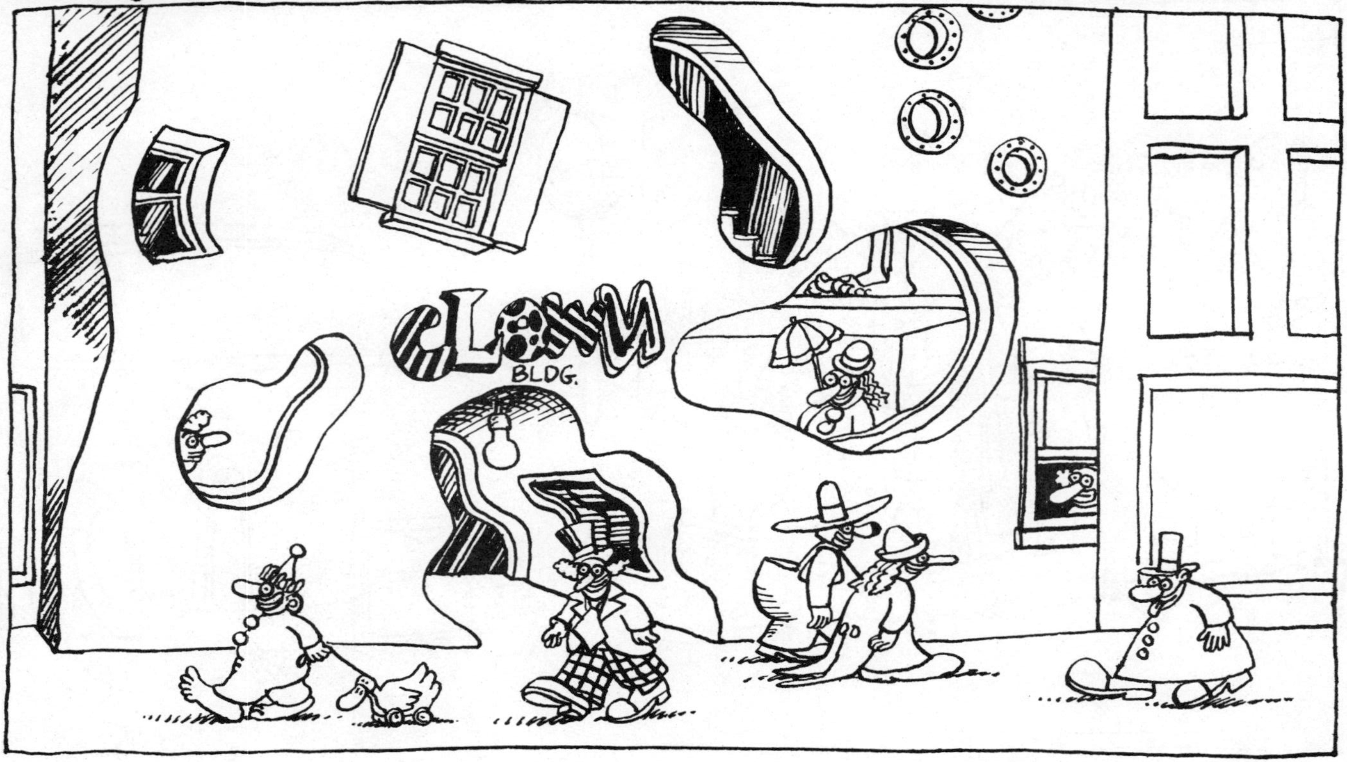
CLOWN
BLDG.

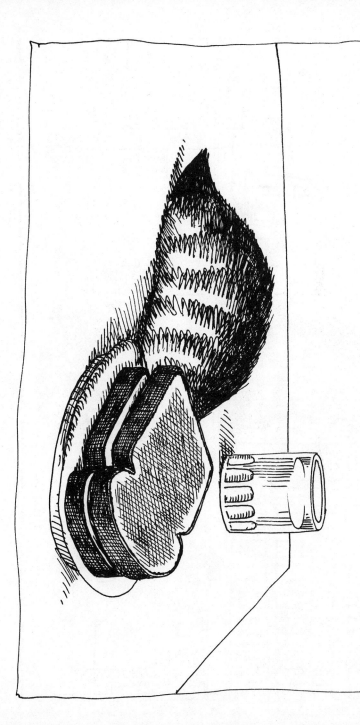

Raccoon on wheat toast

MONUMENT TO THE UNKNOWN TEN FOOT POLE

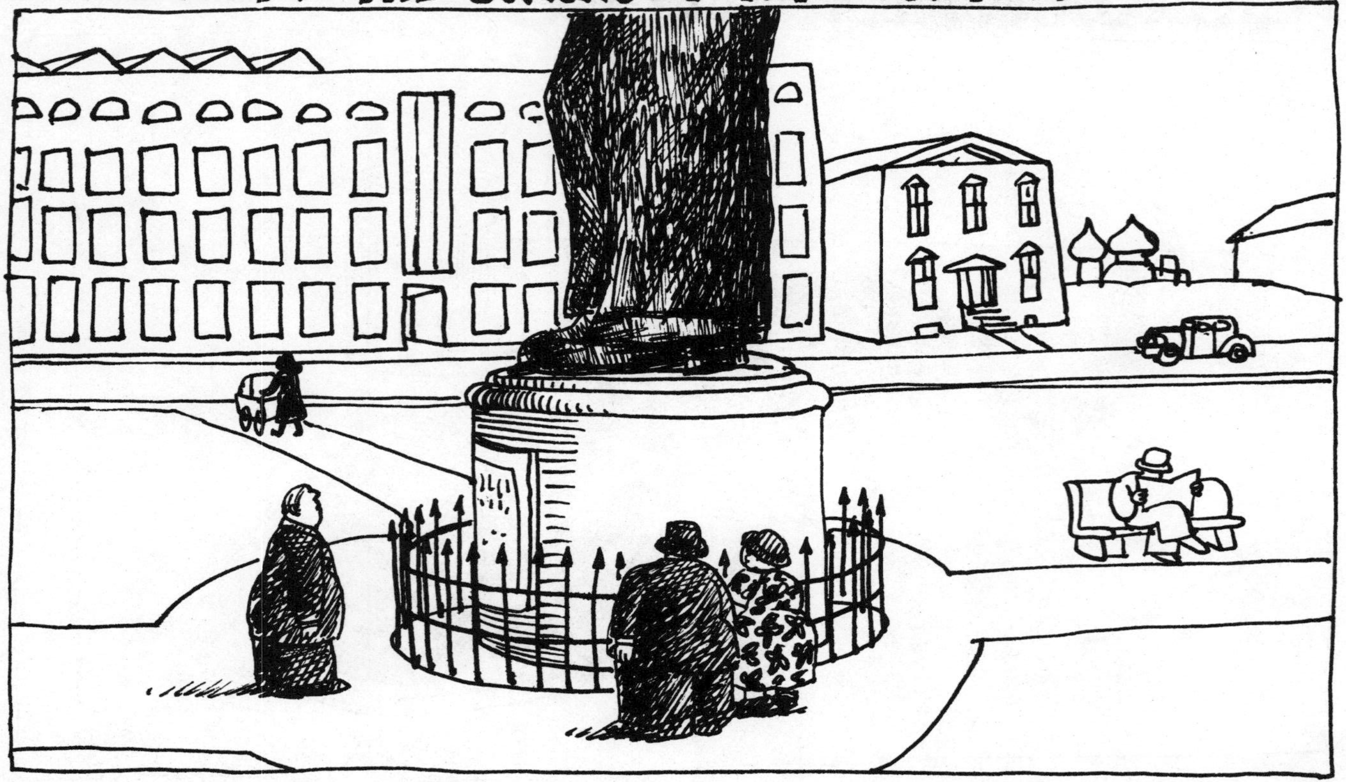

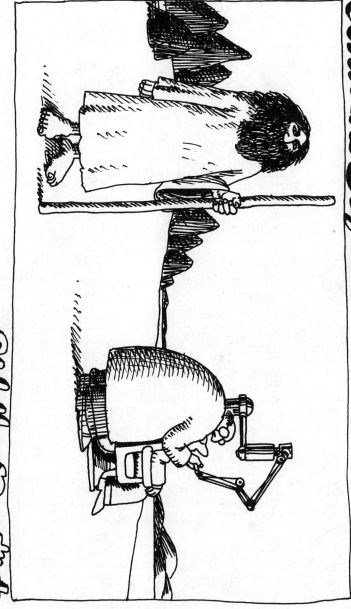

John the Baptist

Sid the Dentist

Inglese

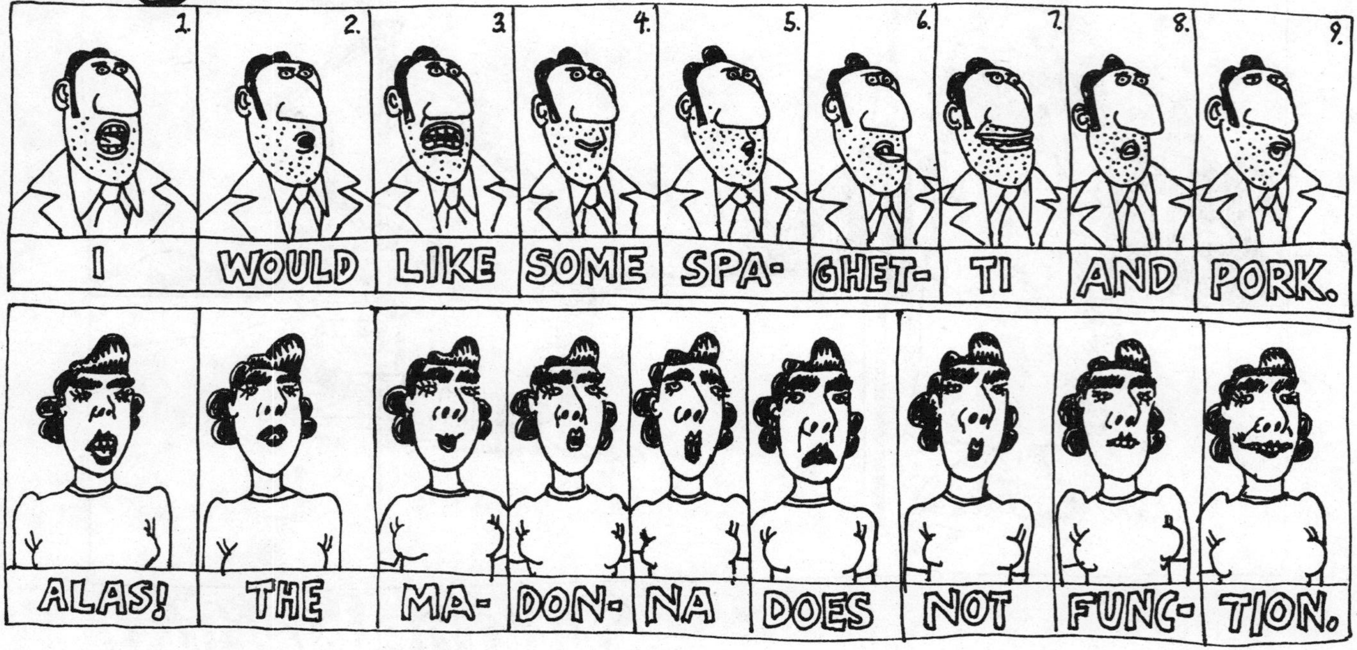

1.
2.
3.
4.
5.
6.
7.
8.
9.
I
WOULD
LIKE
SOME
SPA-
GHET-
TI
AND
PORK.
ALAS!
THE
MA-
DON-
NA
DOES
NOT
FUNC-
TION.

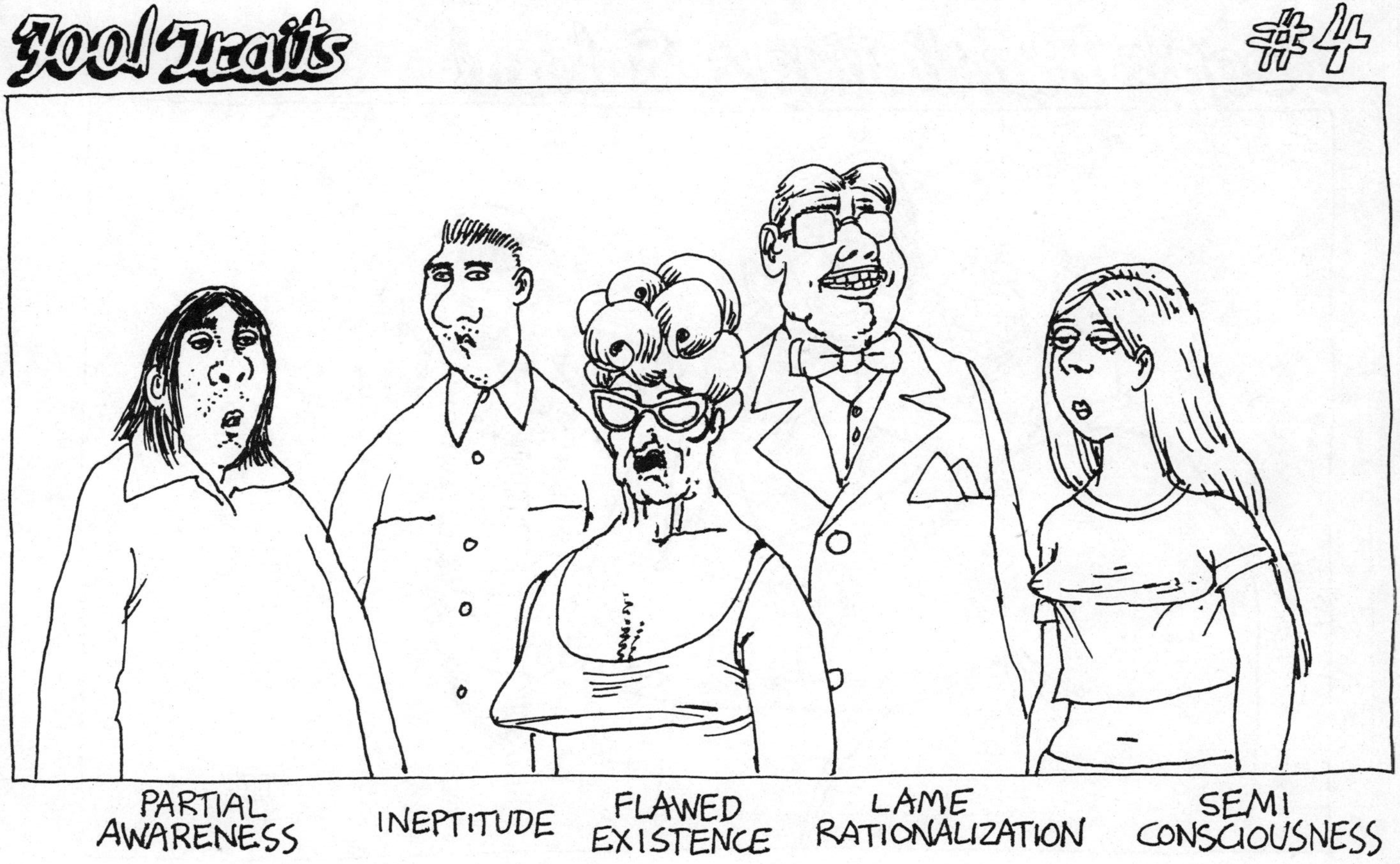
Fool Traits
#4
PARTIAL AWARENESS
INEPTITUDE
FLAWED EXISTENCE
LAME RATIONALIZATION
SEMI CONSCIOUSNESS

People Humiliating A Salami

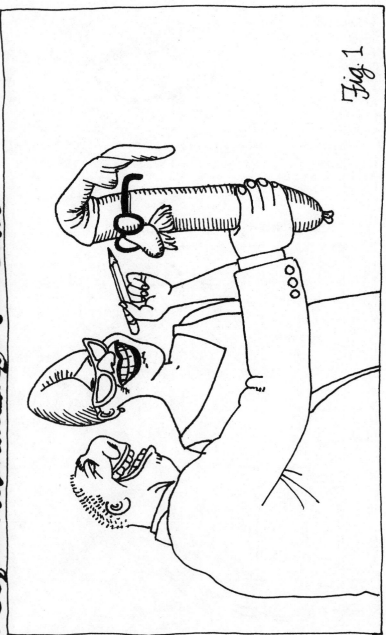

Fig. 1

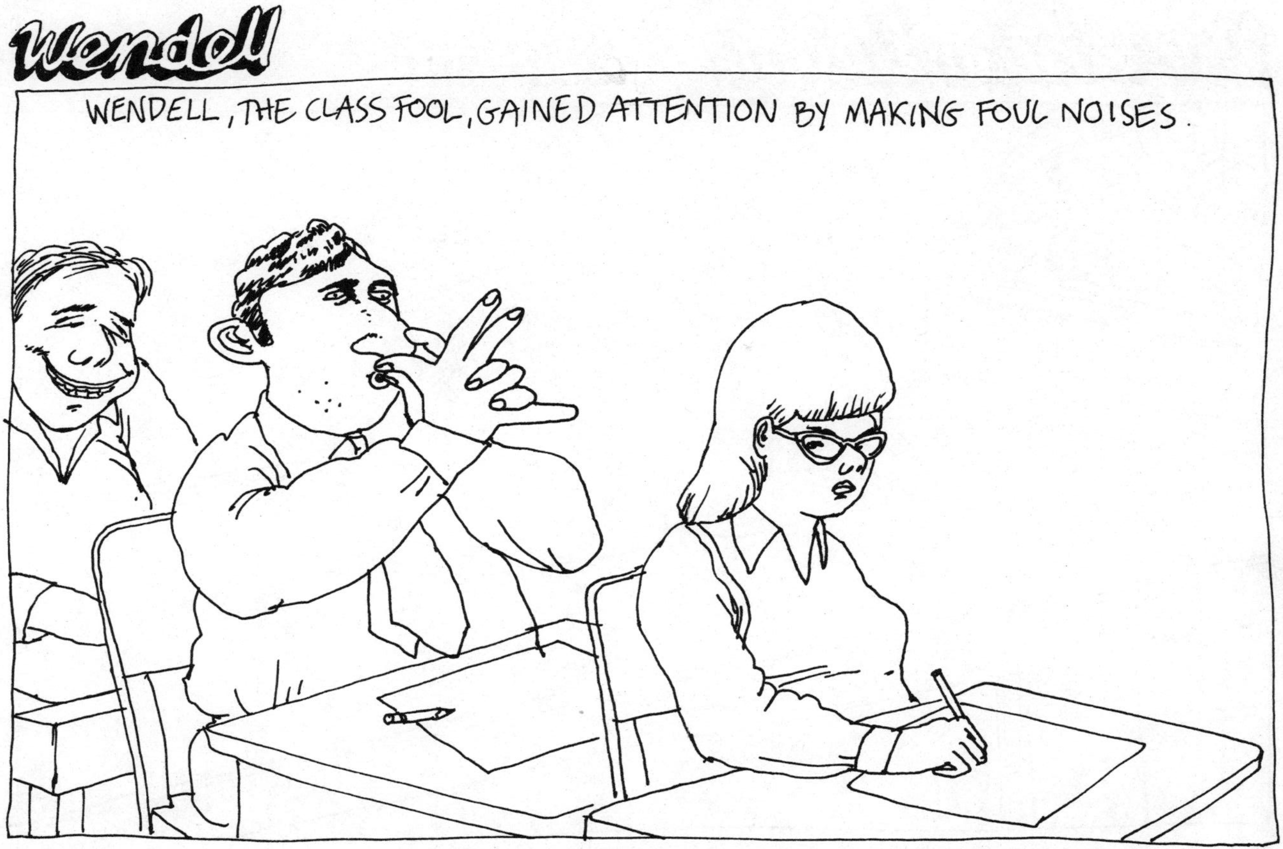
Wendell
WENDELL, THE CLASS FOOL, GAINED ATTENTION BY MAKING FOUL NOISES.

Merchandising

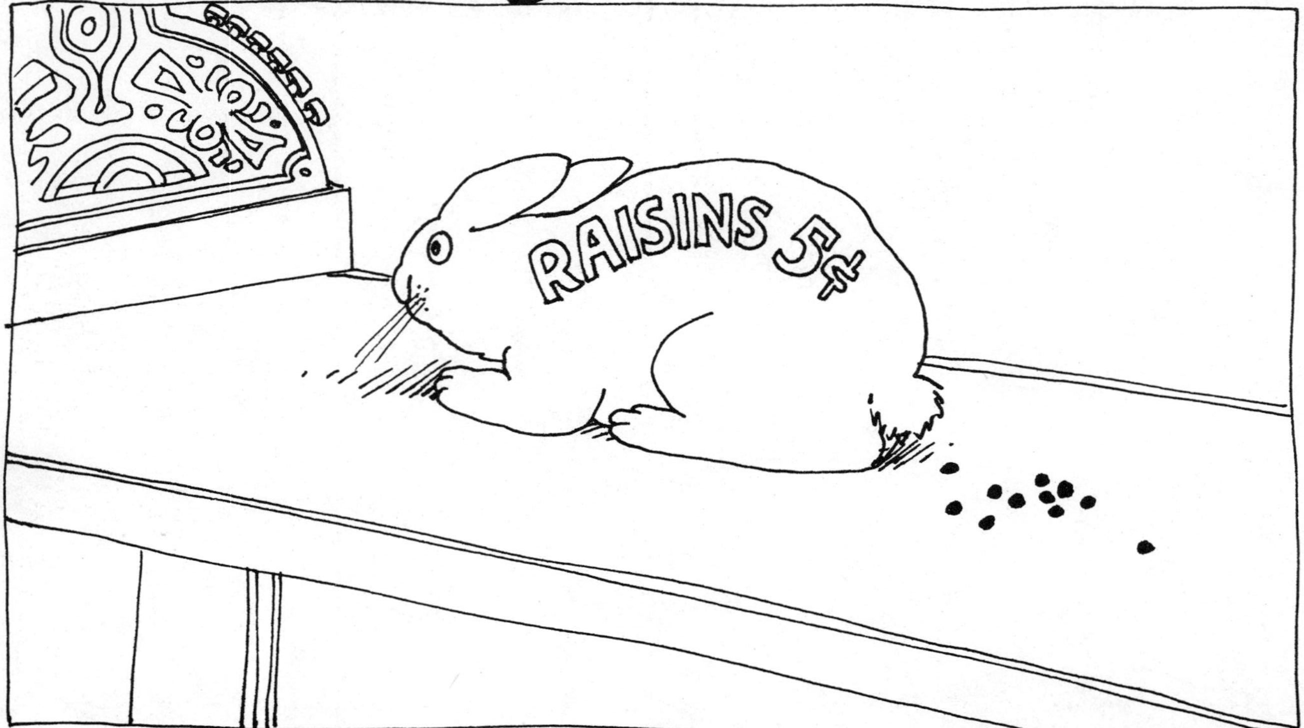
RAISINS 5¢

At the Stripe Works

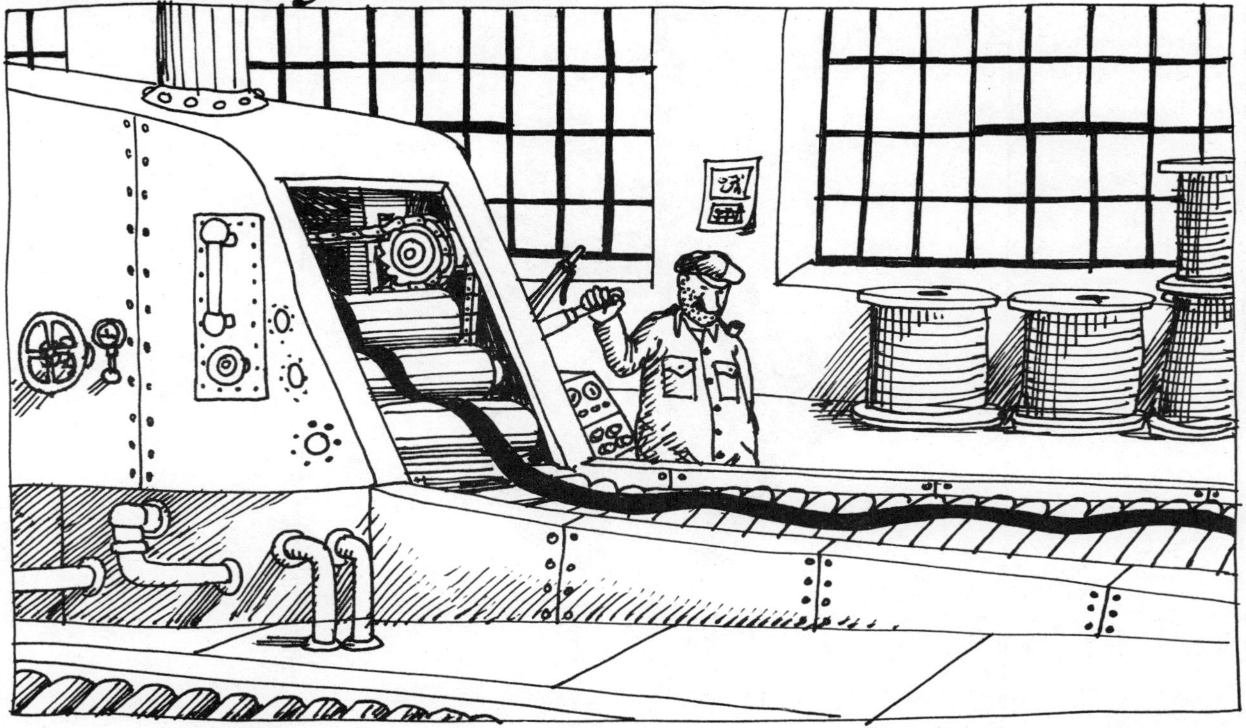

Natural History

AUTOMOTIVE MAN

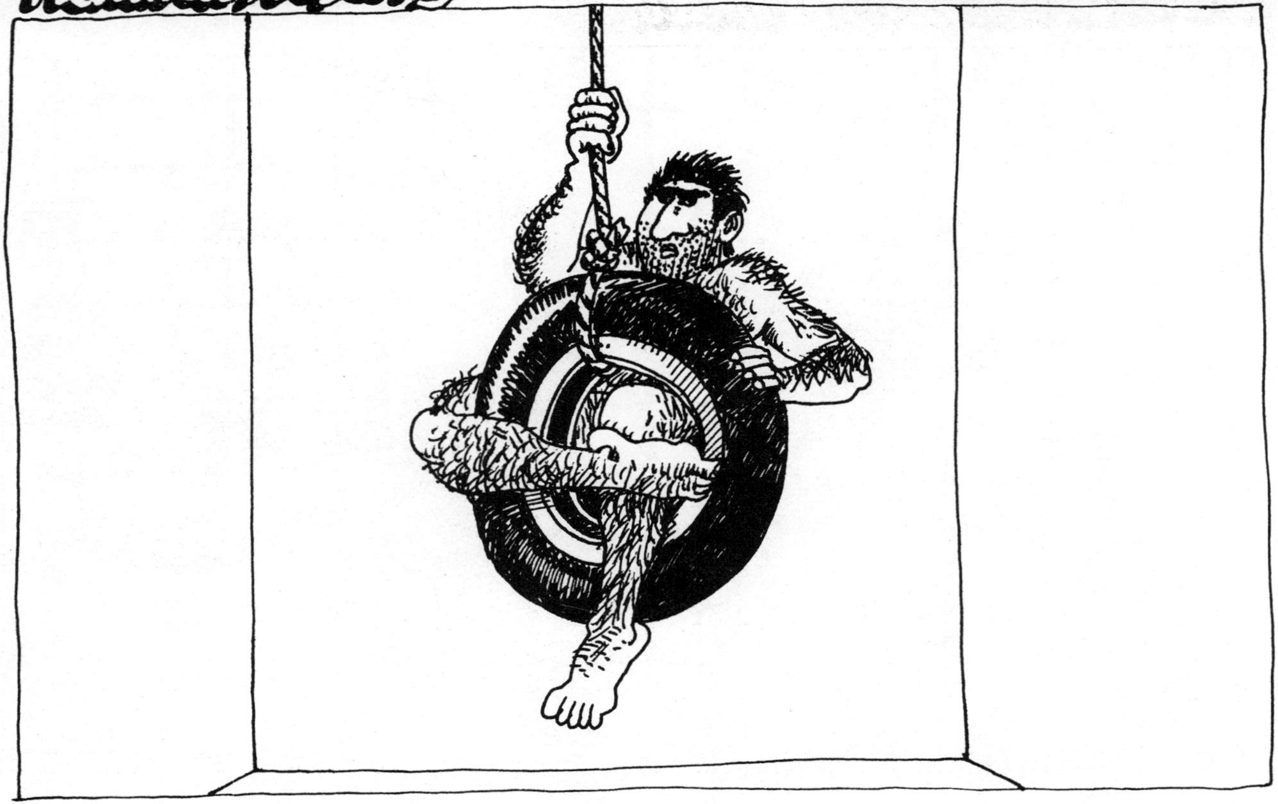

Primitive Accountants

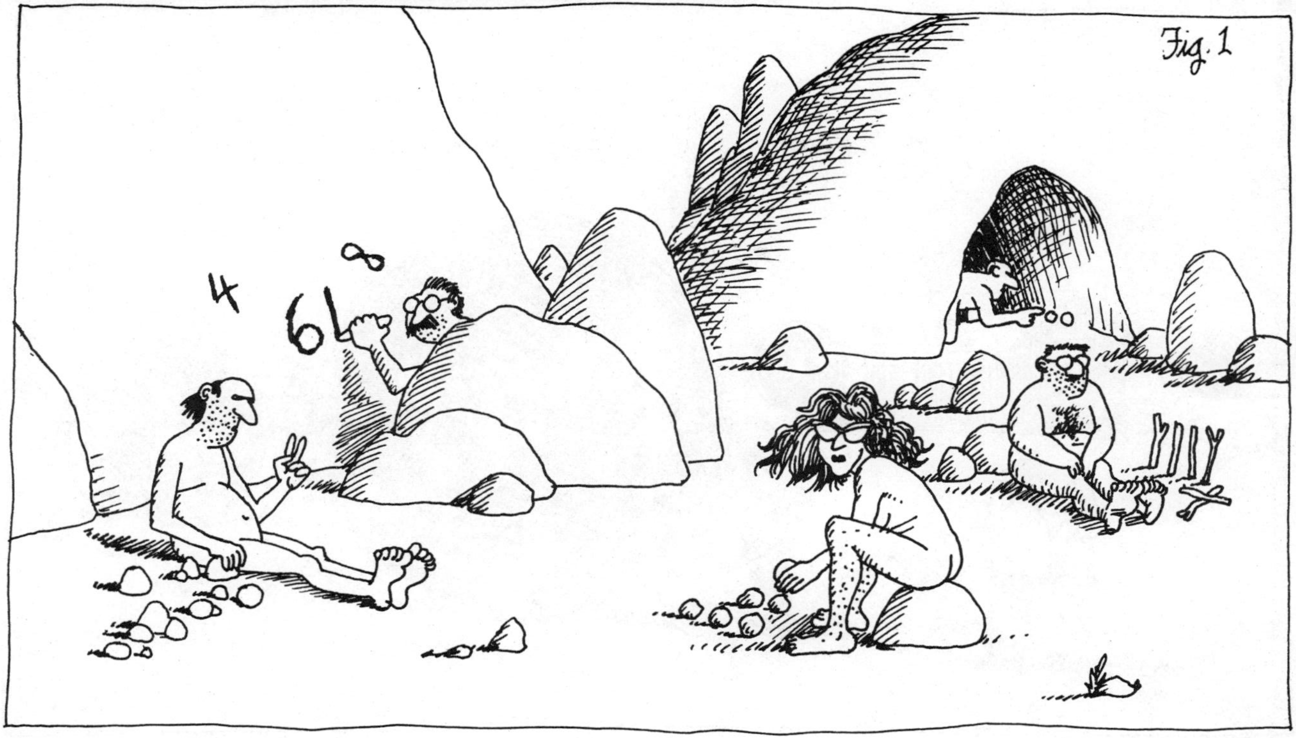

Fig. 1

Great Balls of Fur

HELENA, MONTANA

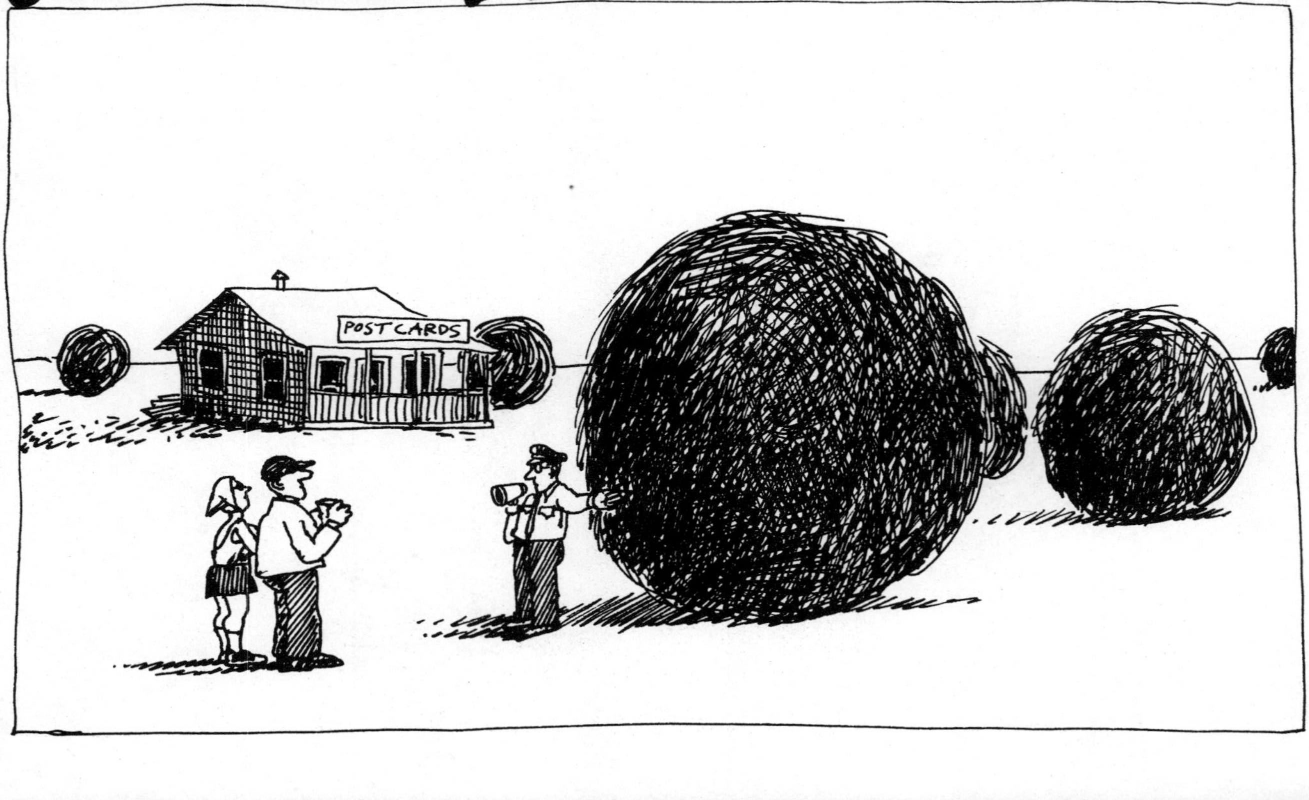
POST CARDS

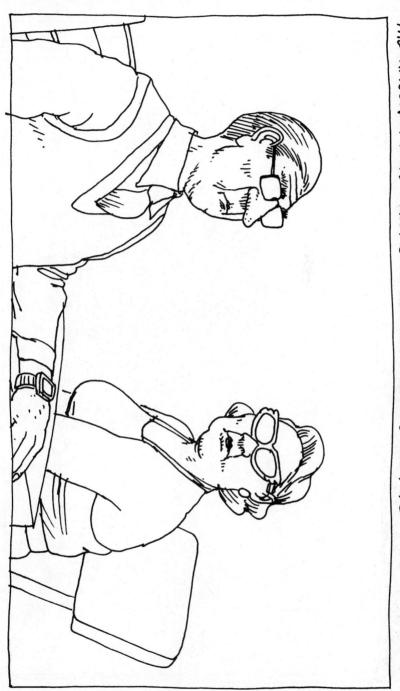

THE WAGON OF LOVE BREAKS UNDER THE BAGGAGE OF LIFE

Chapter One • ARNOLD MEETS TWO OTHER ARNOLDS

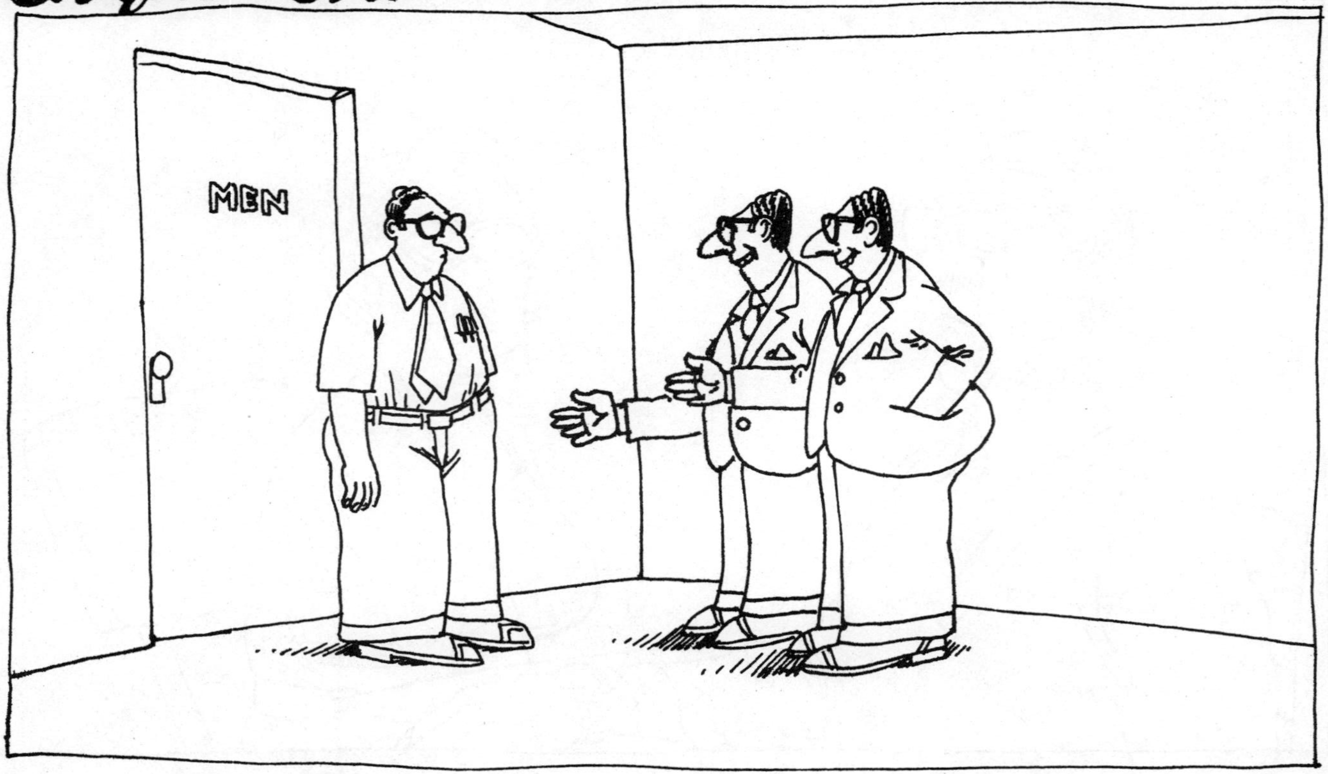
MEN

THE NINE WARNING SIGNALS OF CHRISTMAS

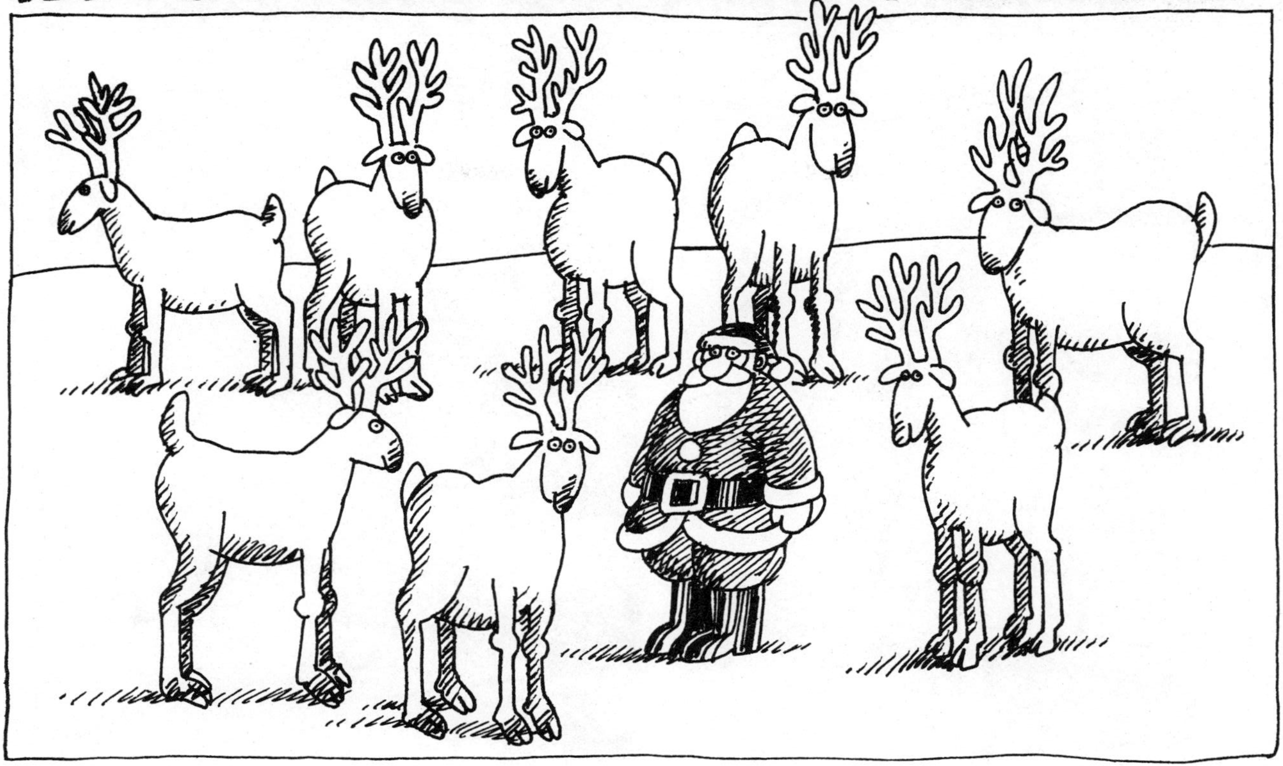

The Inventor & His Device

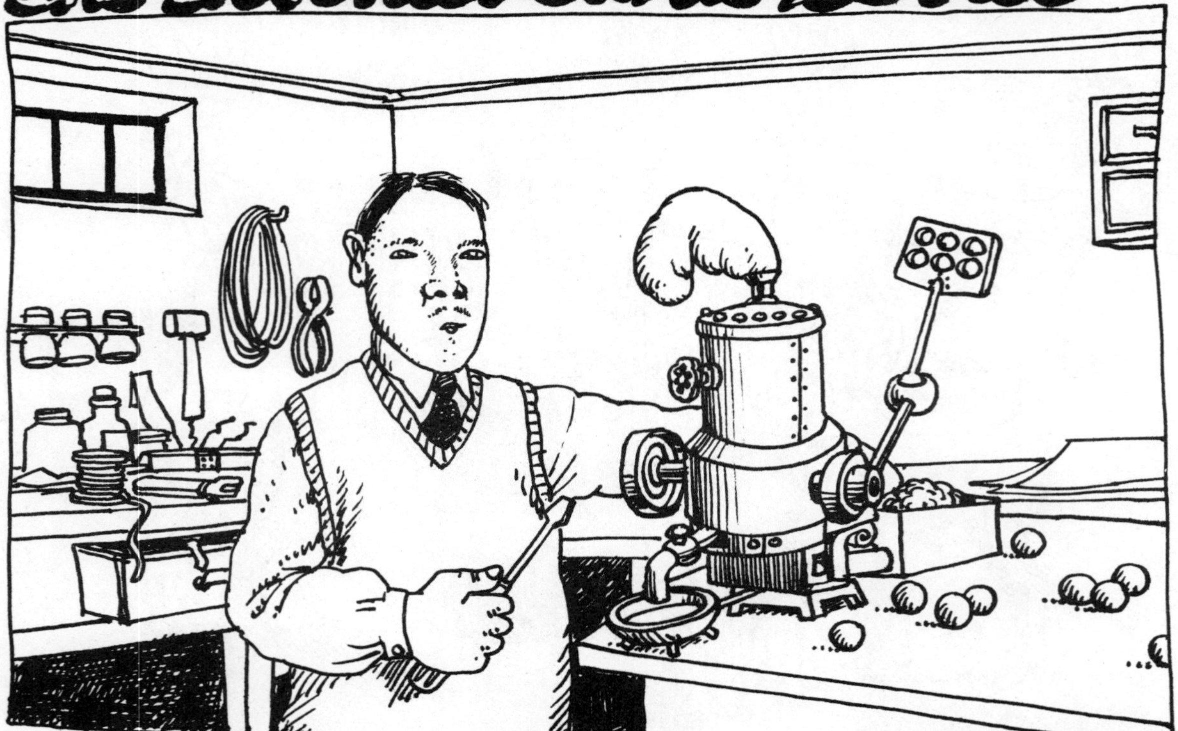

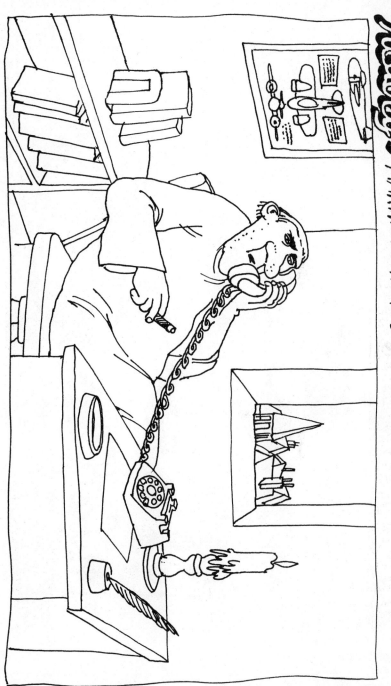

History MARTIN LUTHER DECLINES STATEHOOD

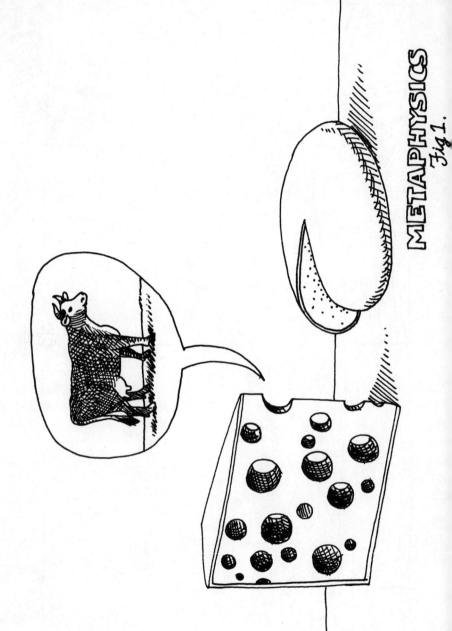

METAPHYSICS
Fig 1.

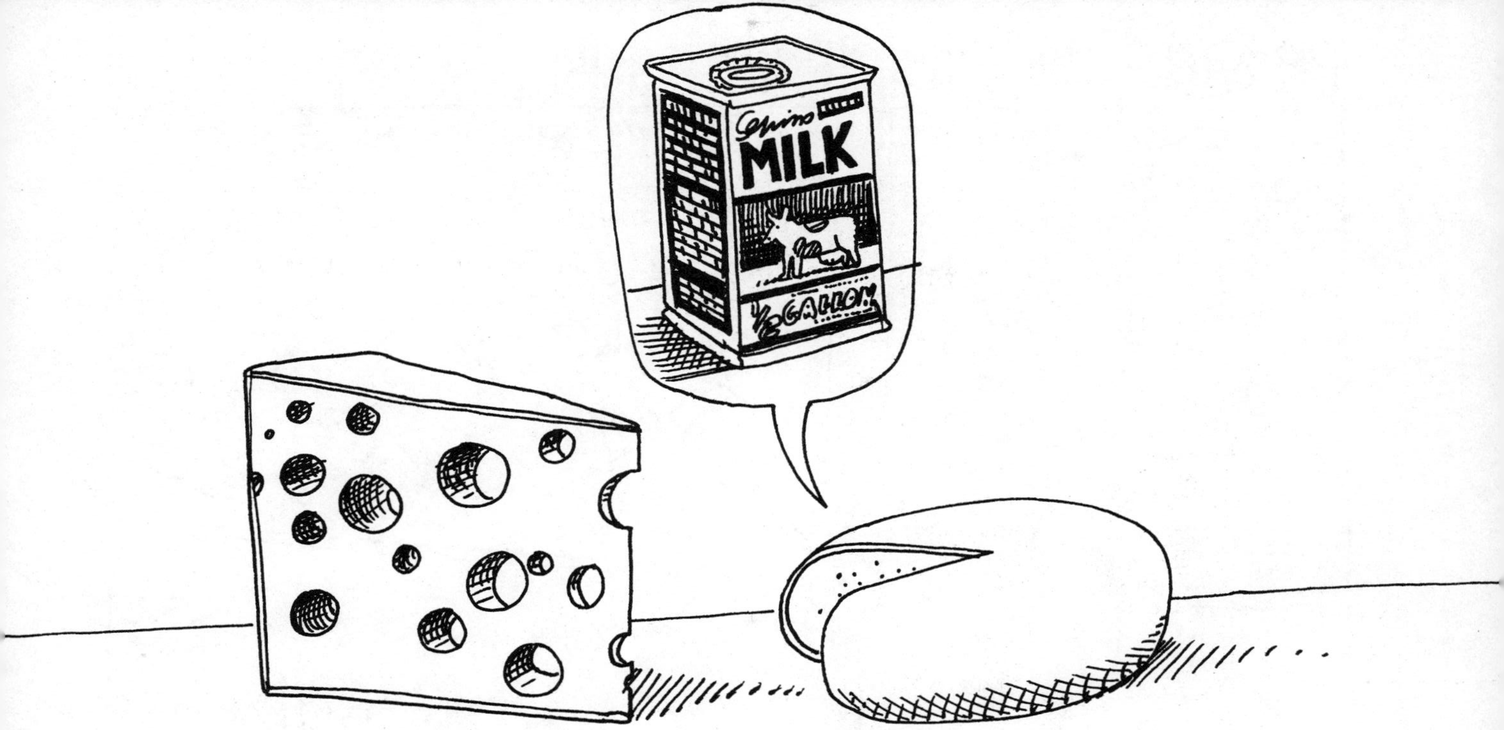
MILK
½ GALLON

METAPHYSICS
Fig 2.

PROVING THE EXISTENCE OF FISH

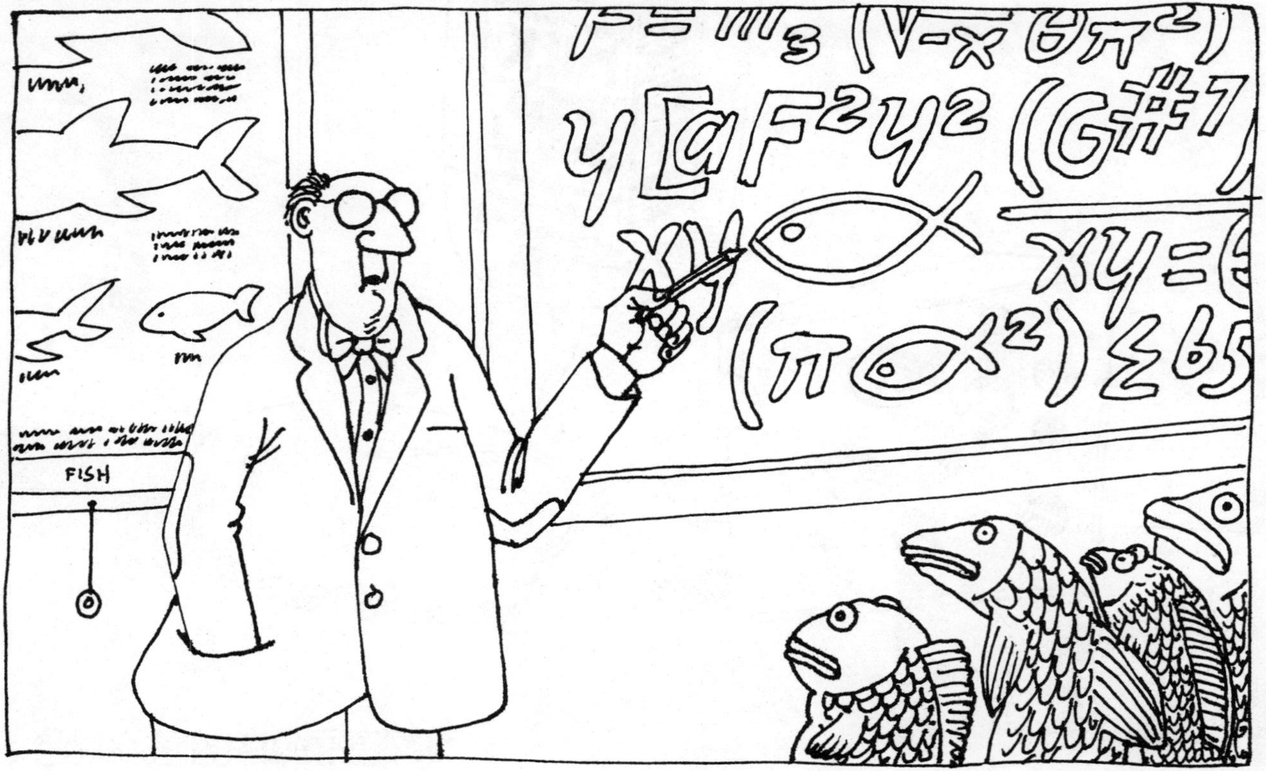
FISH

How They Get Watermelon #8

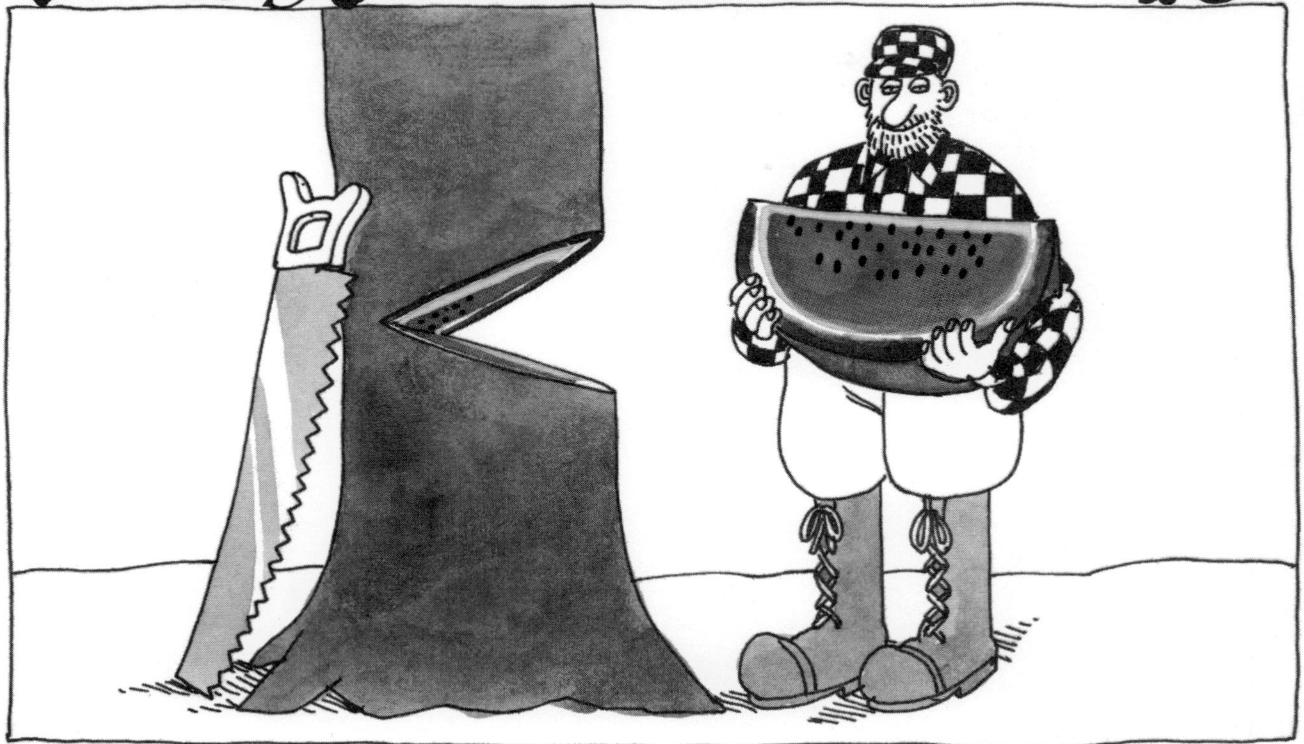

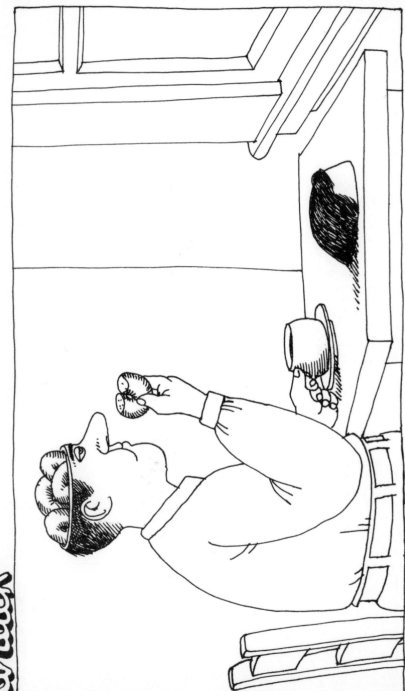

Snack

Dick Sees Spot Run

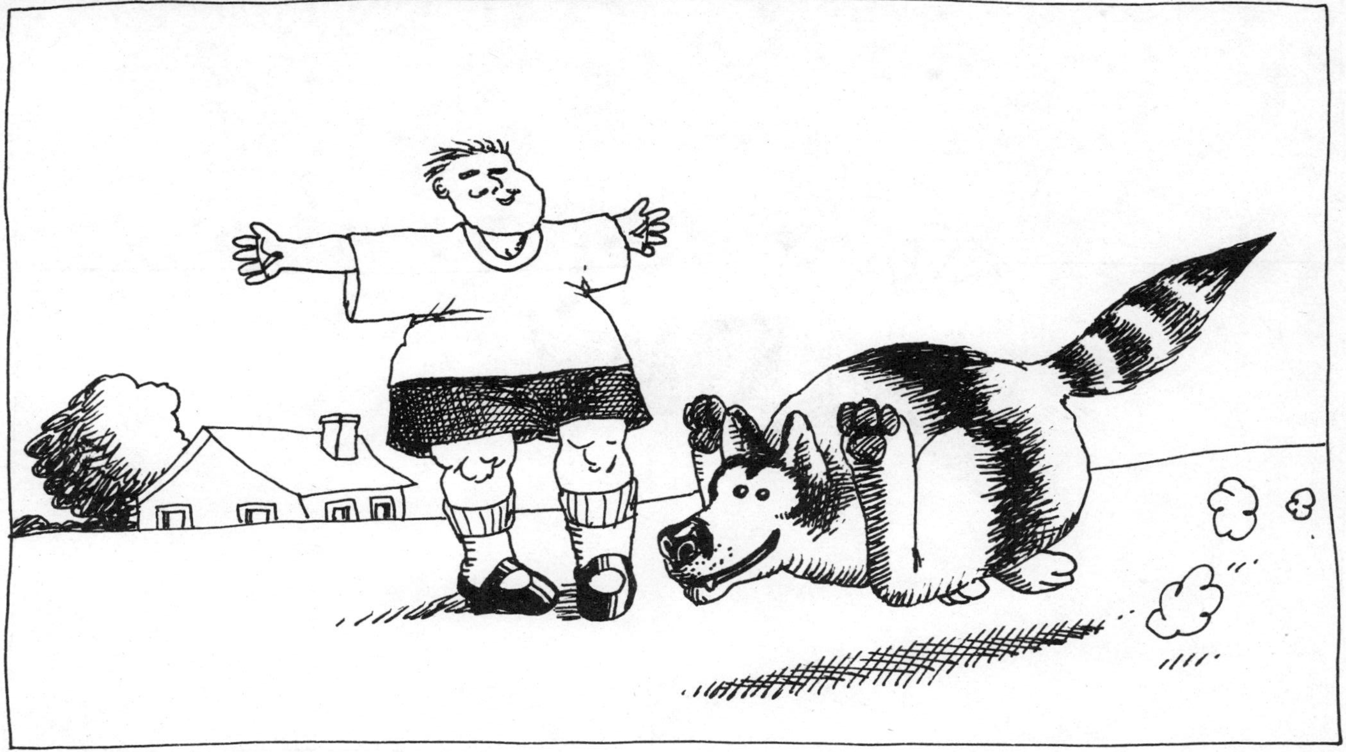

DIRTY FAT PERSON SITS ON PRESIDENT'S FACE

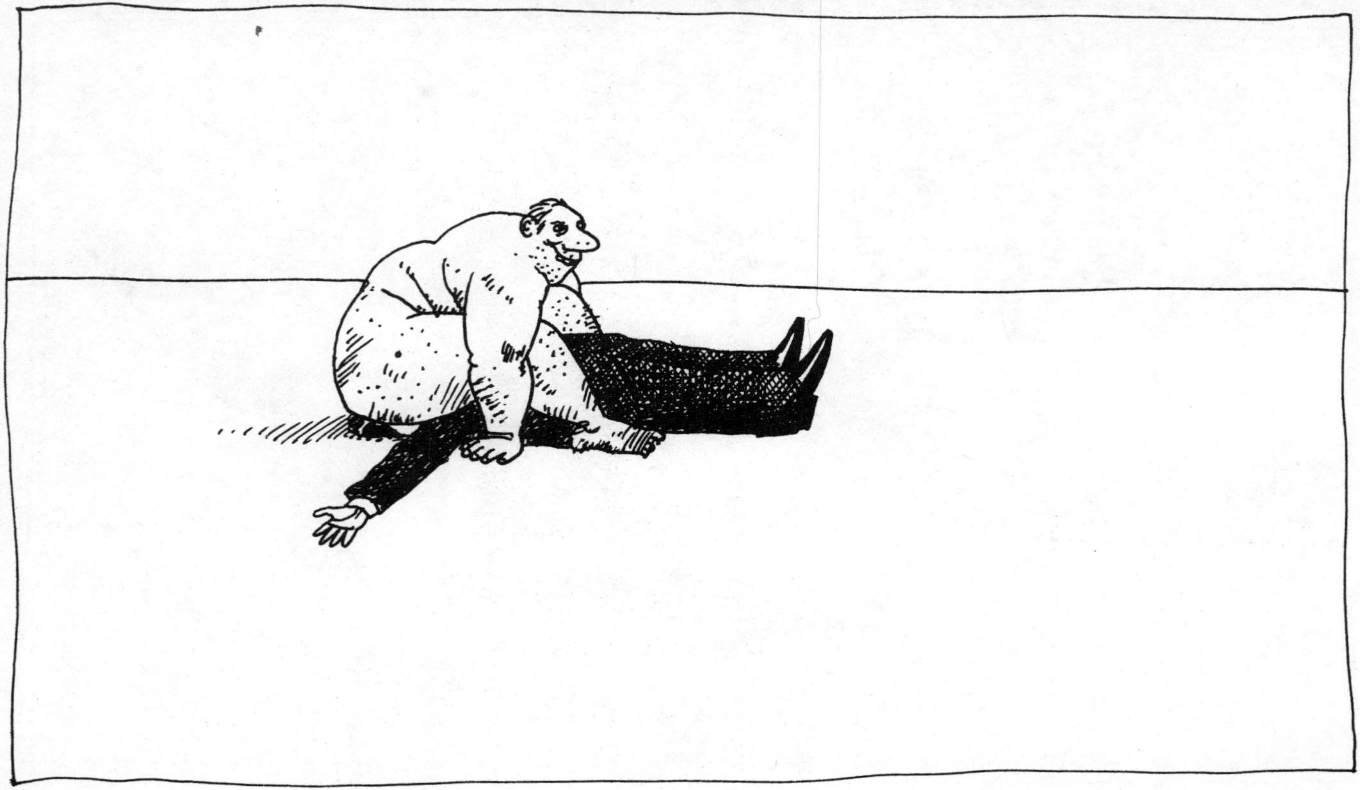

Our Founder

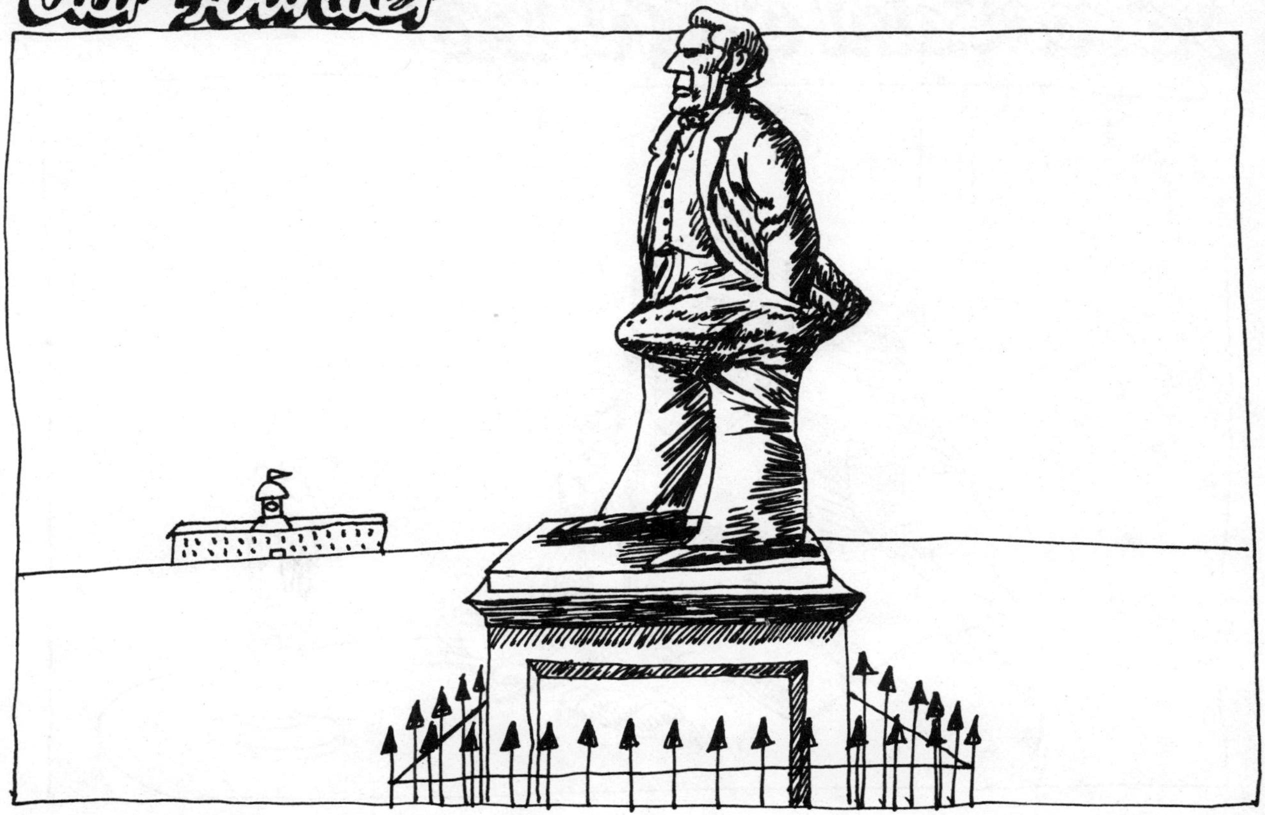

Patron Saint of Crullers

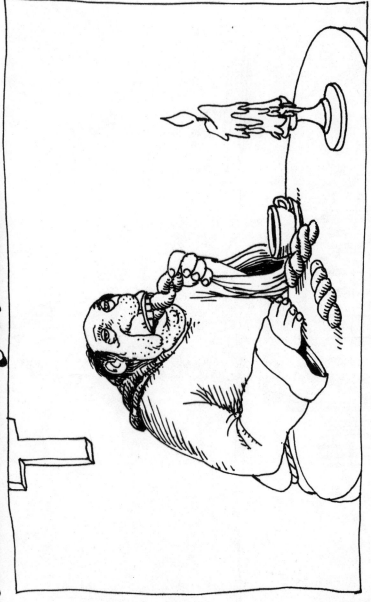

Deformed Car Salesmen

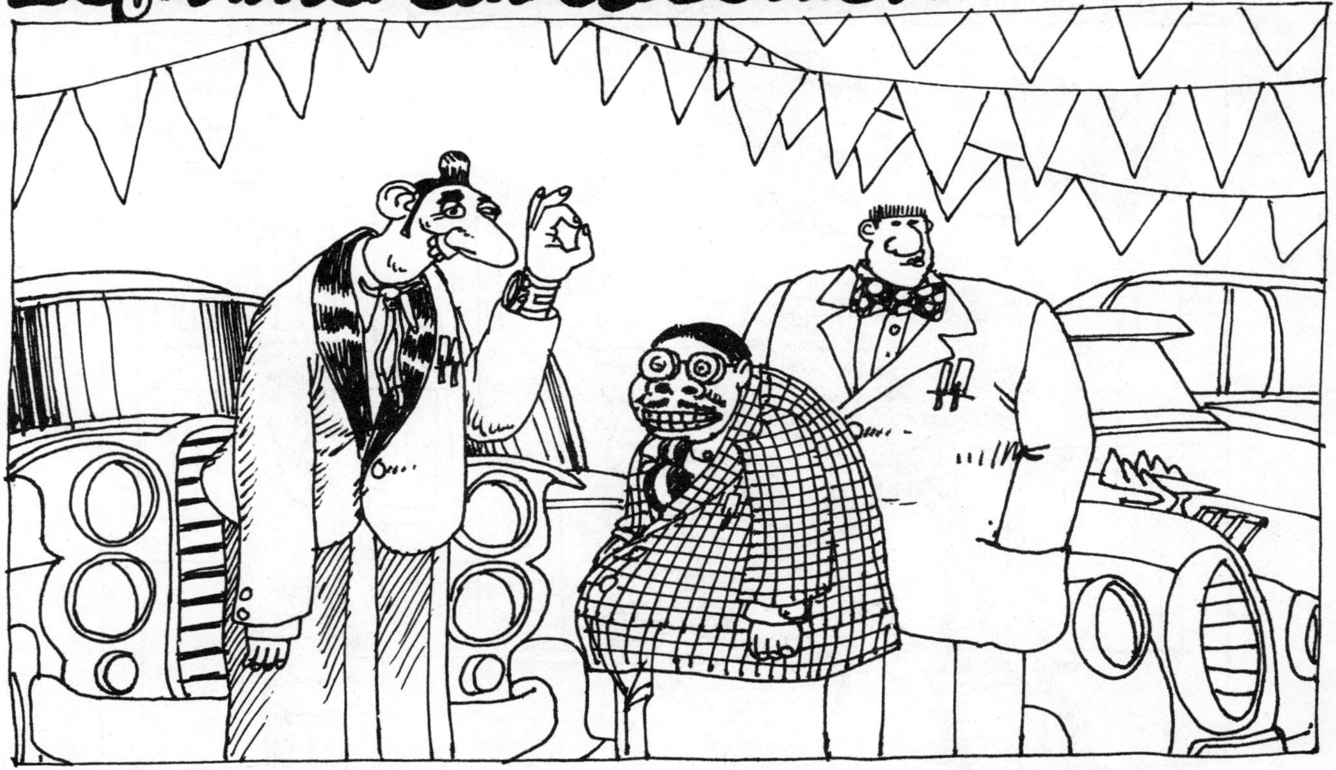

THE IMPROVED GAS TURBAN

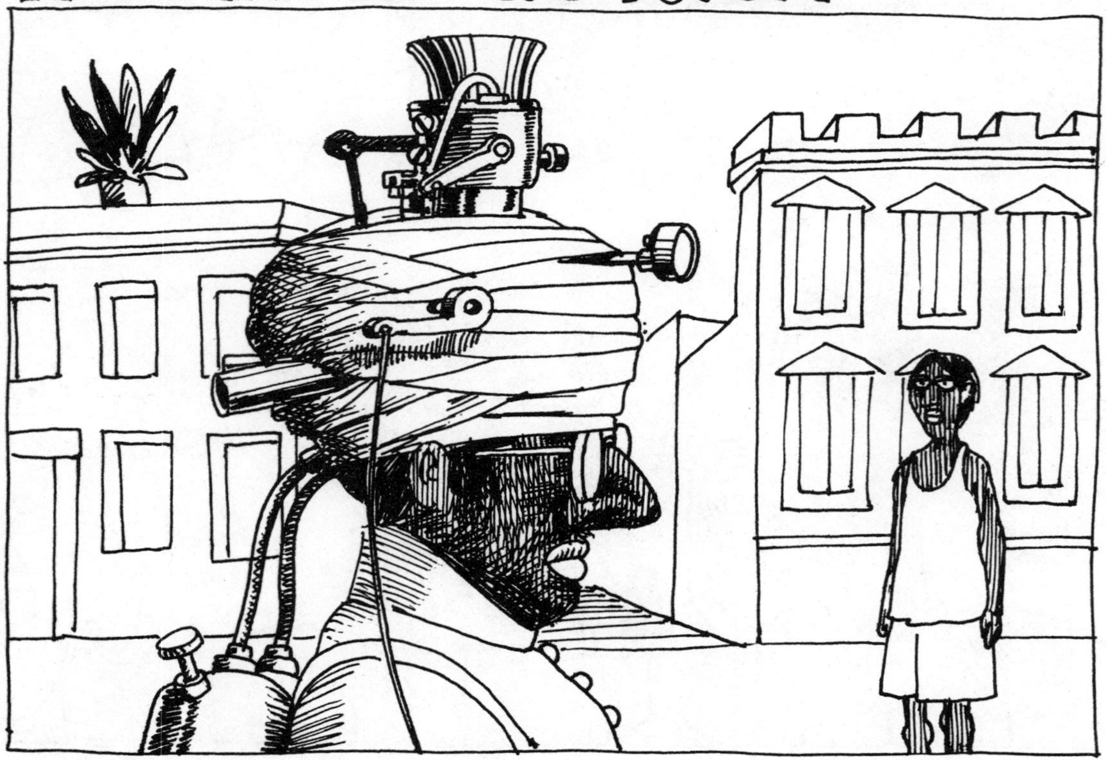

Wheedling on the Plains

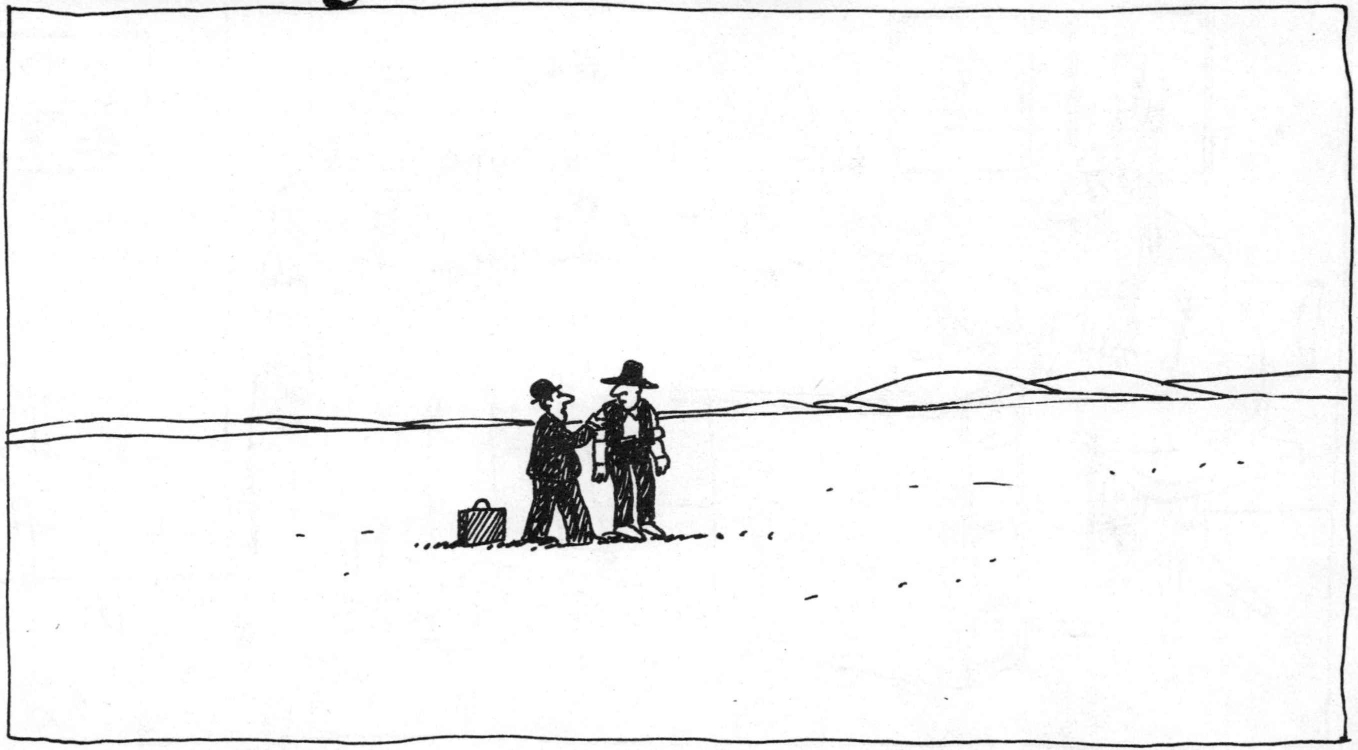

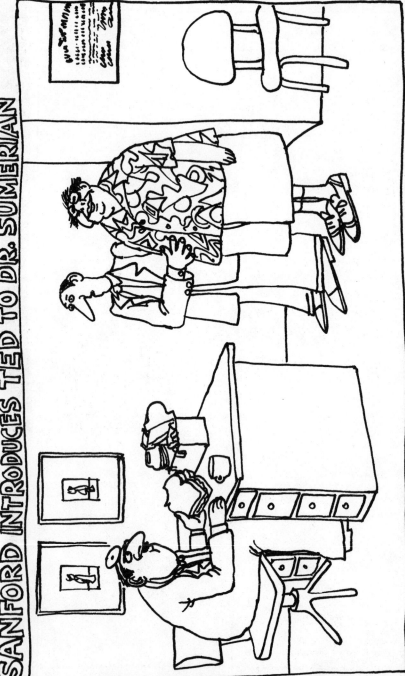

SANFORD INTRODUCES TED TO DR. SUMERIAN

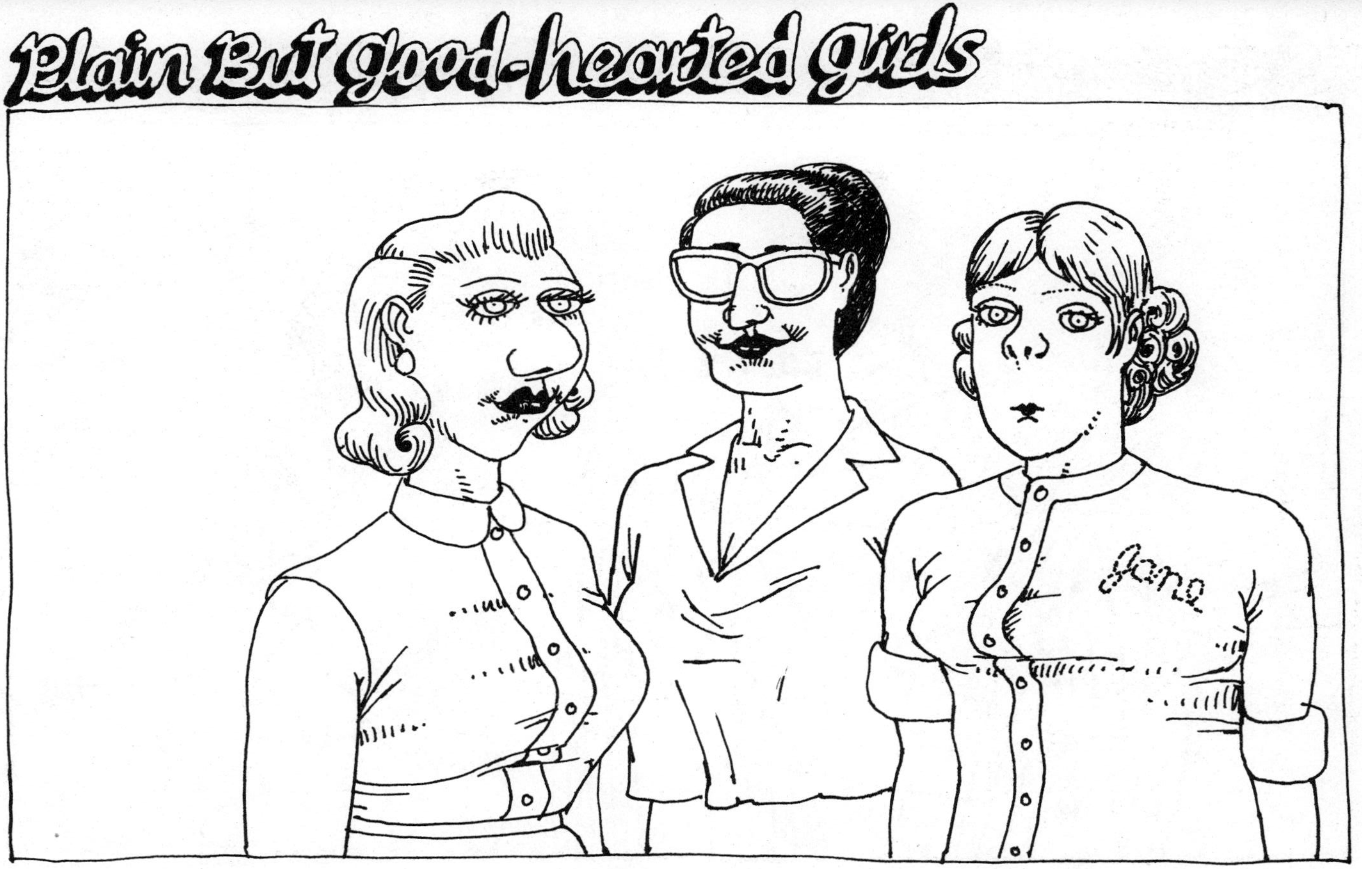
Plain But Good-hearted girls
Jane

Short on Brains, but a Terrific Dancer

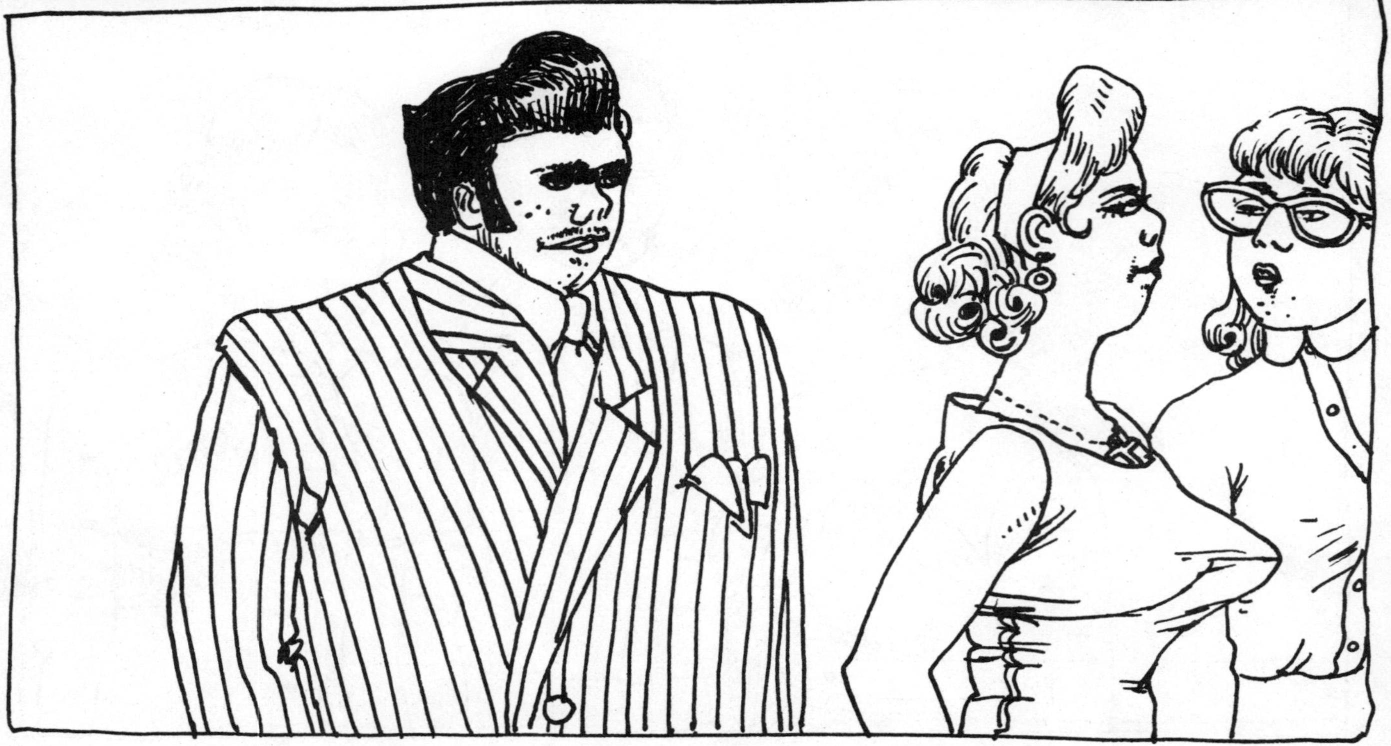

Keeping Bugs Away

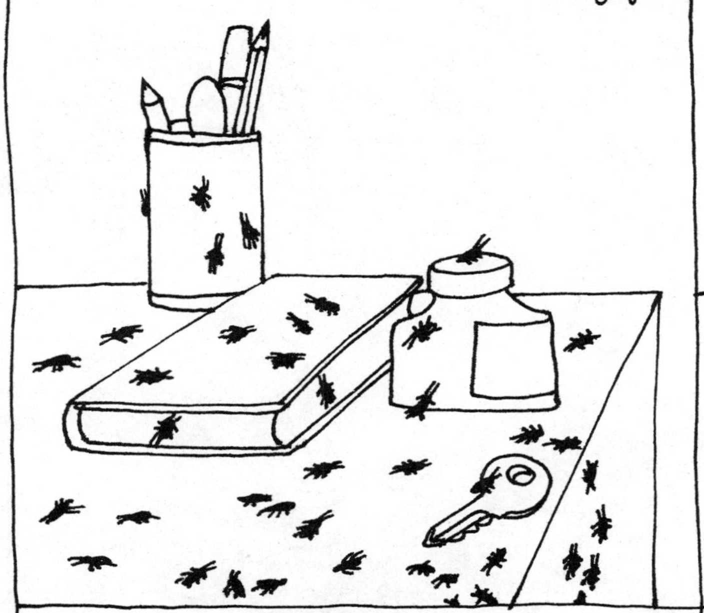
Fig. 1

BUGS

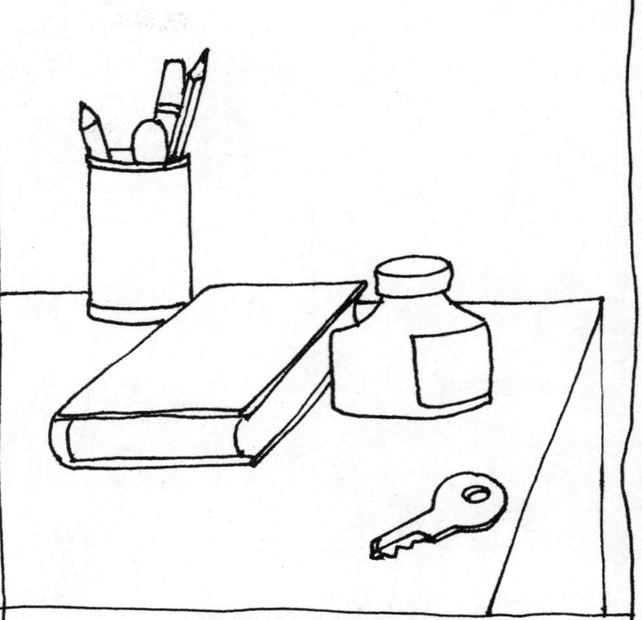
Fig. 2

BUGS KEPT AWAY

Bach

DUM, DUM, DUM,... DUM DE DE DE DE DE DE DUM.. DUM DE, DUM DE, DUM DUM DE DUM DE... DE DE DE DE...

Mozart

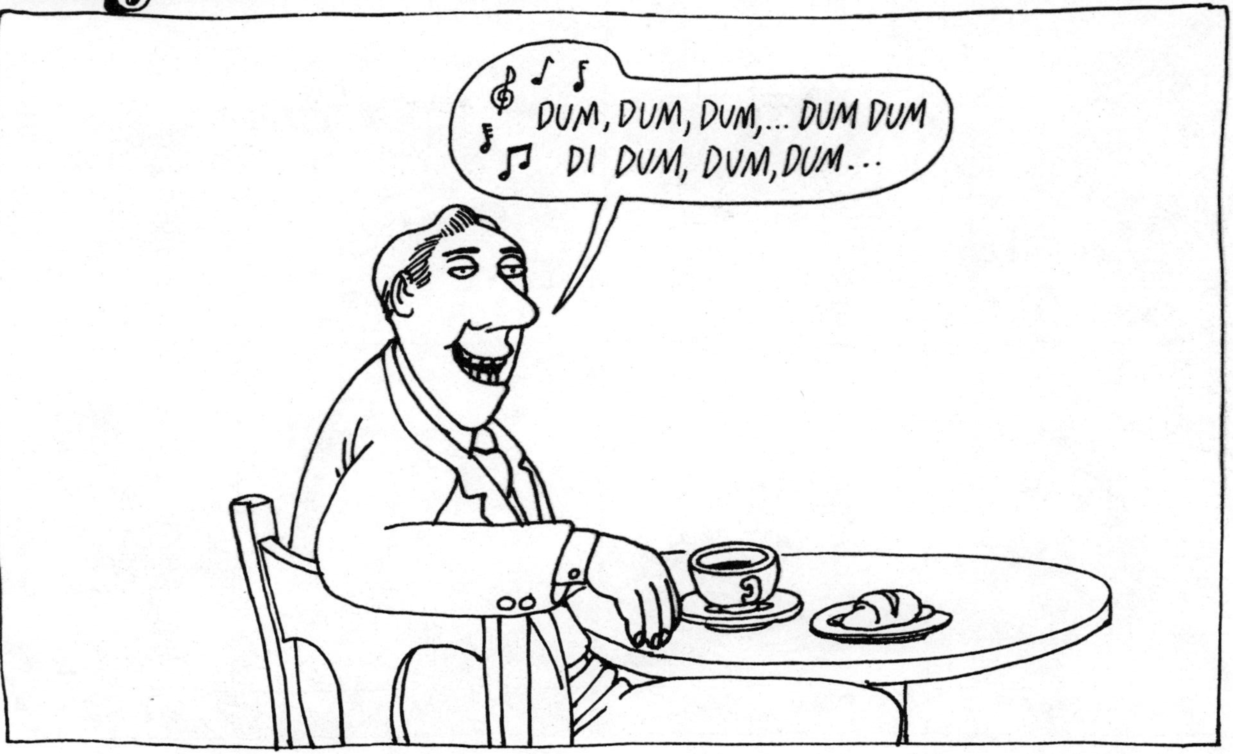
DUM, DUM, DUM,... DUM DUM
DI DUM, DUM, DUM...

Favorite Foods #38

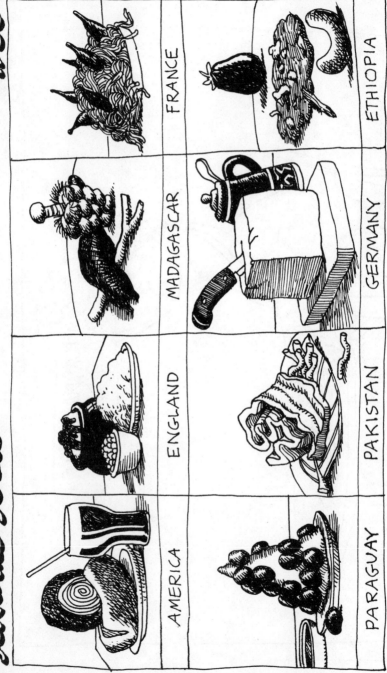

| AMERICA | ENGLAND | MADAGASCAR | FRANCE |
| PARAGUAY | PAKISTAN | GERMANY | ETHIOPIA |

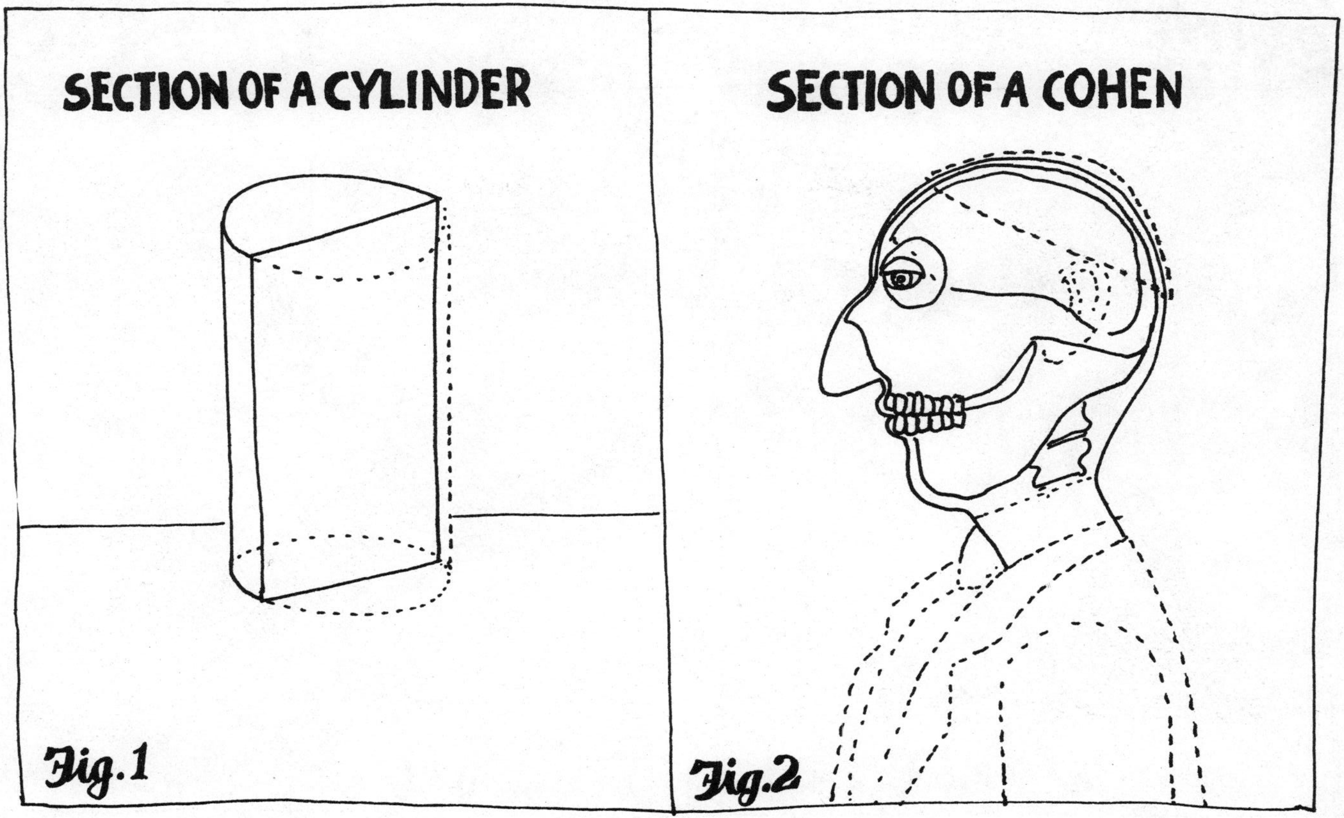
SECTION OF A CYLINDER
Fig. 1
SECTION OF A COHEN
Fig. 2

Fruit

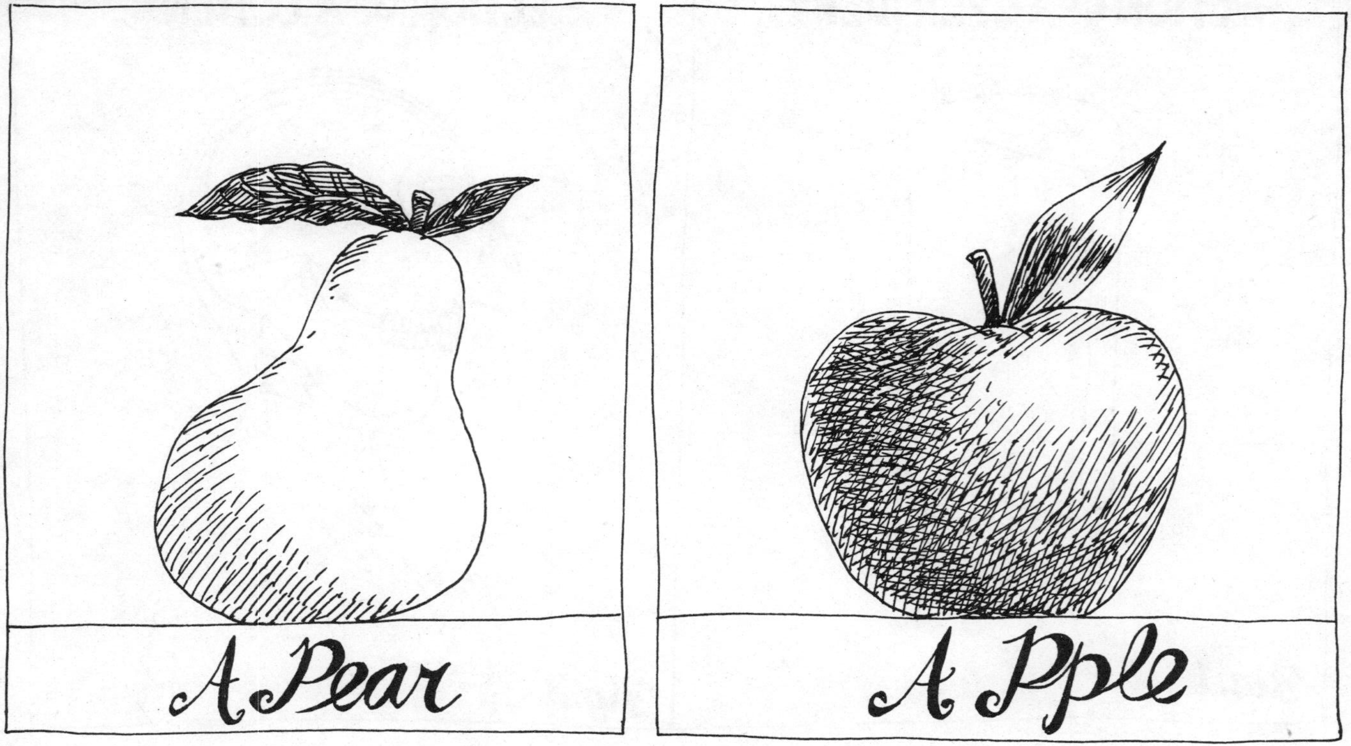
A Pear
A Pple

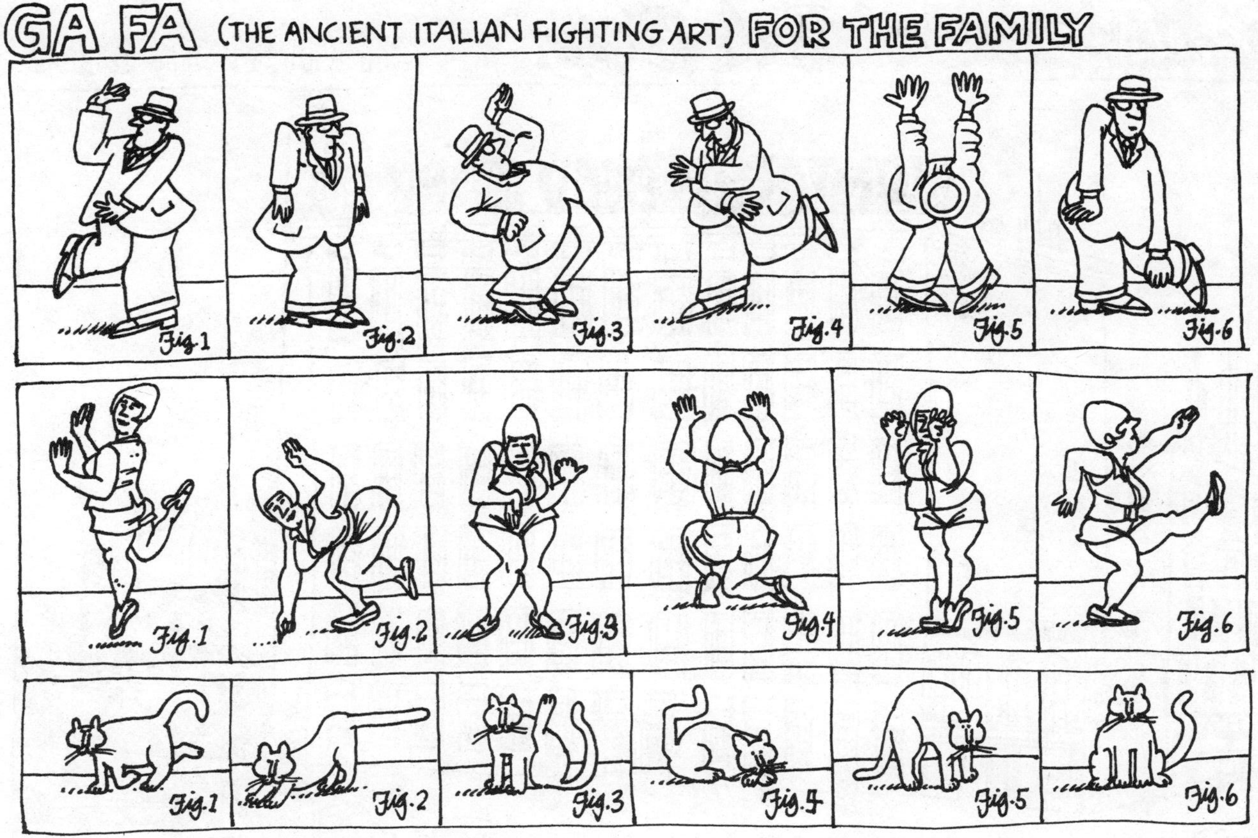
GA FA (THE ANCIENT ITALIAN FIGHTING ART) FOR THE FAMILY
Fig. 1
Fig. 2
Fig. 3
Fig. 4
Fig. 5
Fig. 6
Fig. 1
Fig. 2
Fig. 3
Fig. 4
Fig. 5
Fig. 6
Fig. 1
Fig. 2
Fig. 3
Fig. 4
Fig. 5
Fig. 6

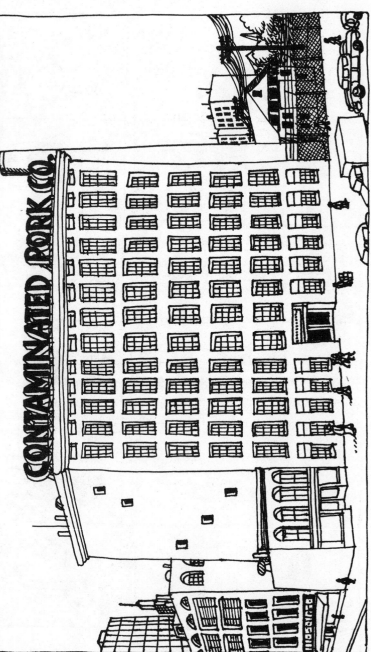
Contaminated Pork Bldg.   CINCINNATI, OHIO

CONTAMINATED PORK CO.

Stick Cleaning Simplified

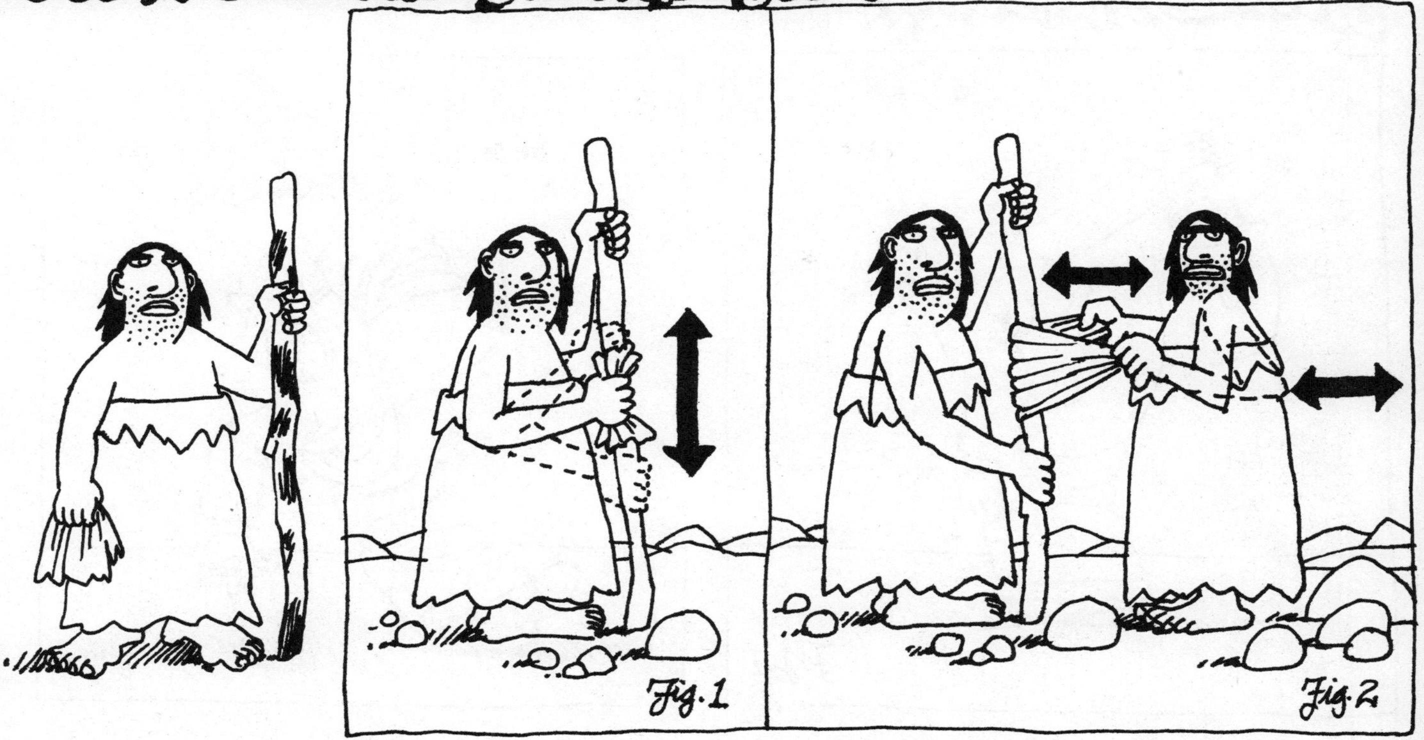

Fig. 1
Fig. 2

Futile Hurling

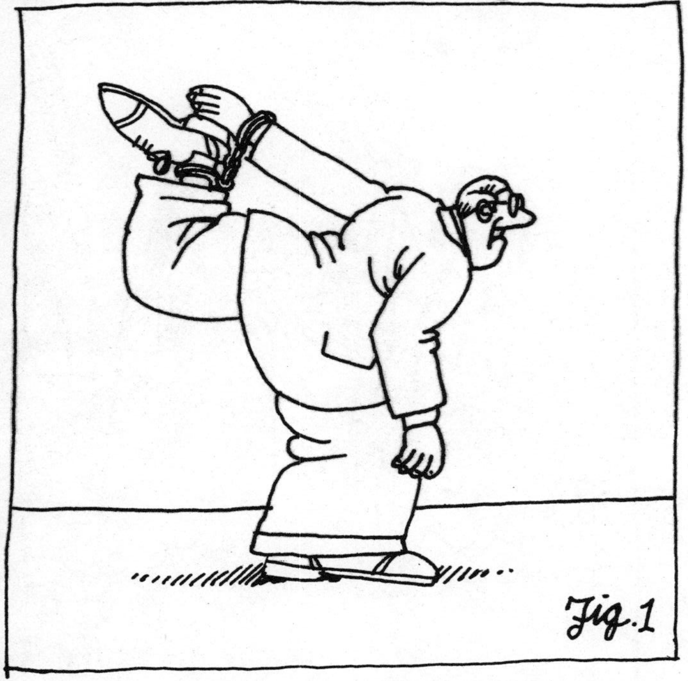

Fig. 1

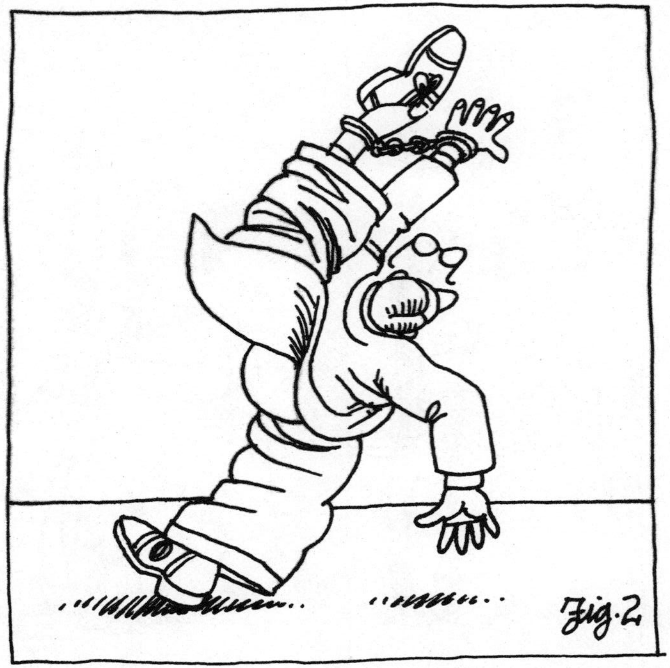

Fig. 2

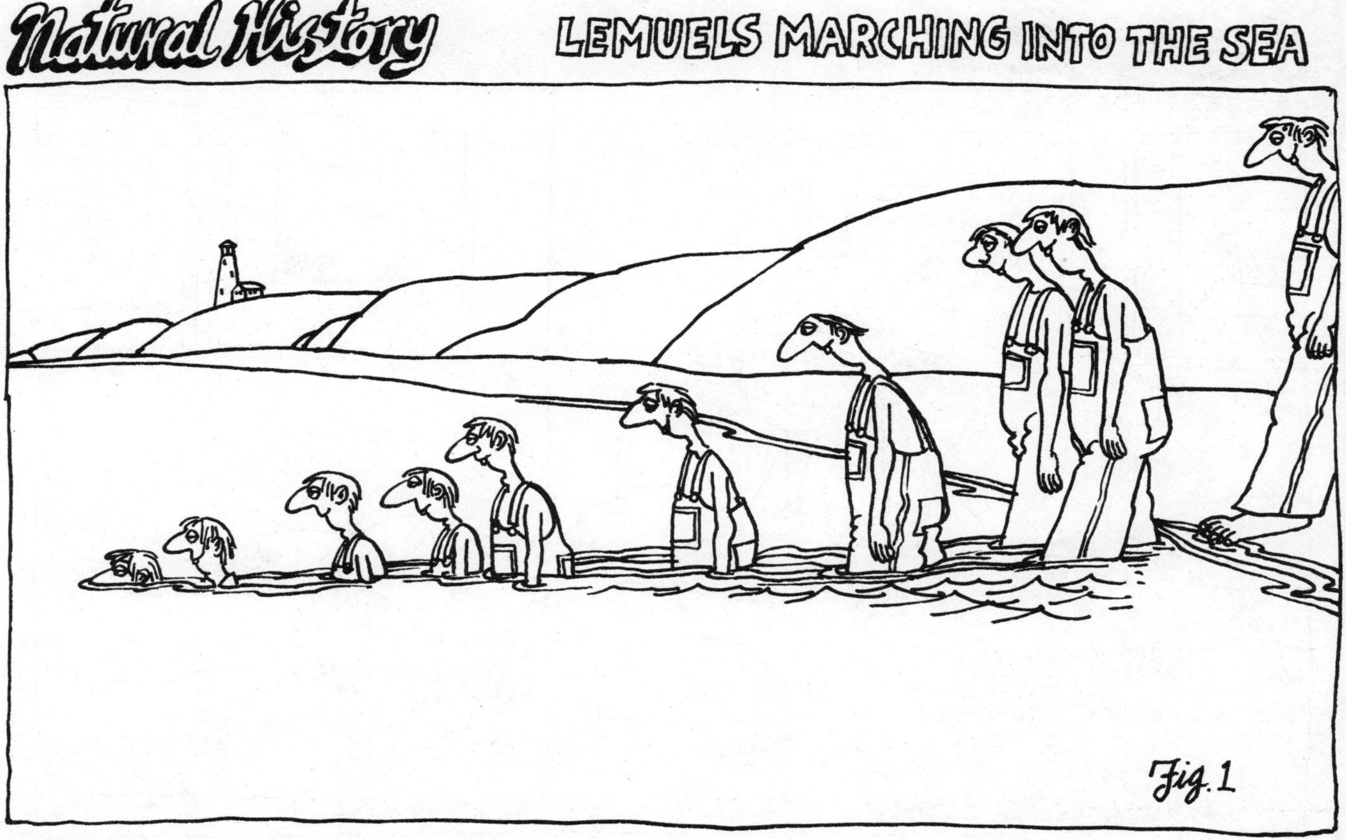
Natural History
LEMUELS MARCHING INTO THE SEA
Fig. 1

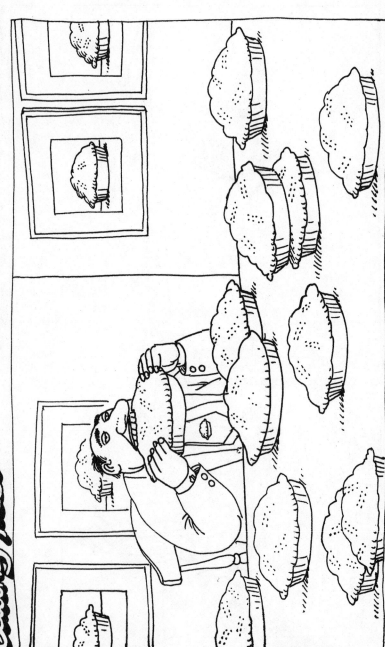

Eating Pies

Carl Meets His Match in Ramon

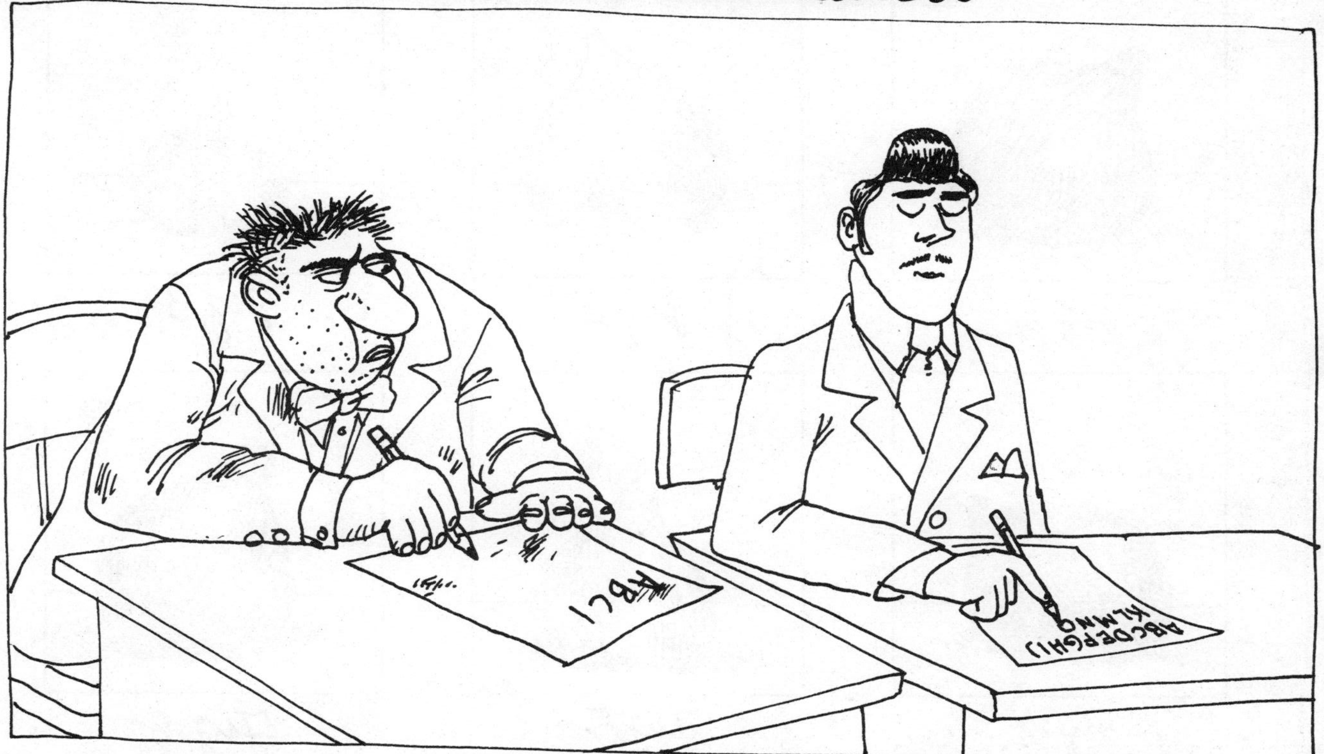
ABCDEFGHIJ
KLMNO

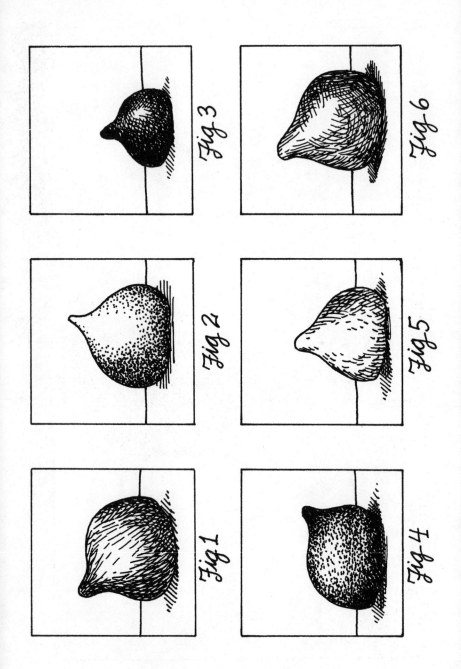

Fig 3

Fig 2

Fig 1

Fig 6

Fig 5

Fig 4

Psychology

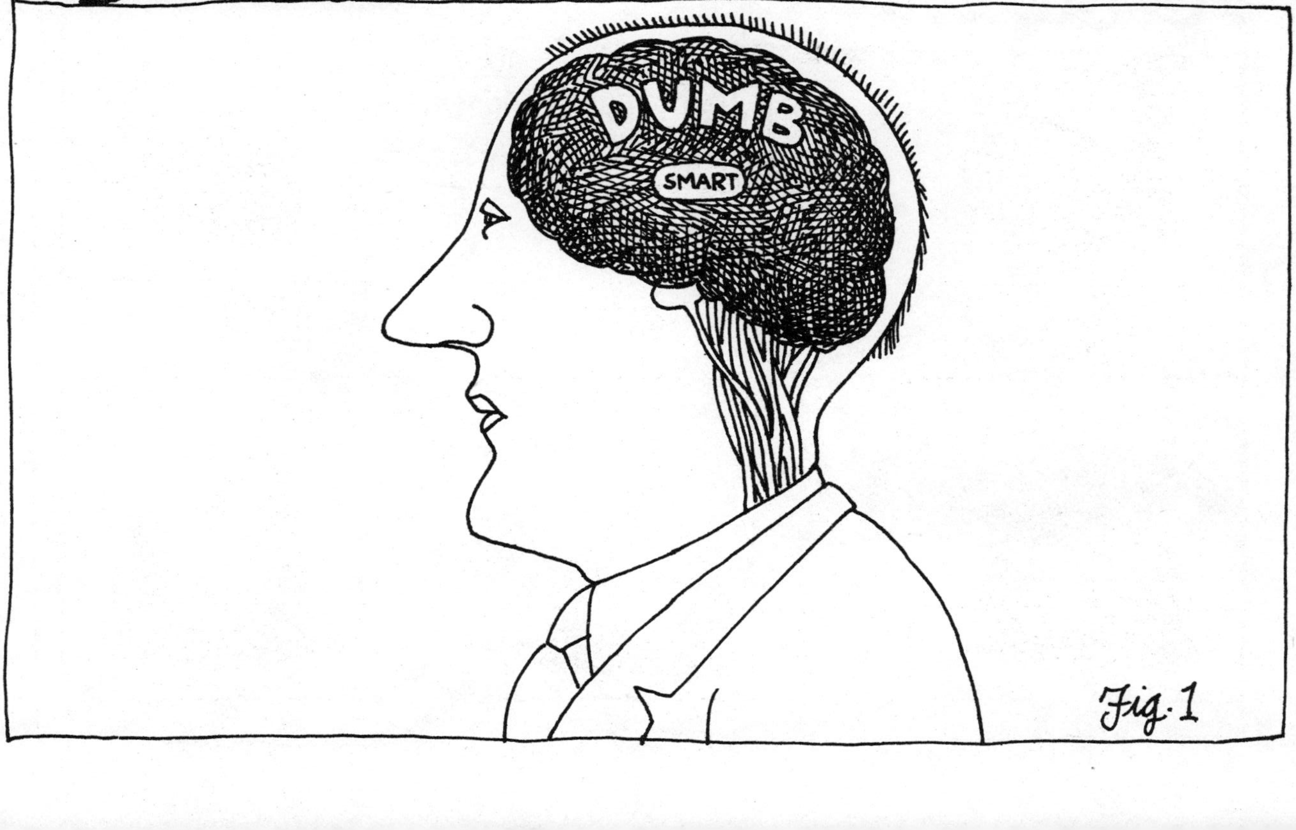
DUMB
SMART

Fig. 1

Porcupine Joke

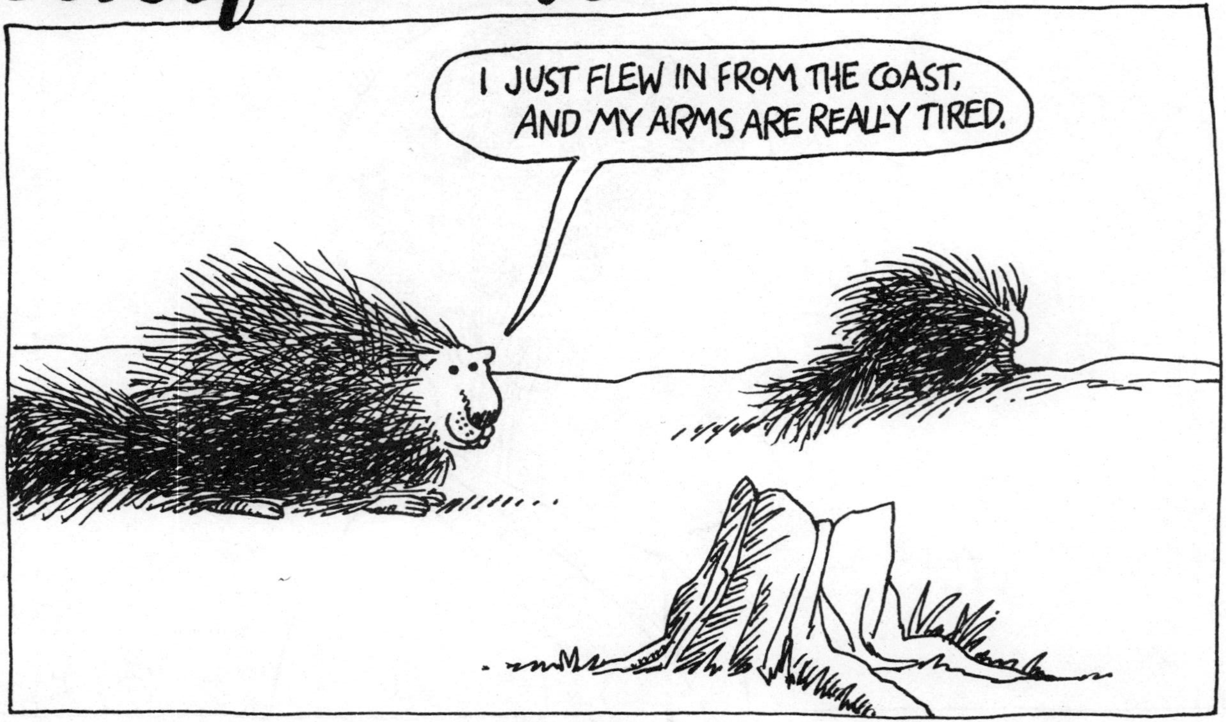
I JUST FLEW IN FROM THE COAST,
AND MY ARMS ARE REALLY TIRED.

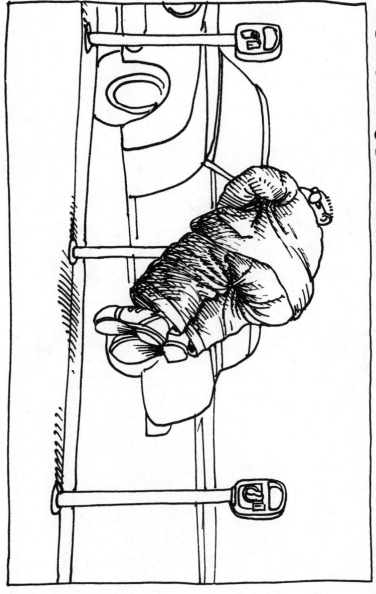

A Meter Violation

BIZARRE PRACTICES #83

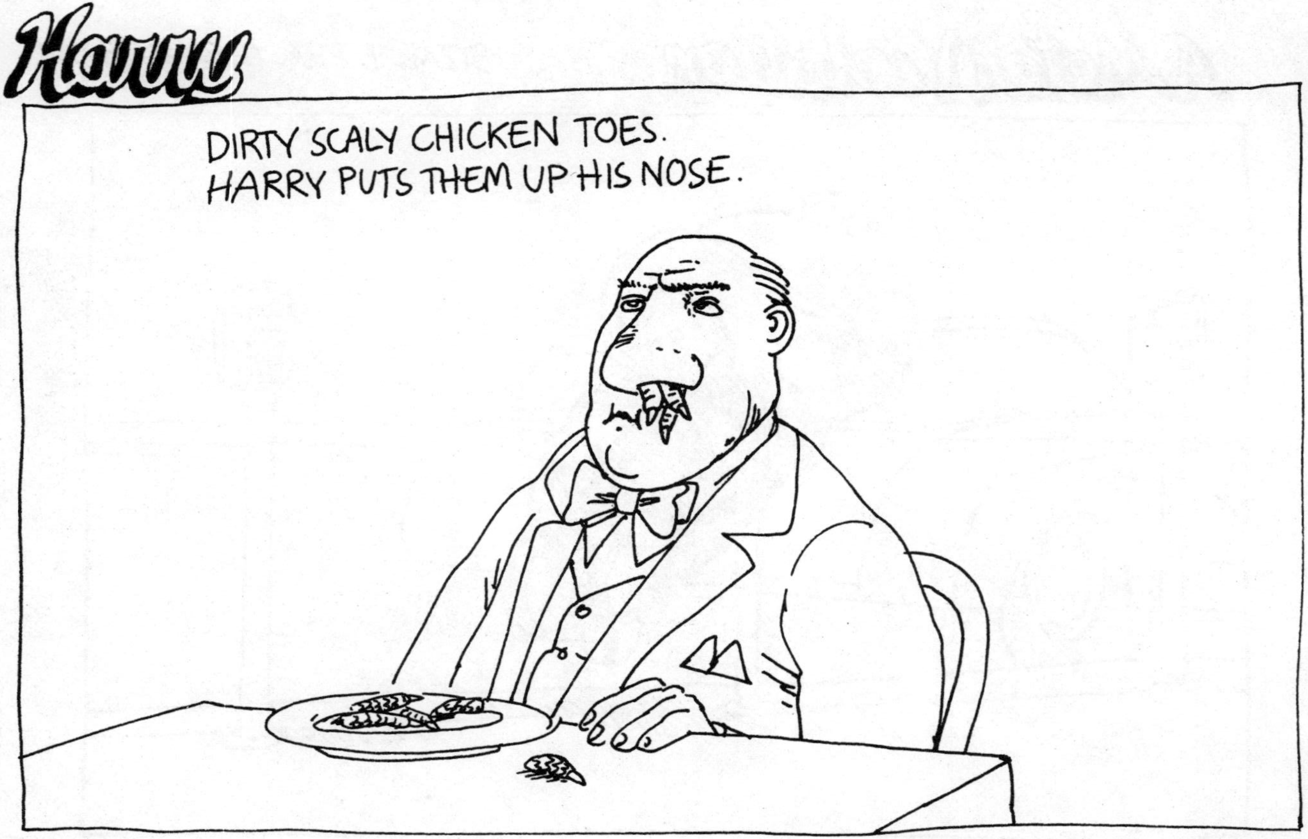
Harry
DIRTY SCALY CHICKEN TOES.
HARRY PUTS THEM UP HIS NOSE.

The Nixon Monument

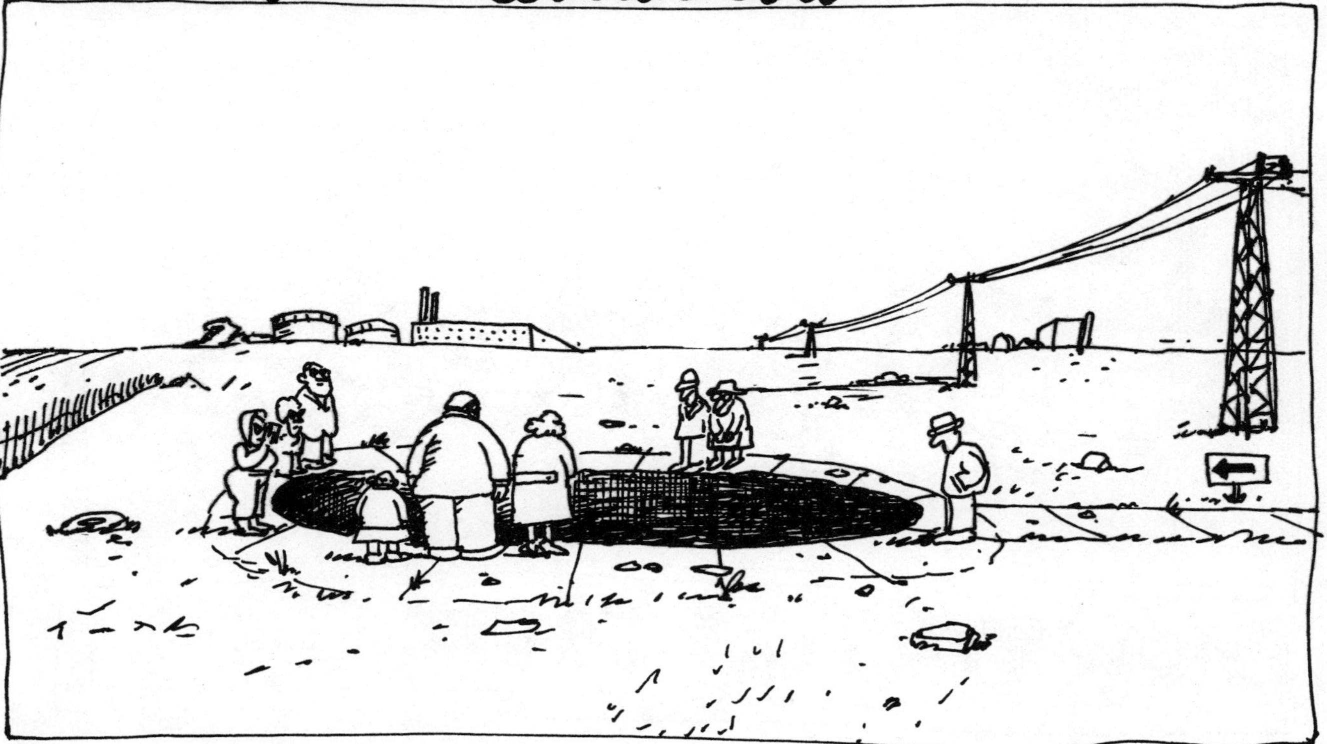

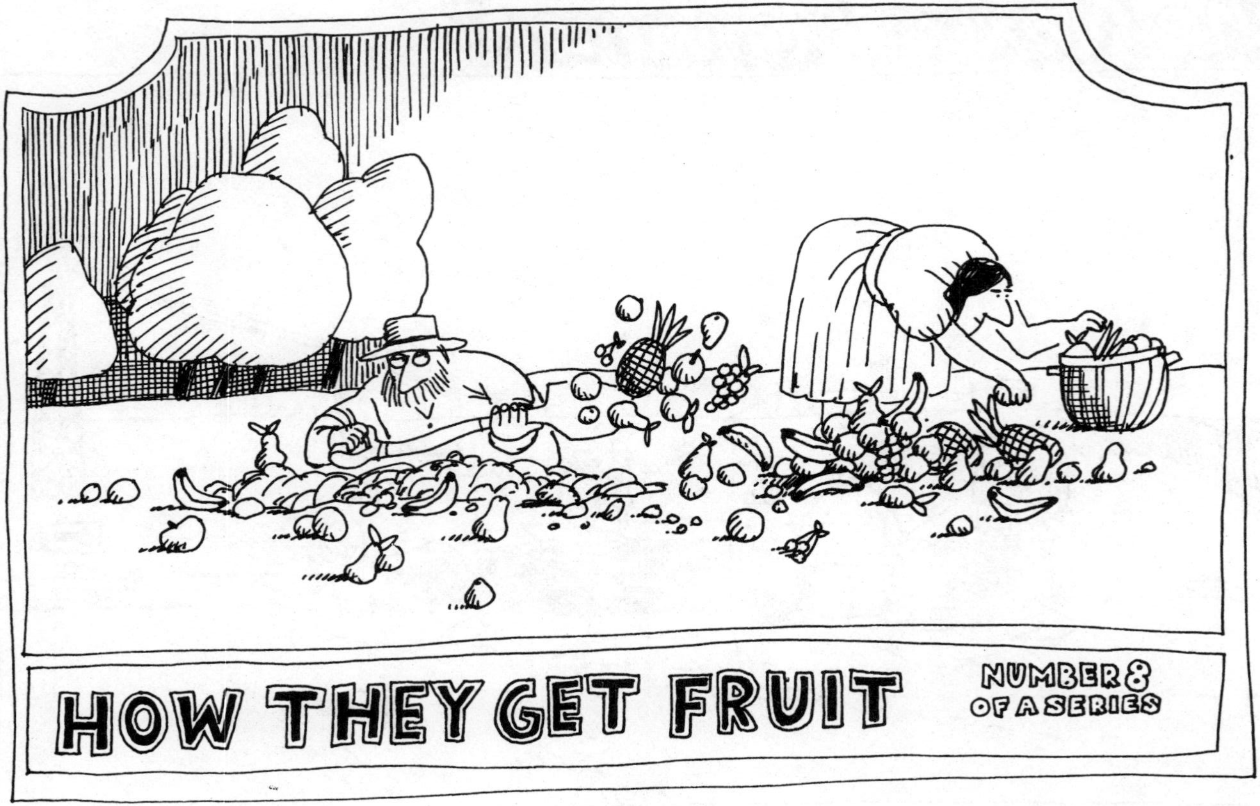
HOW THEY GET FRUIT
NUMBER 8
OF A SERIES

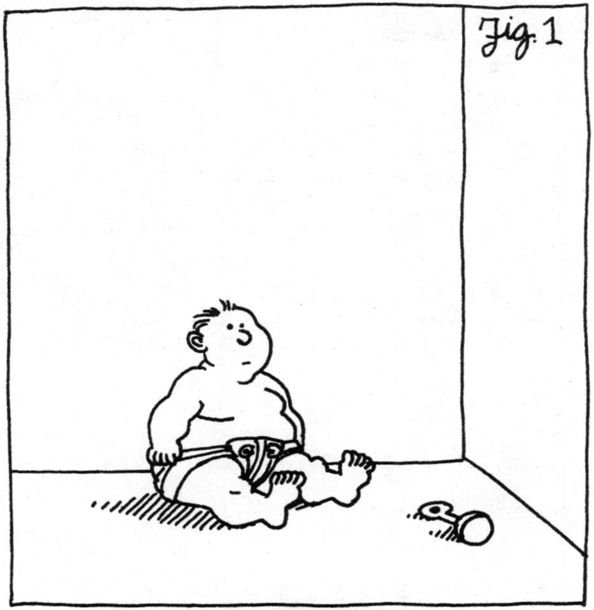
Fig. 1

BEFORE

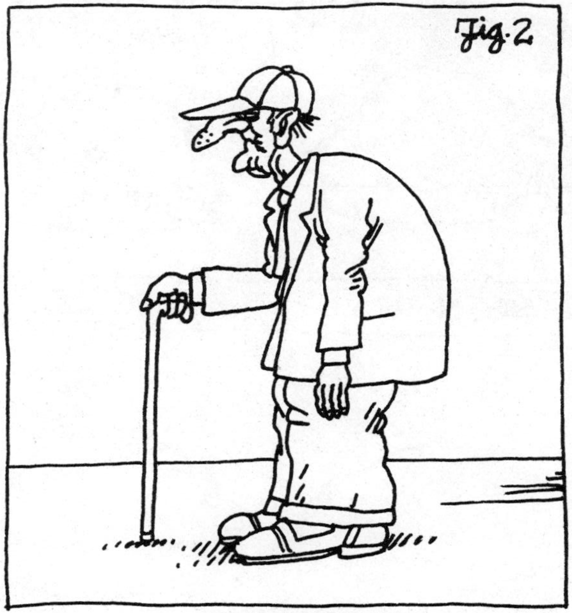
Fig. 2

AFTER

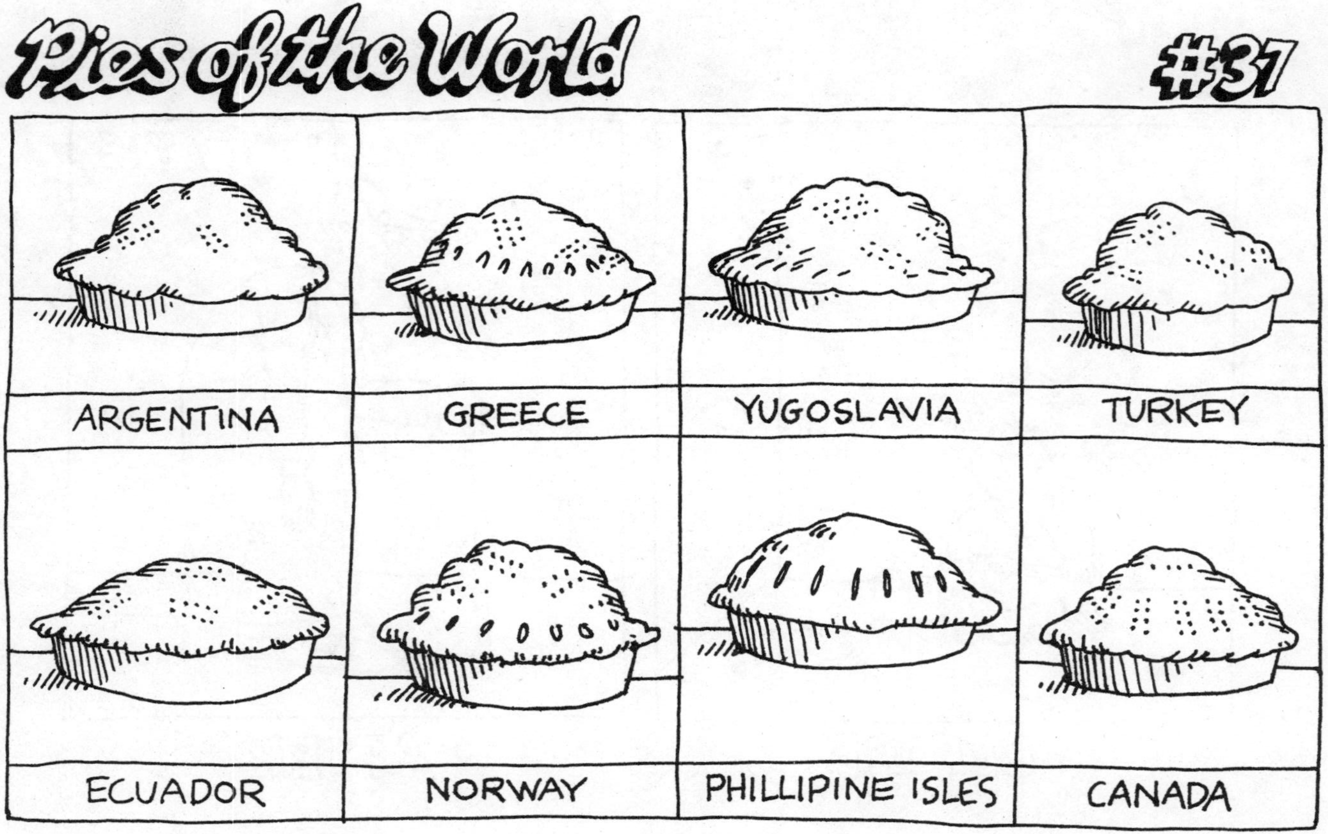
Pies of the World
#37
ARGENTINA
GREECE
YUGOSLAVIA
TURKEY
ECUADOR
NORWAY
PHILLIPINE ISLES
CANADA

god

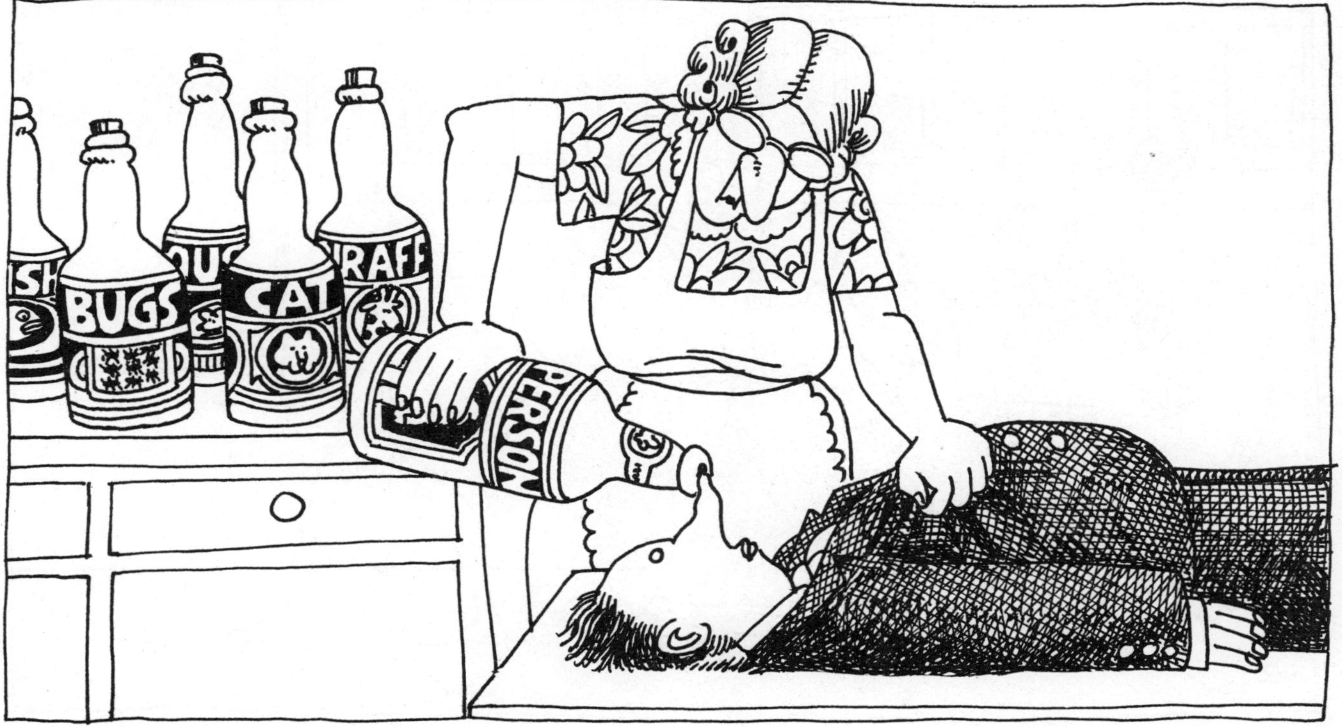
BUGS
CAT
PERSON

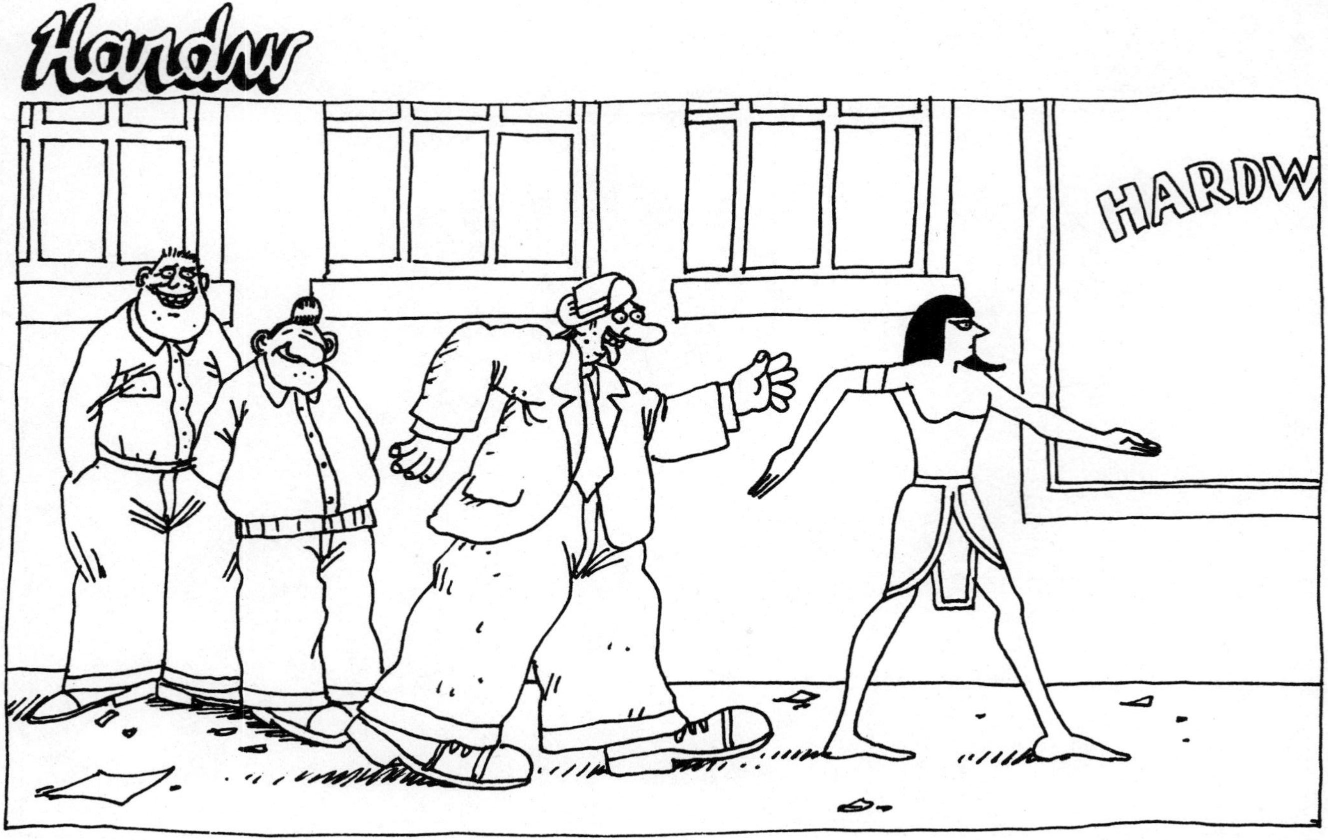
Hardw
HARDW

Wiggly Man

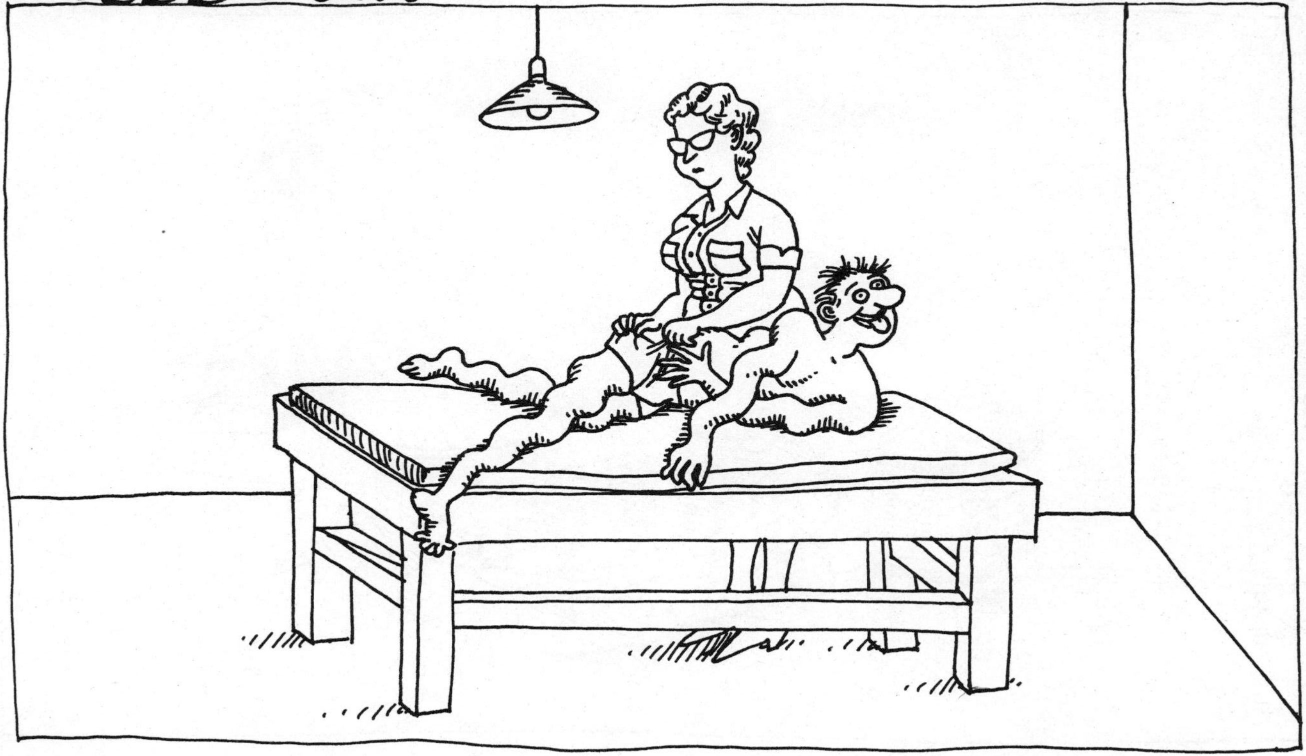

The Original Venison Receiver

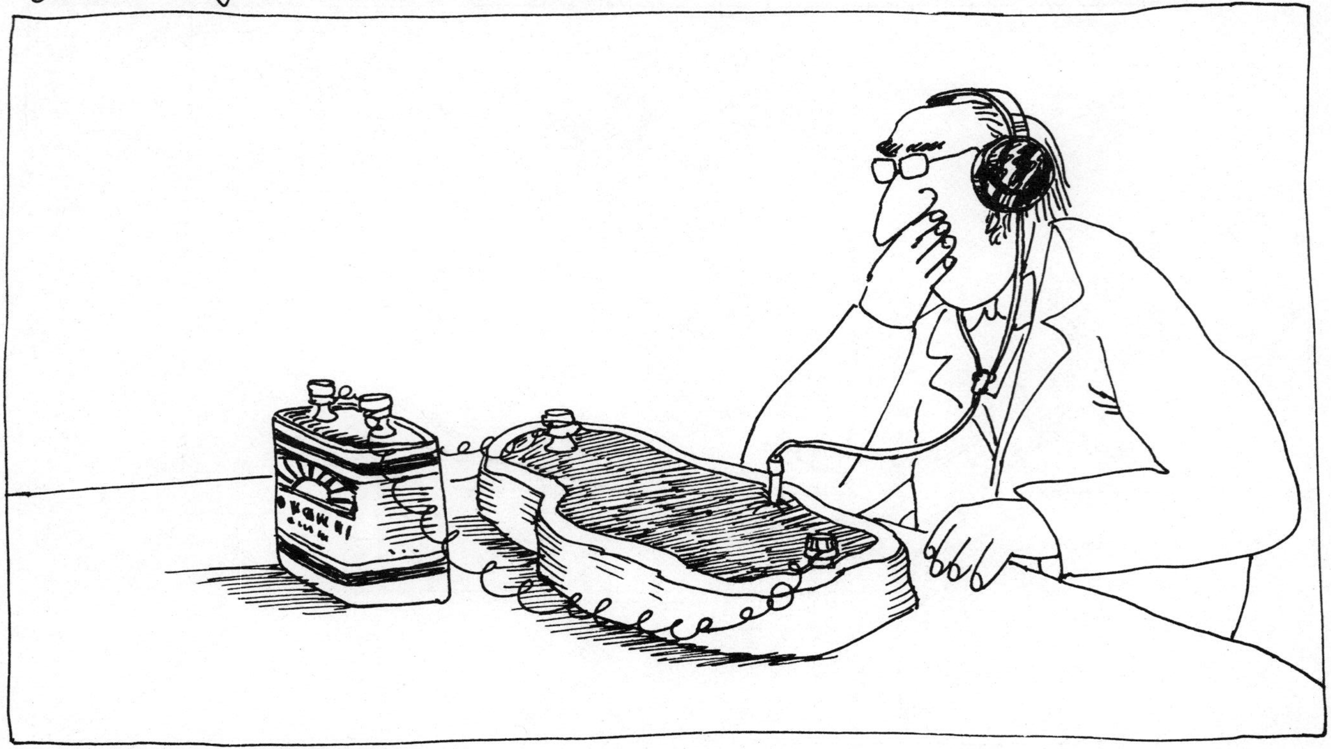

T.S., Eliot

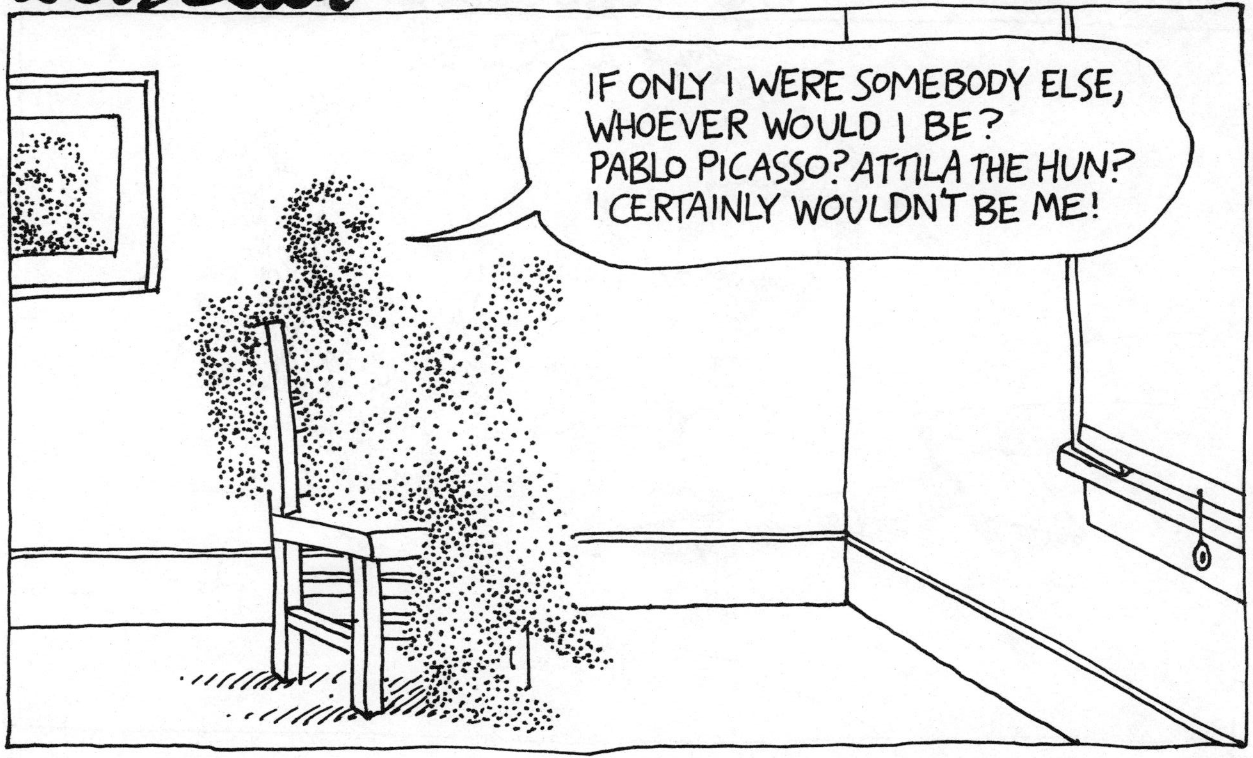
IF ONLY I WERE SOMEBODY ELSE,
WHOEVER WOULD I BE?
PABLO PICASSO? ATTILA THE HUN?
I CERTAINLY WOULDN'T BE ME!

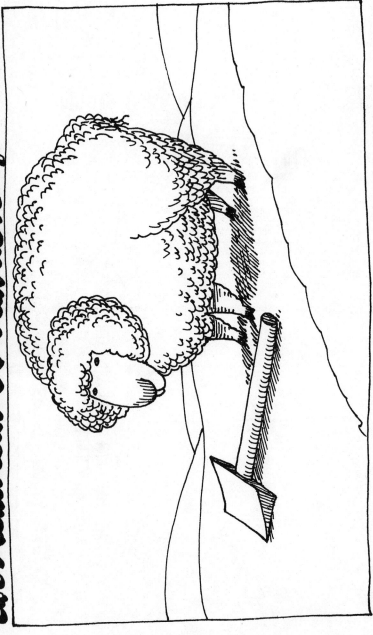

Un-Natural Ax with a Sheep

Flesh Bulbs

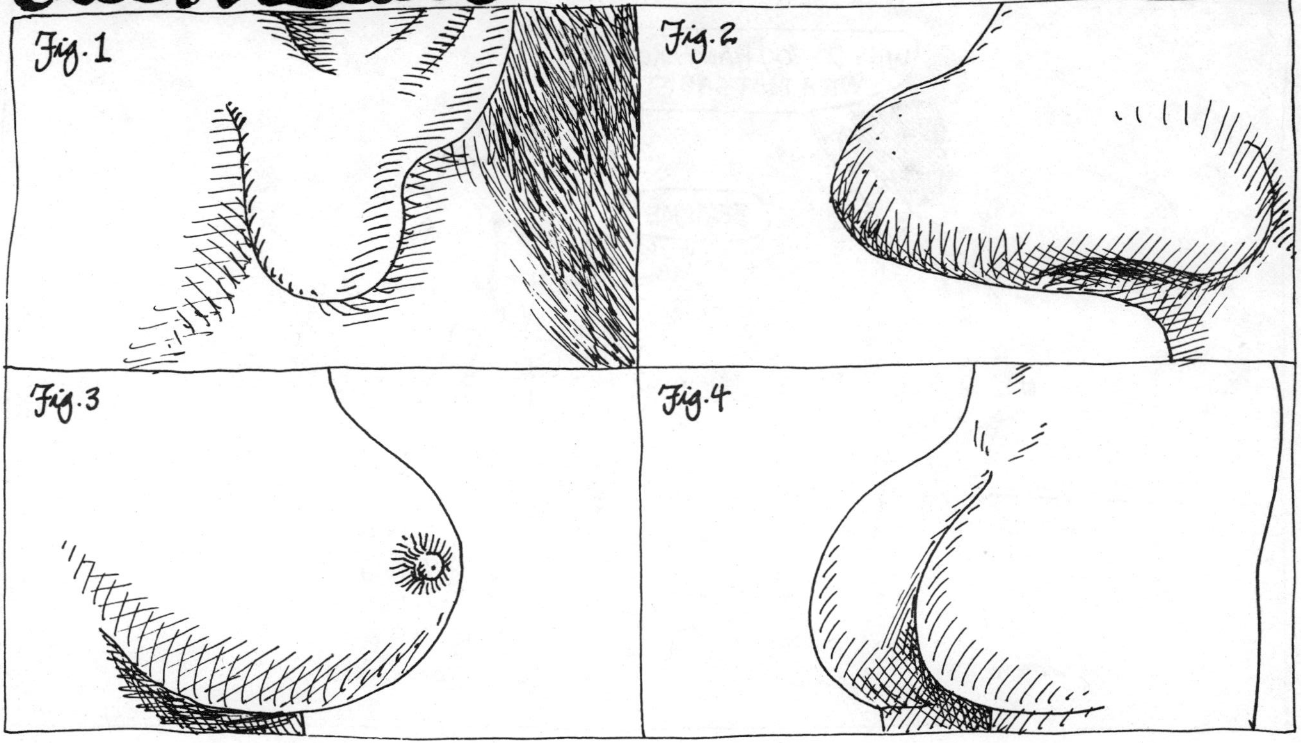
Fig. 1
Fig. 2
Fig. 3
Fig. 4

Q.&A.

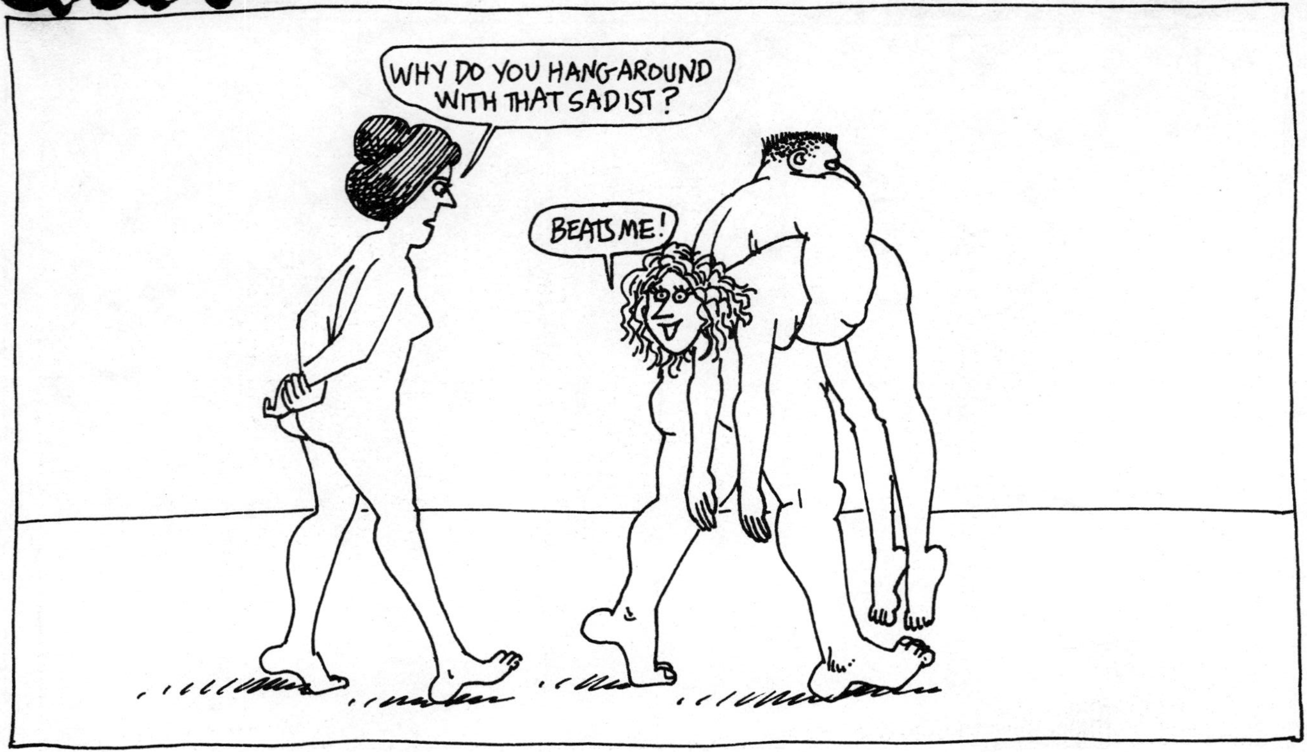
WHY DO YOU HANG-AROUND WITH THAT SADIST?
BEATS ME!

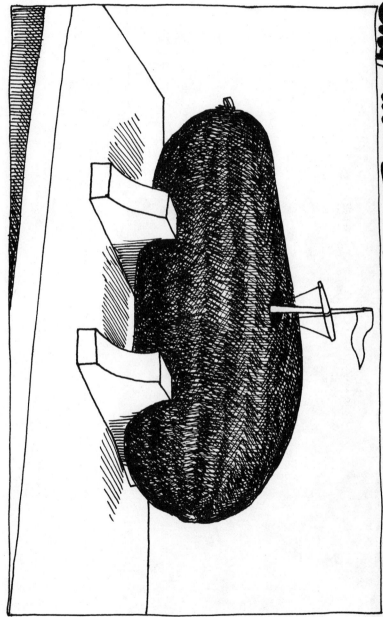

Ship in a Zucchini

PALERMO, SICILY

Humorous Drawing

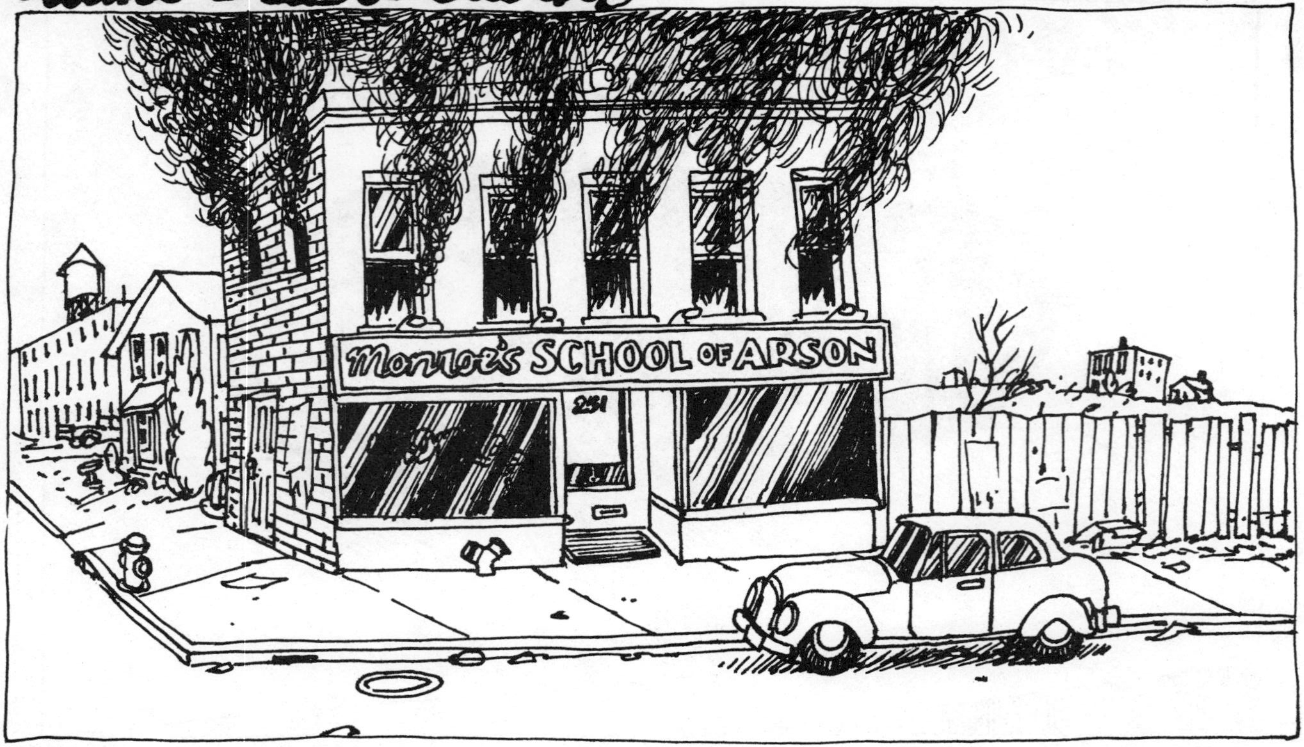

Monroe's SCHOOL OF ARSON
2131

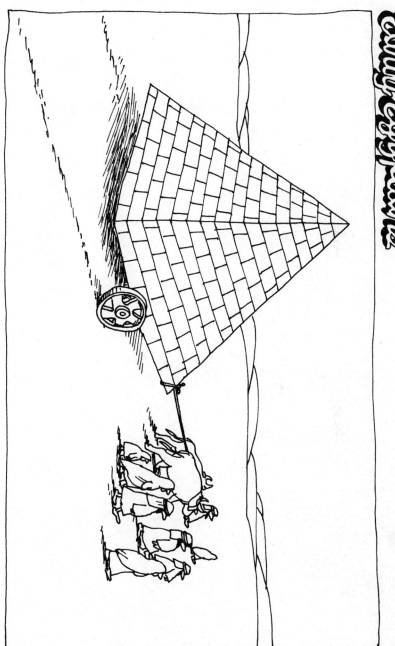

Early Egyptians

FOUR USELESS MOTIONS

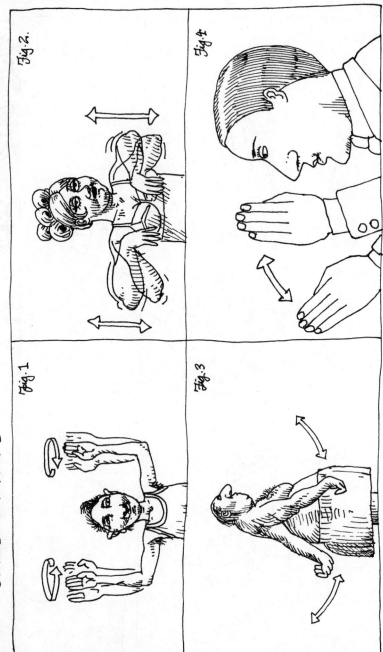

Fig. 1.   Fig. 2.

Fig. 3.   Fig. 4.

The Venetian Deaf

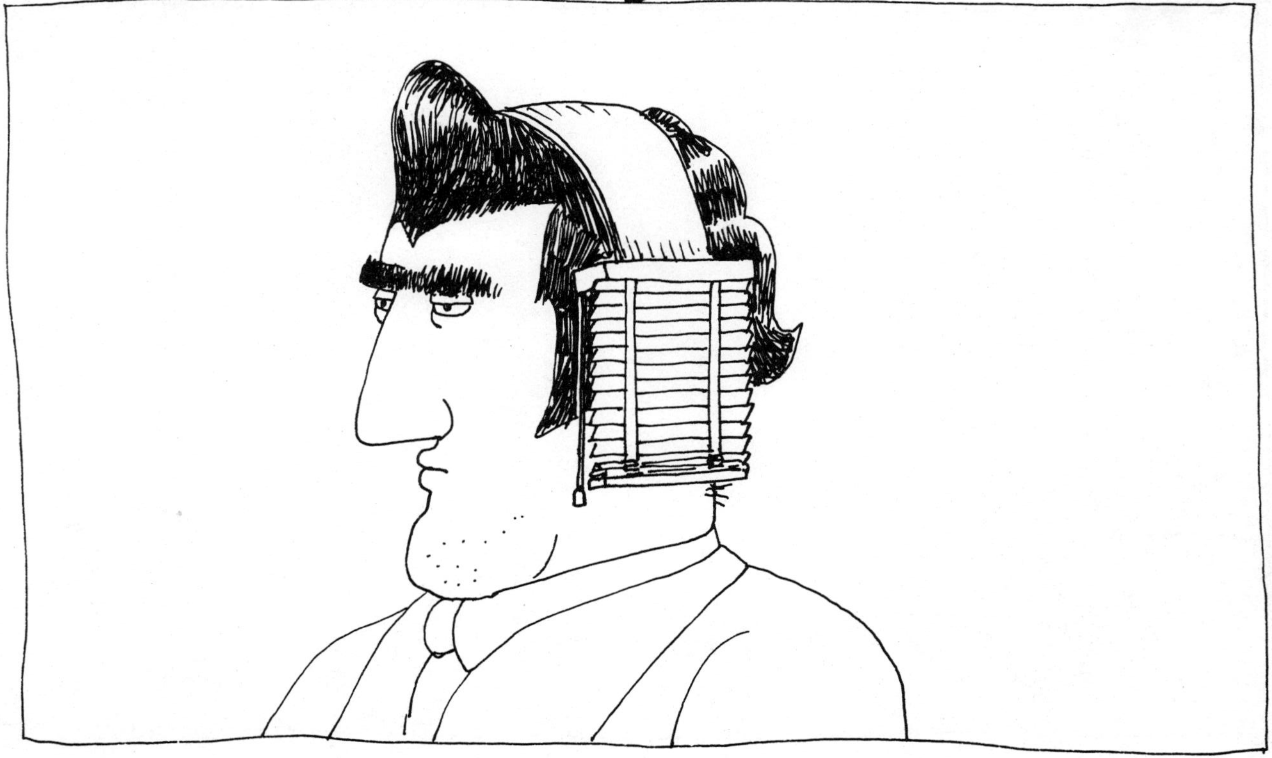

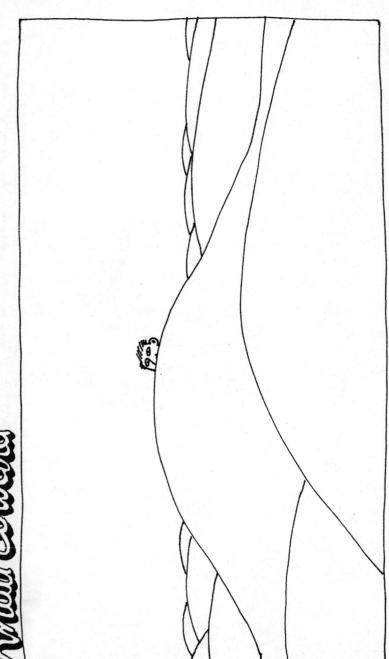

Knoll Coward

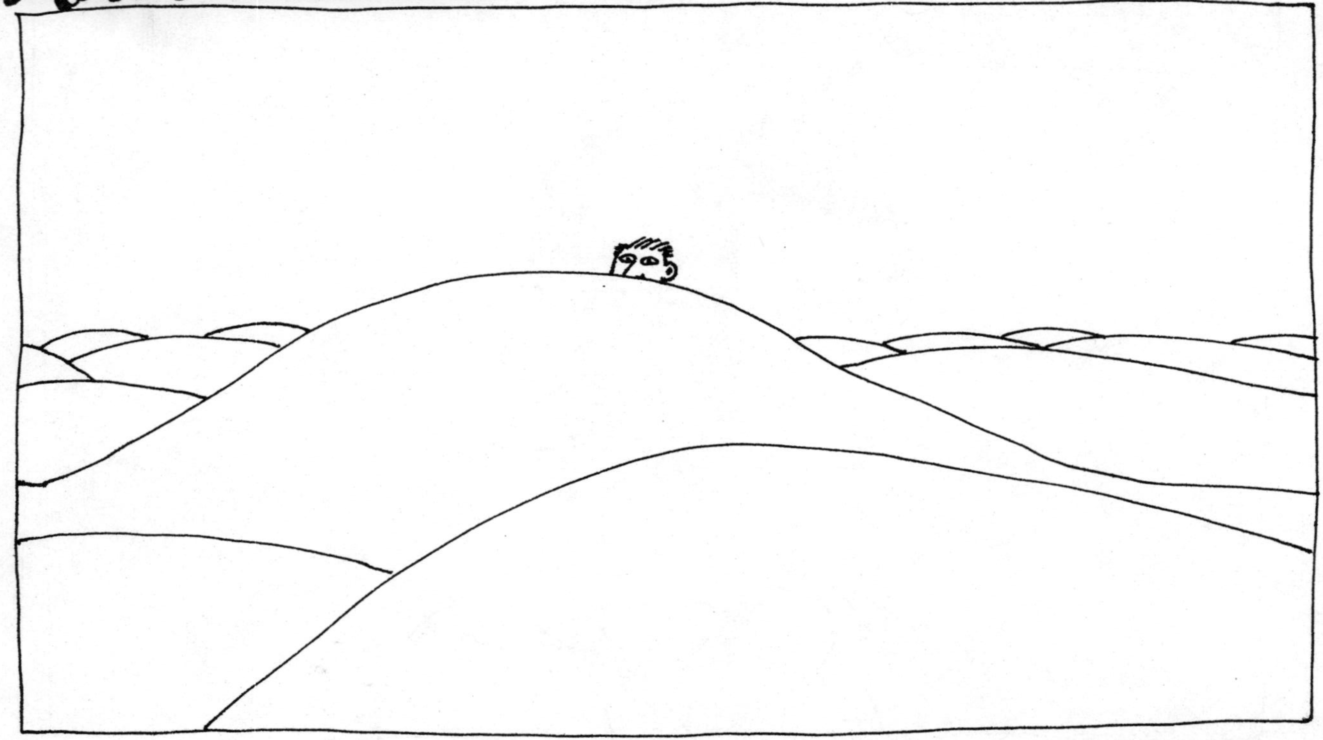

Bad Pun disturbing a Rhyme

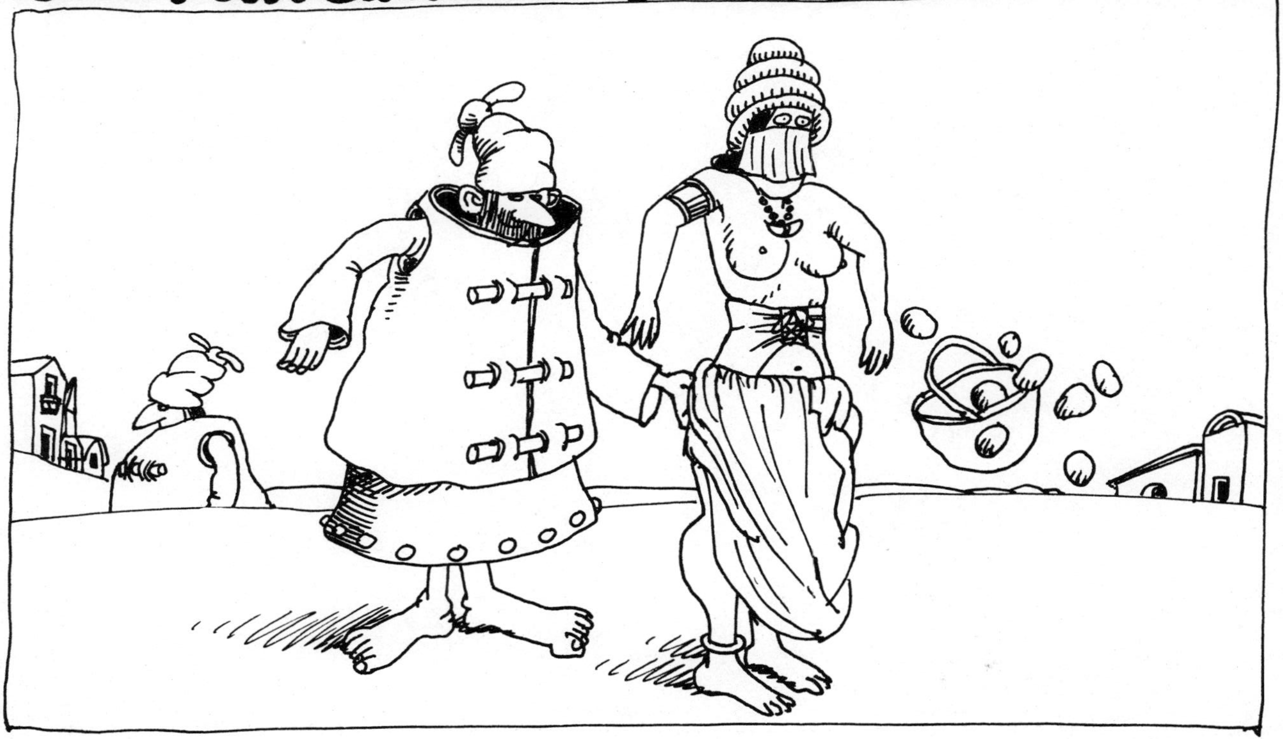

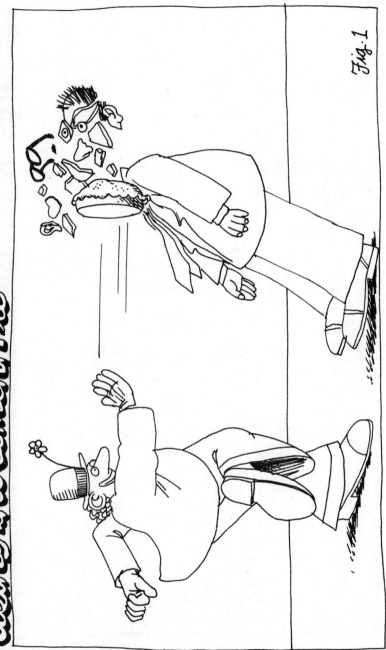

Using the Cement Pie

Fig. 1

Genghis & Sylvia Khan

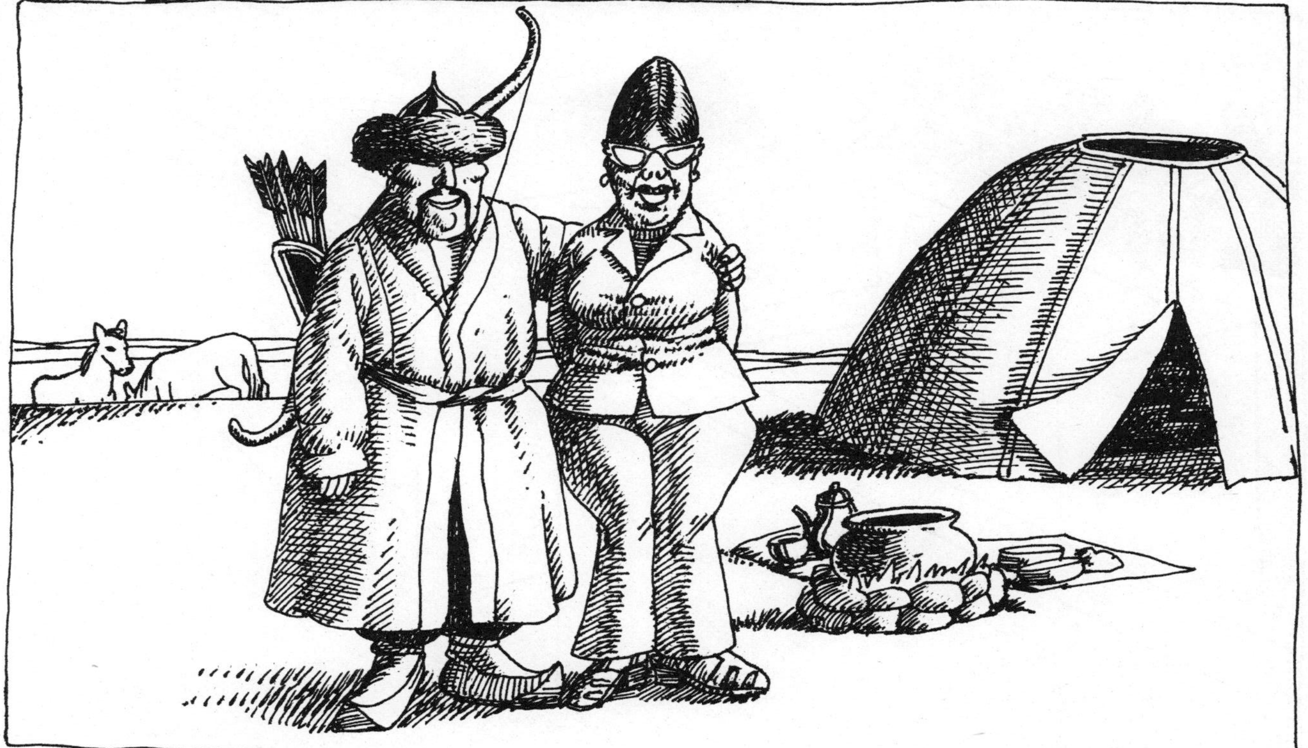

Simple Maze

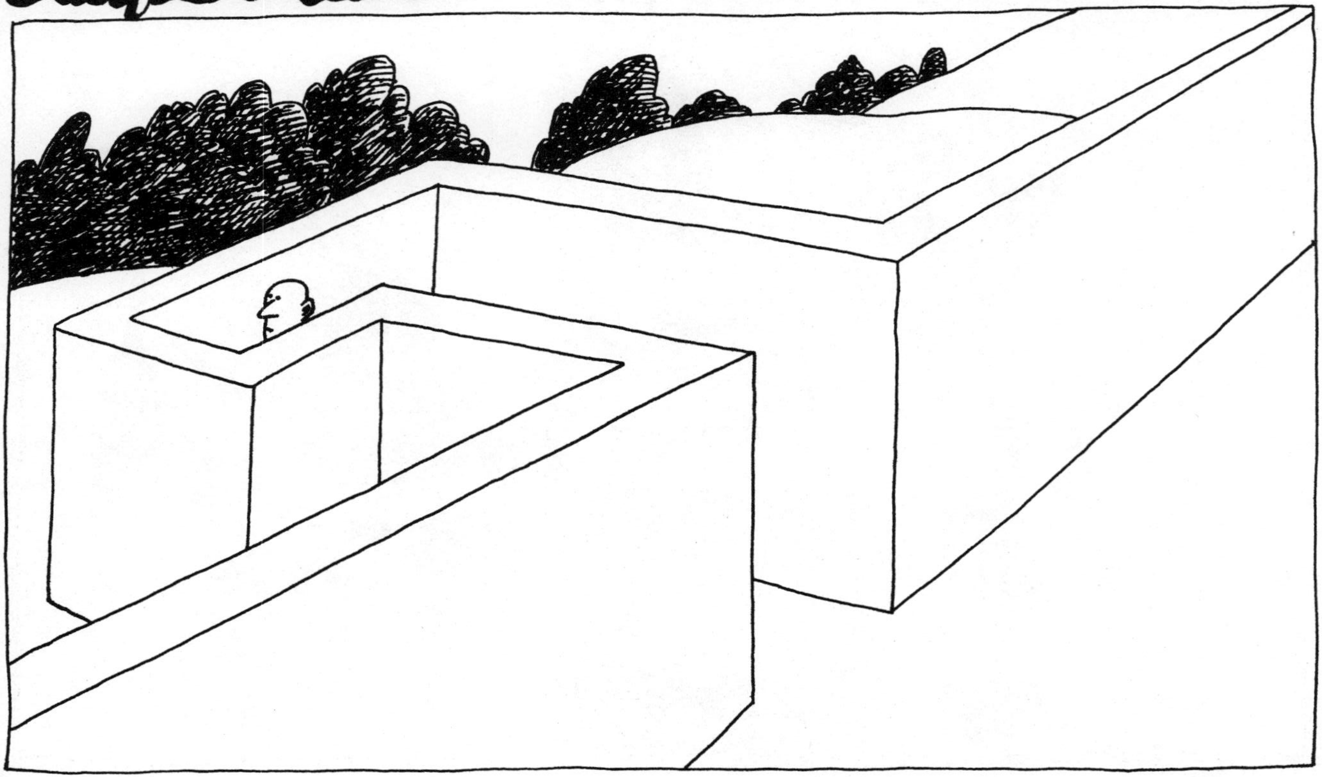

Chapter VII

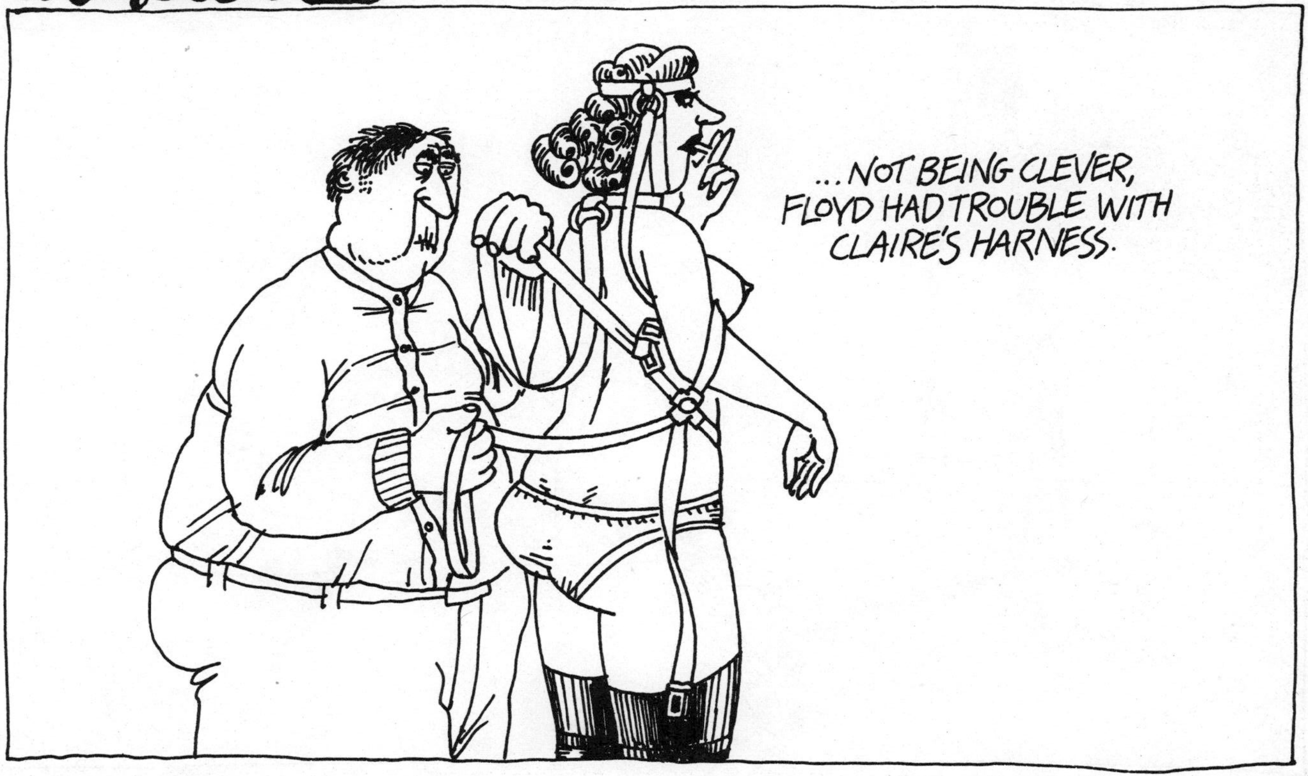
...NOT BEING CLEVER, FLOYD HAD TROUBLE WITH CLAIRE'S HARNESS.

ORTHOPEDIC SHOES

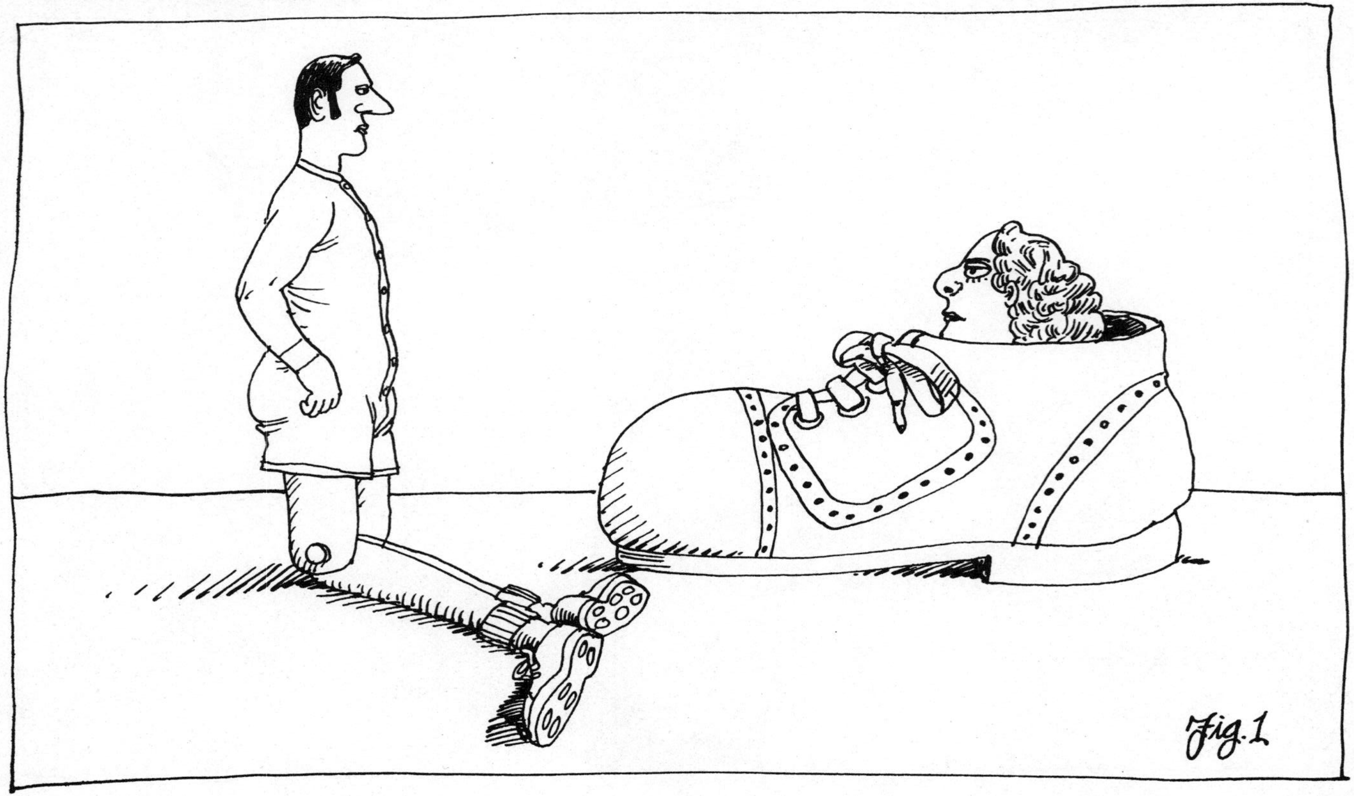
Fig. 1

Never eat anything bigger than your head.

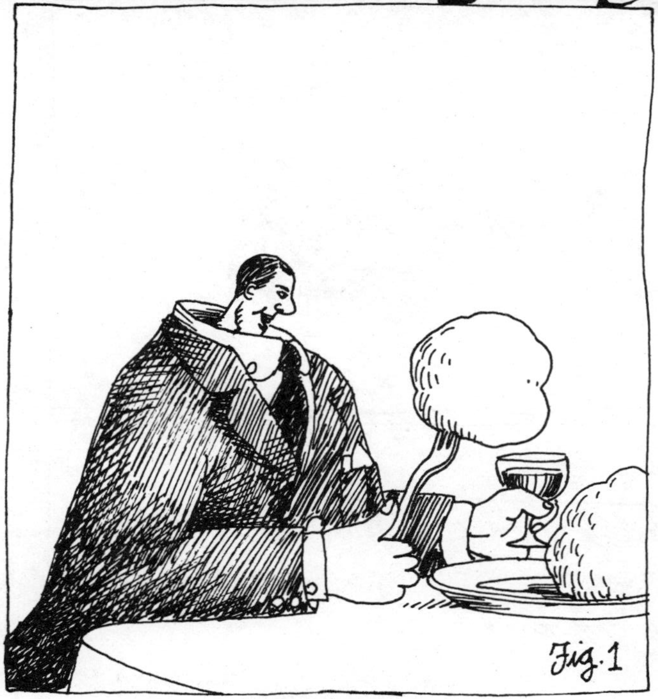
Fig. 1

WRONG

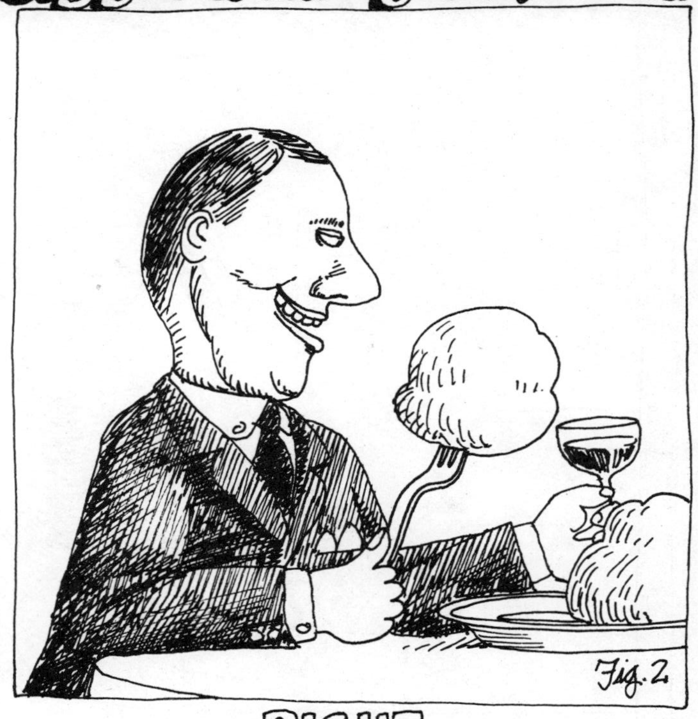
Fig. 2

RIGHT

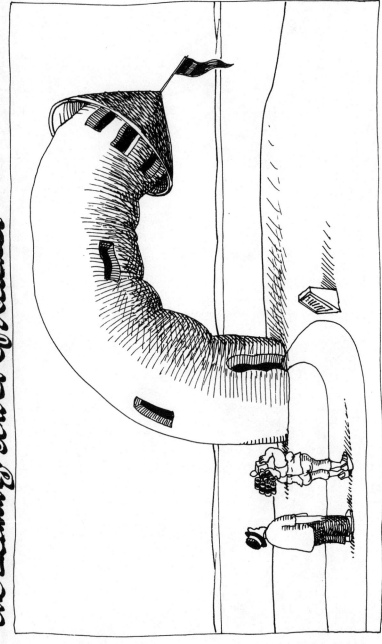

The Leaning Tower of Rubber

Chapter IX

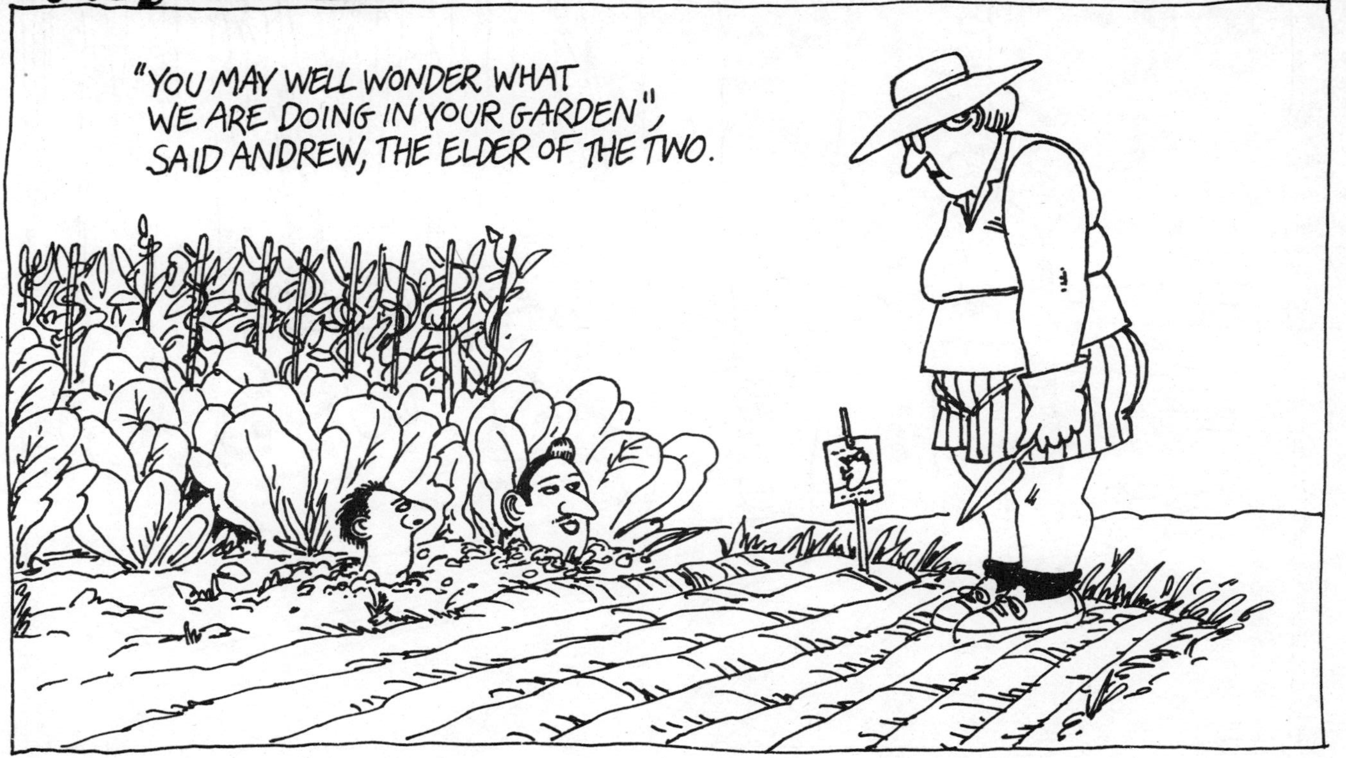
"YOU MAY WELL WONDER WHAT
WE ARE DOING IN YOUR GARDEN",
SAID ANDREW, THE ELDER OF THE TWO.

Victor Grows More Suspicious Hourly

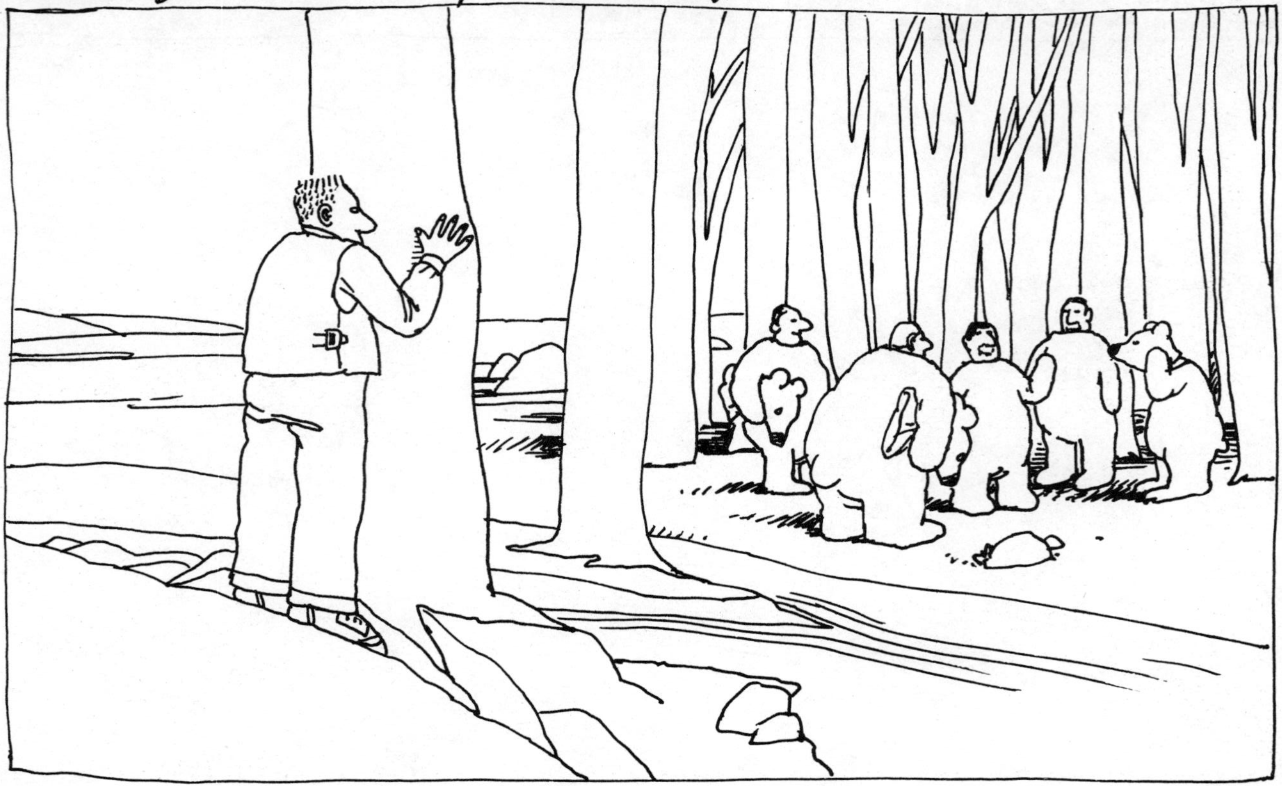

Old Country Pie

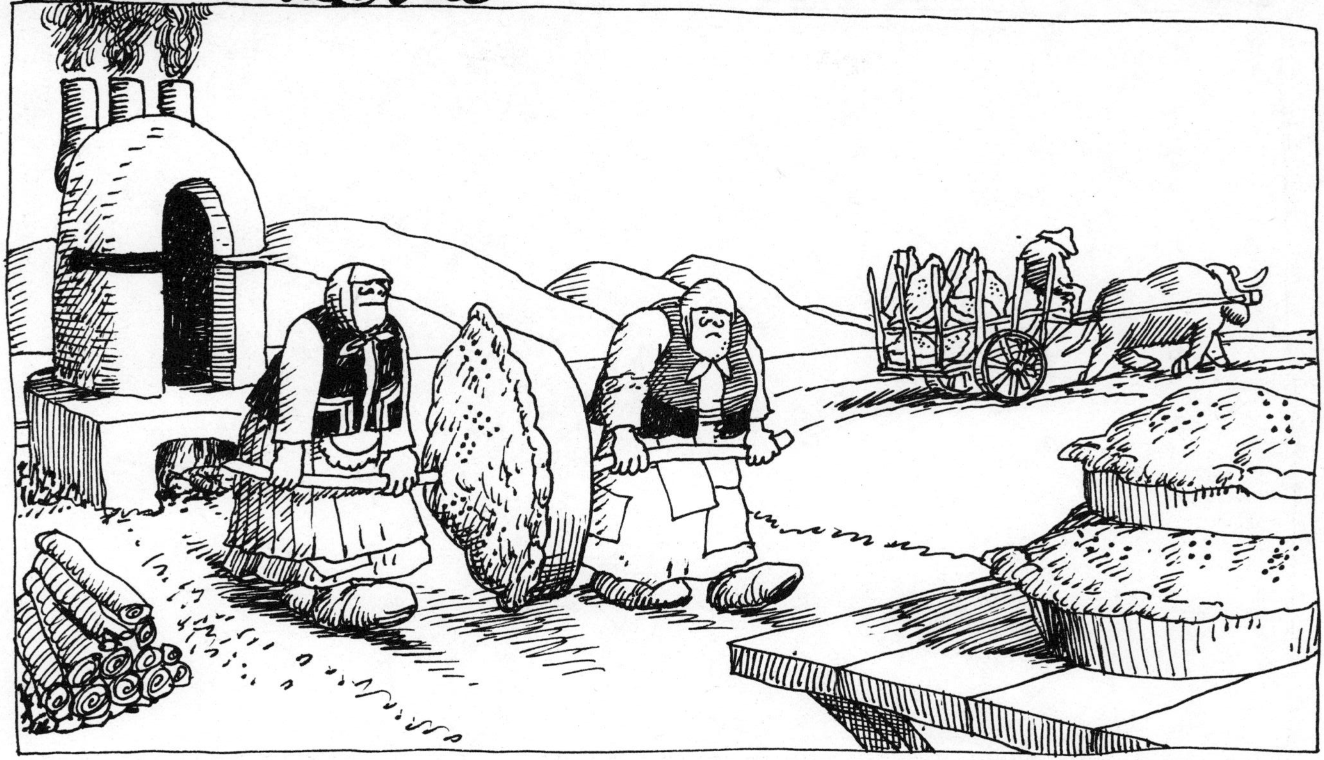

The Unfortunate Child

Superstitions • KISS A DUCK TO CHANGE YOUR LUCK

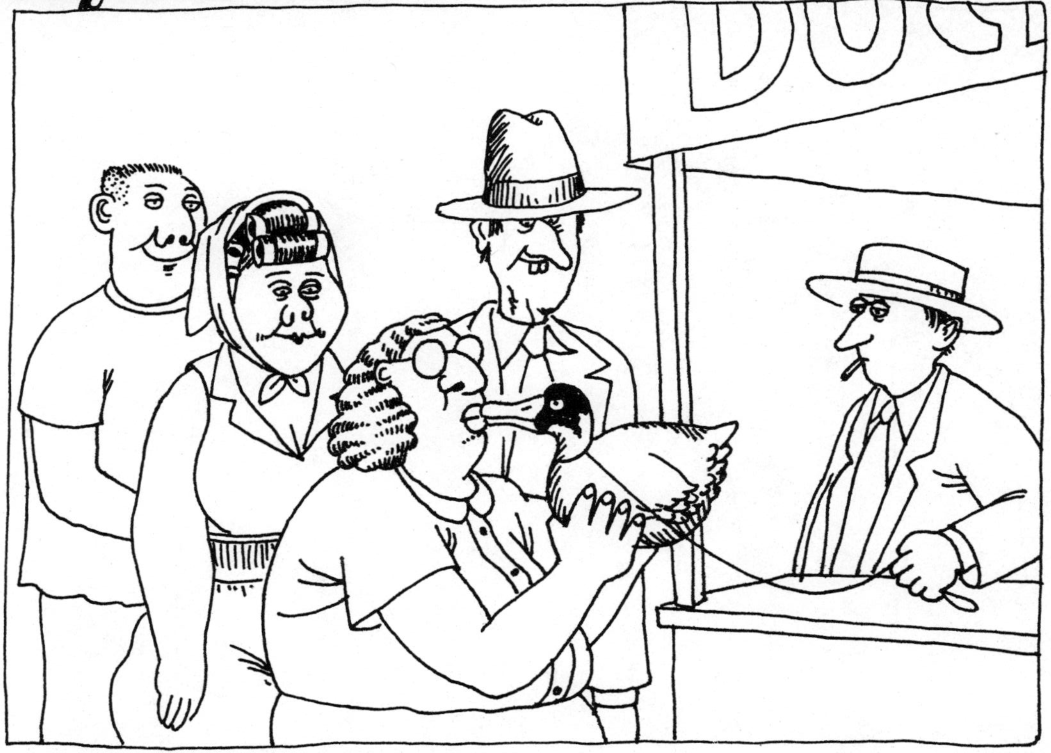
DUC

Mental Floss

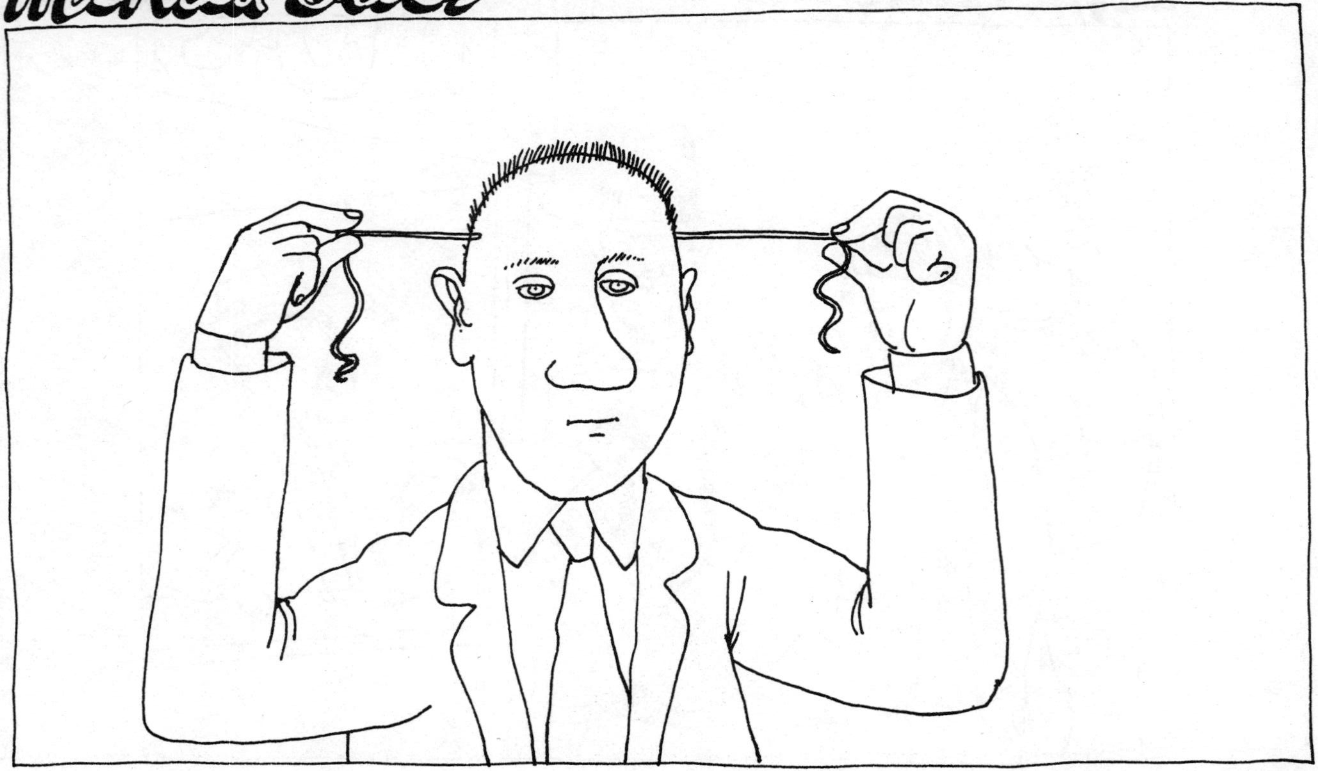

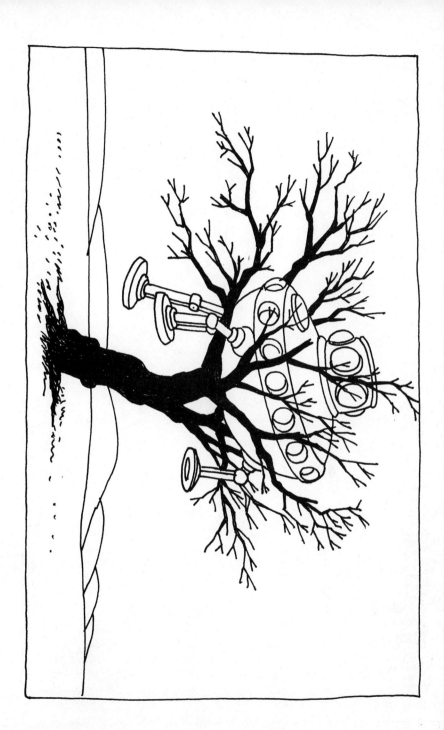

Map Filth

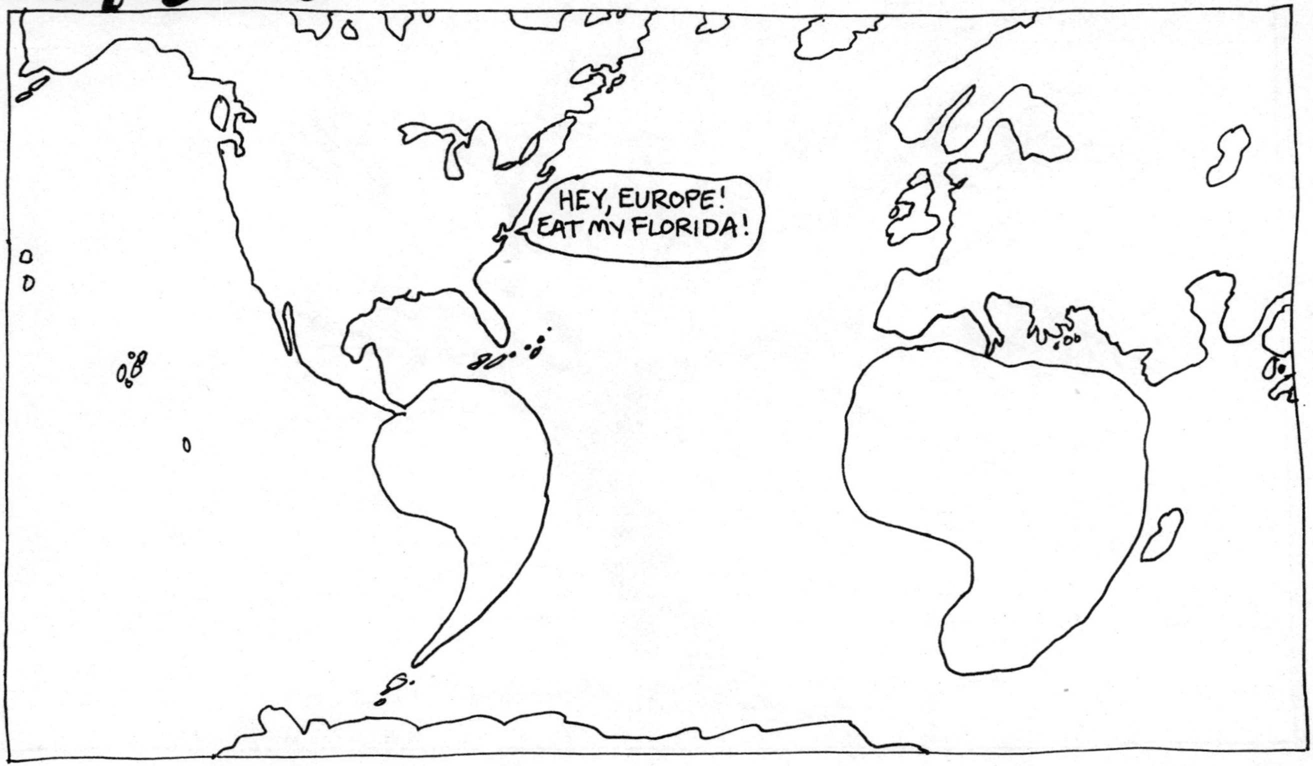
HEY, EUROPE!
EAT MY FLORIDA!

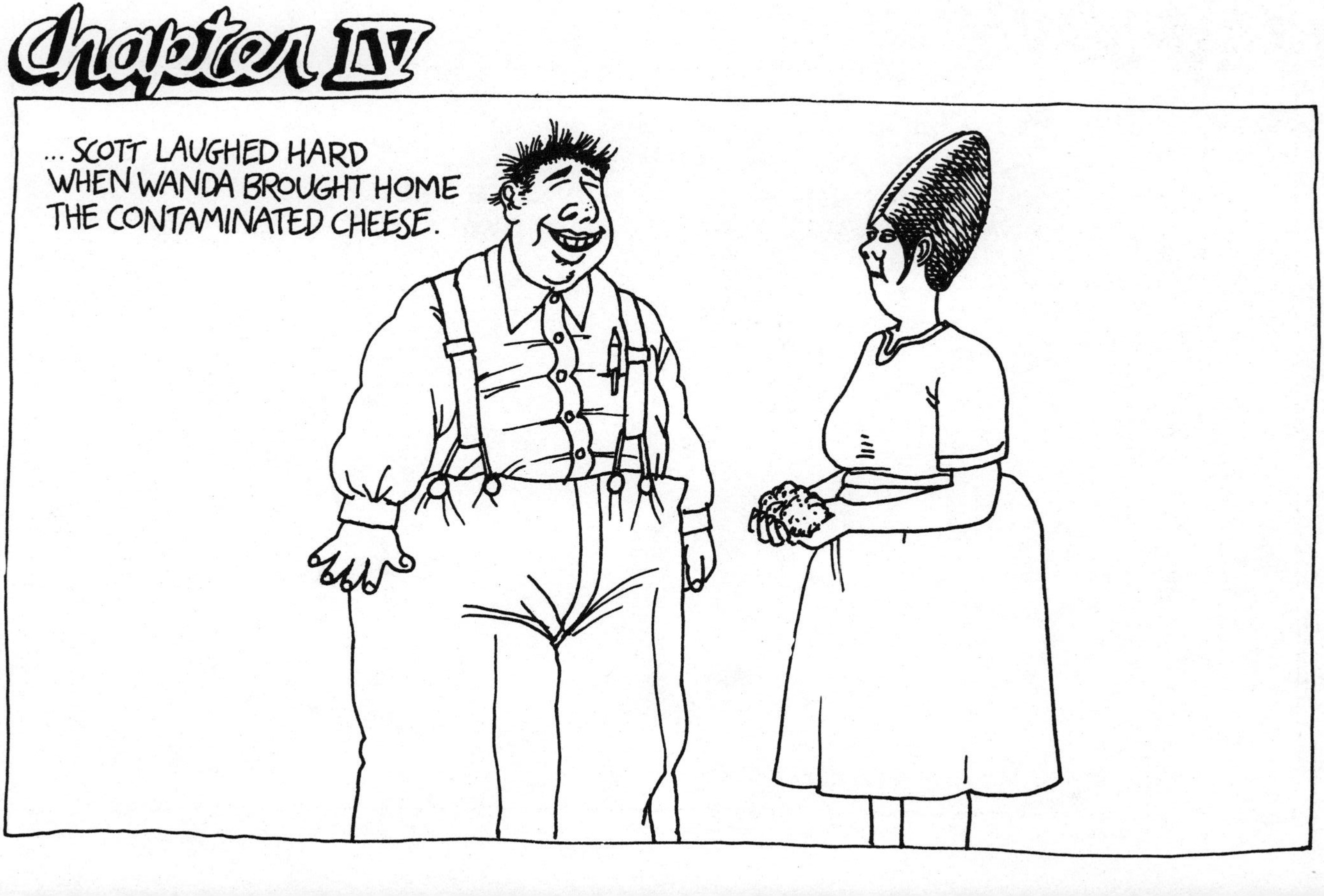
chapter IV
... SCOTT LAUGHED HARD
WHEN WANDA BROUGHT HOME
THE CONTAMINATED CHEESE.

Chapter VIII

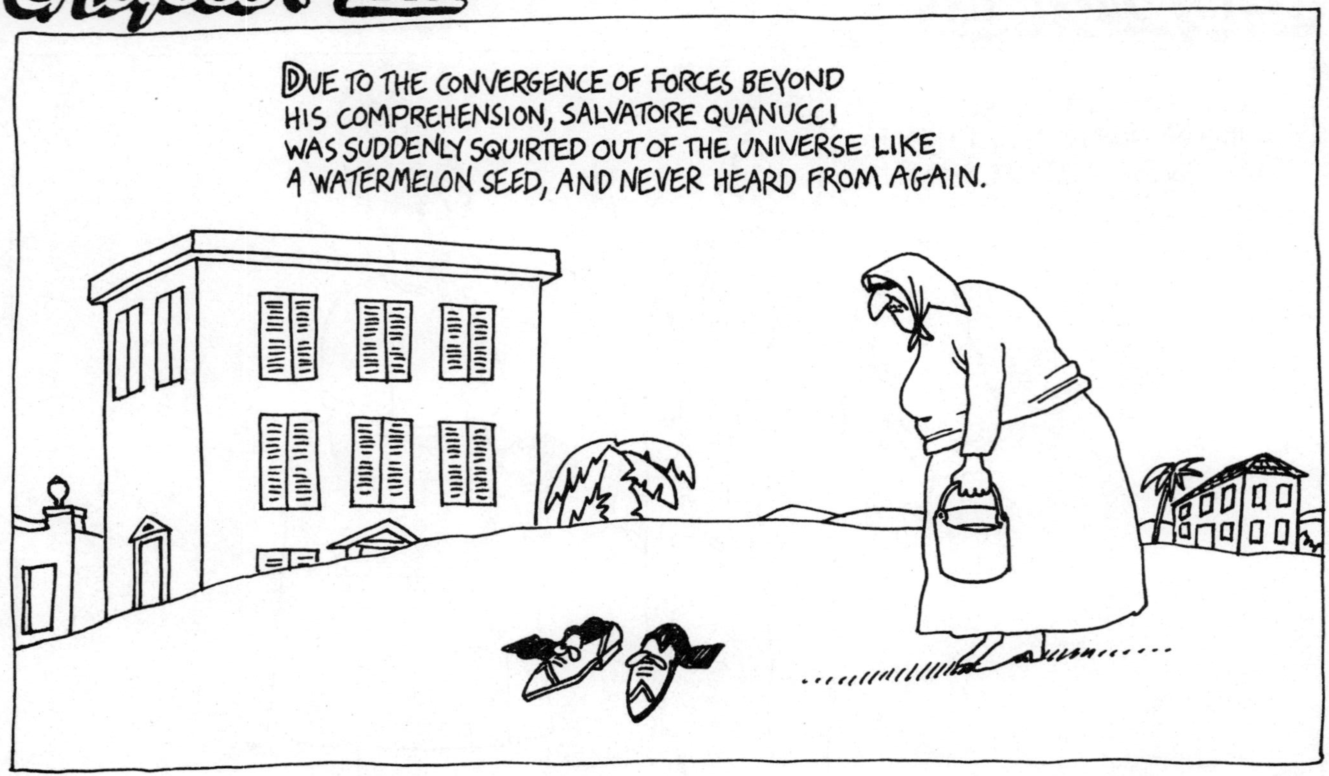
DUE TO THE CONVERGENCE OF FORCES BEYOND
HIS COMPREHENSION, SALVATORE QUANUCCI
WAS SUDDENLY SQUIRTED OUT OF THE UNIVERSE LIKE
A WATERMELON SEED, AND NEVER HEARD FROM AGAIN.

STENCIL

Pencil
GOOD KING WENCIL
Model
waddle
MARQUIS DE SADL!

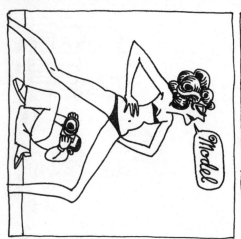

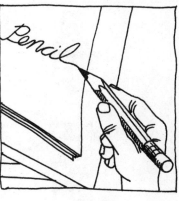

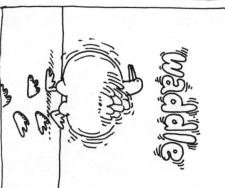

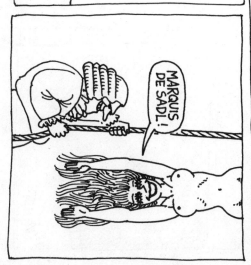

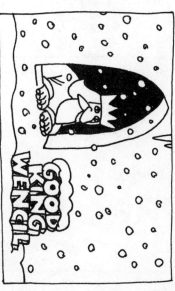

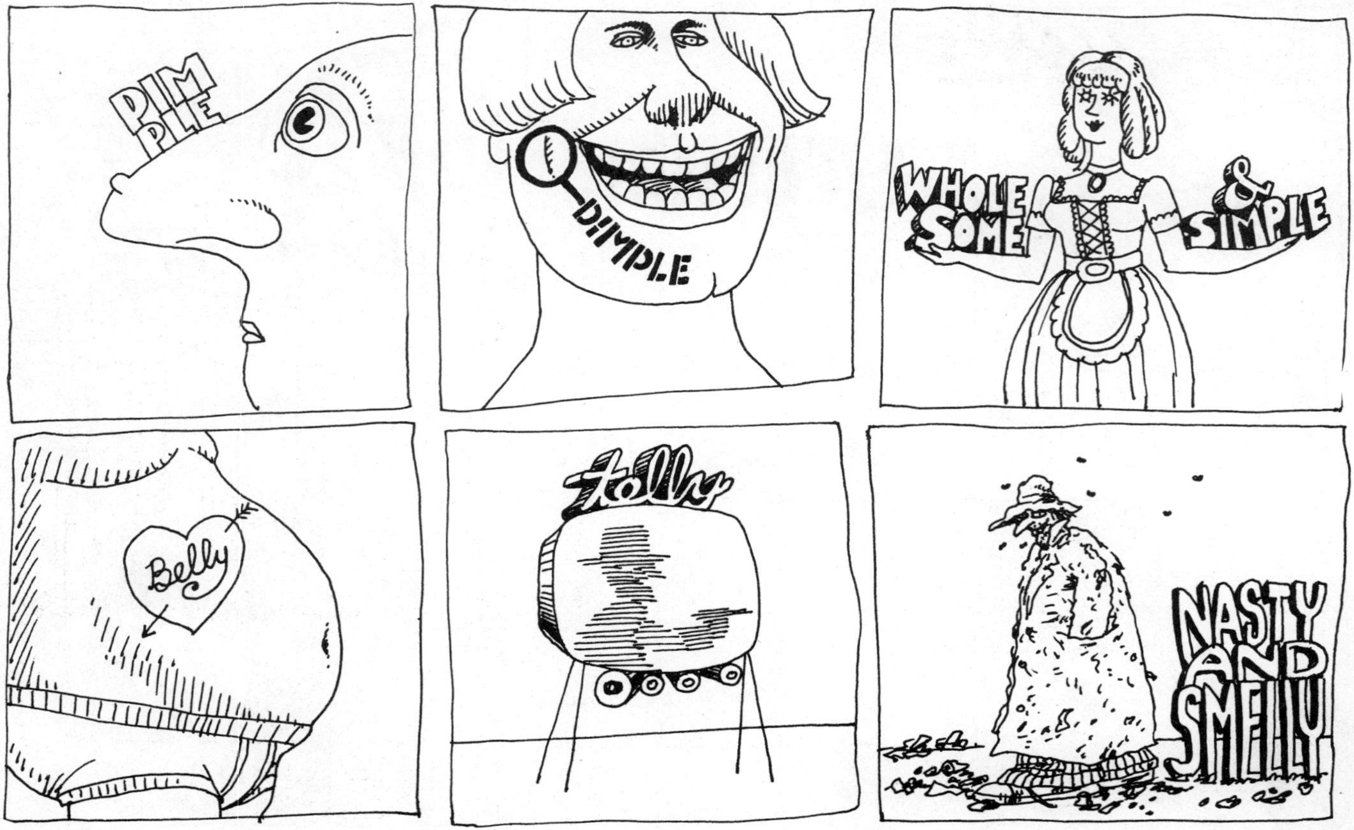
PIMPLE
DIMPLE
WHOLE SOME
& SIMPLE
Belly
telly
NASTY AND SMELLY

Inglese

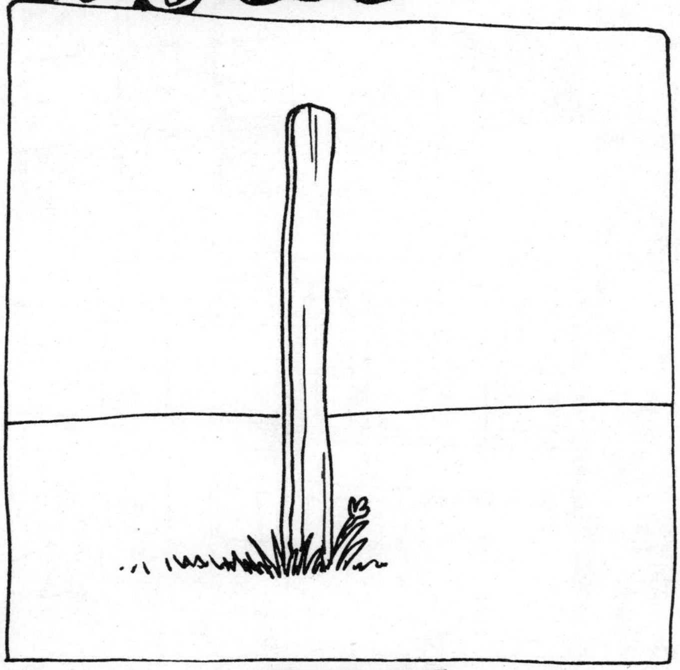

FENT

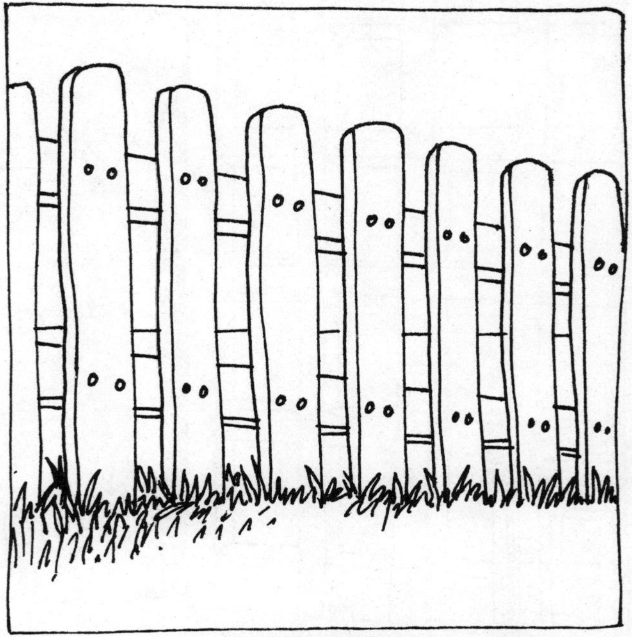

FENTS

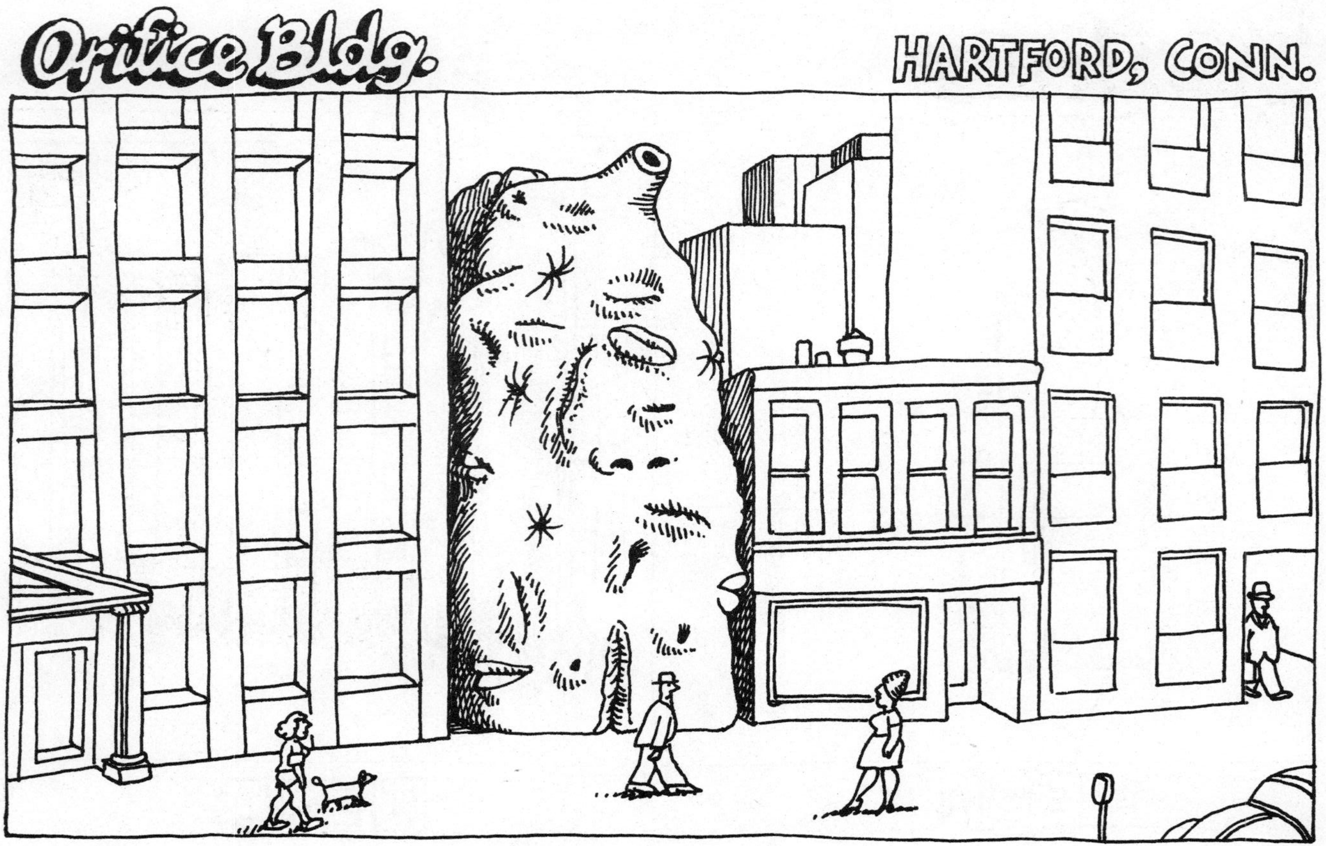
Orifice Bldg.
HARTFORD, CONN.

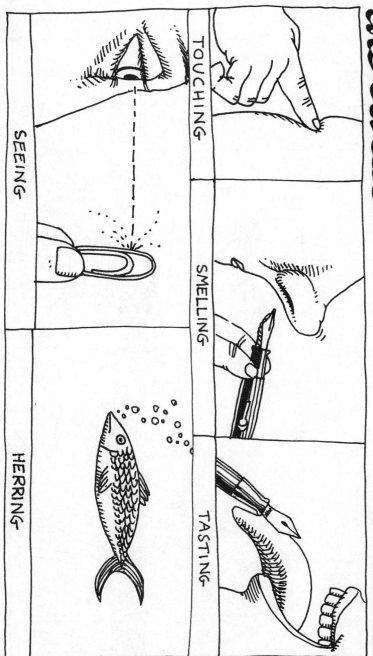

The Senses

TOUCHING

SEEING

SMELLING

HERRING

TASTING

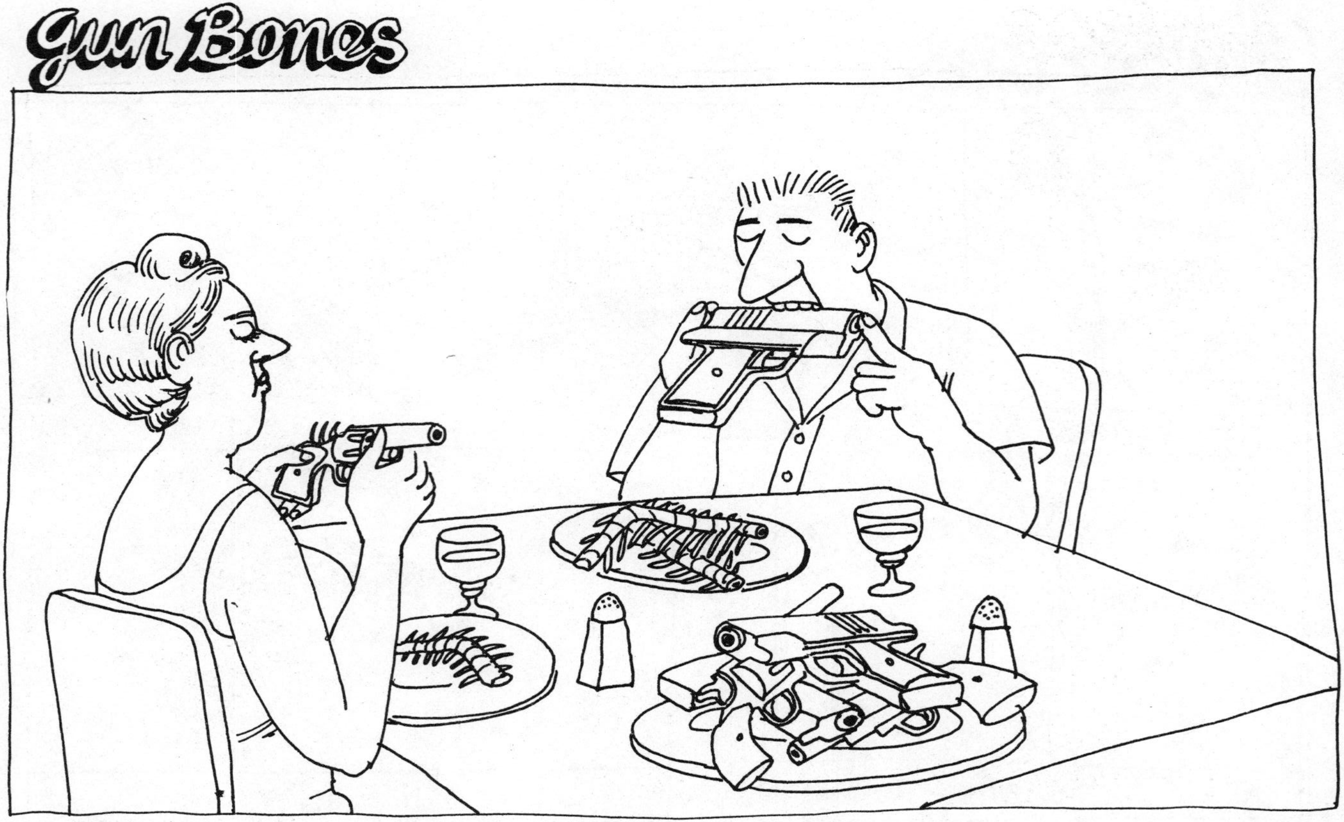
Gun Bones

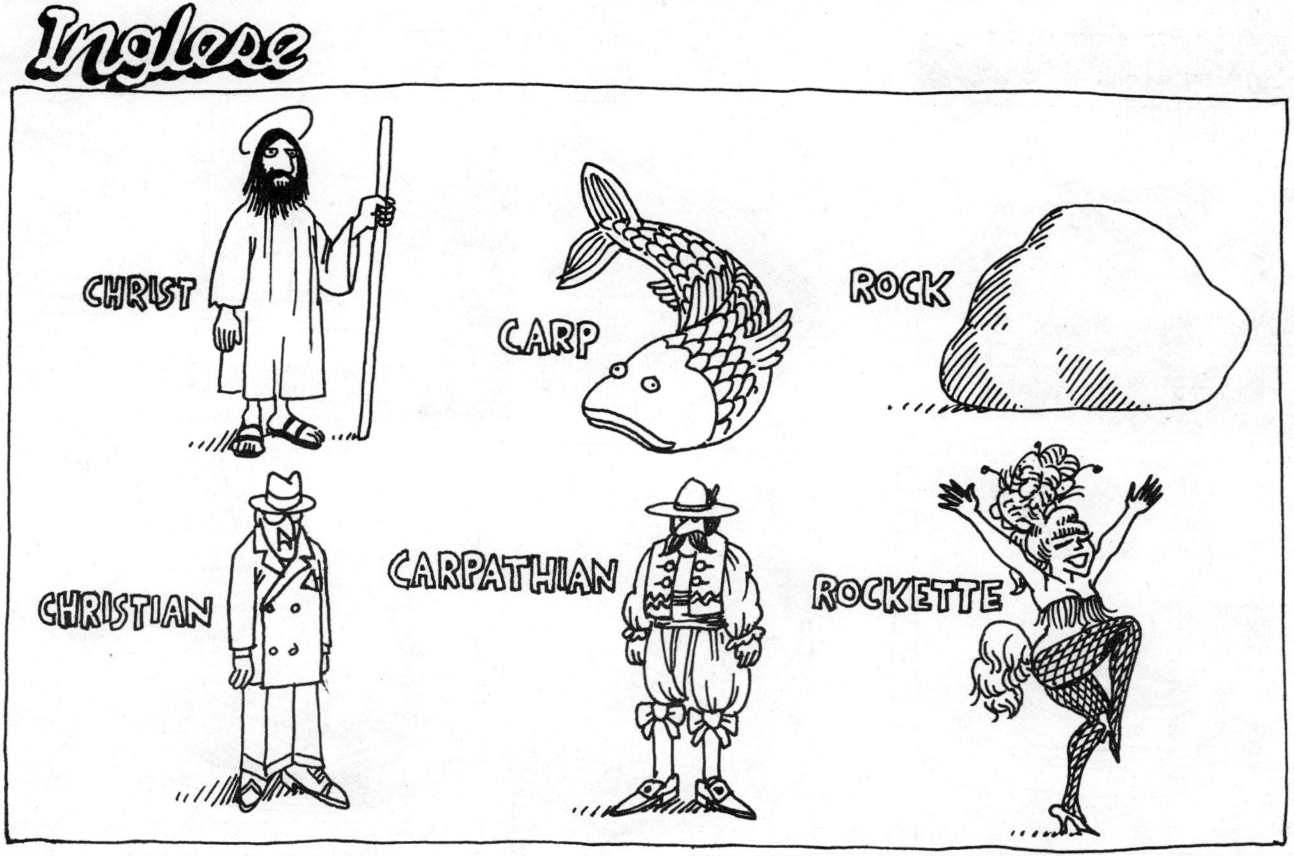
Inglese
CHRIST
CARP
ROCK
CHRISTIAN
CARPATHIAN
ROCKETTE

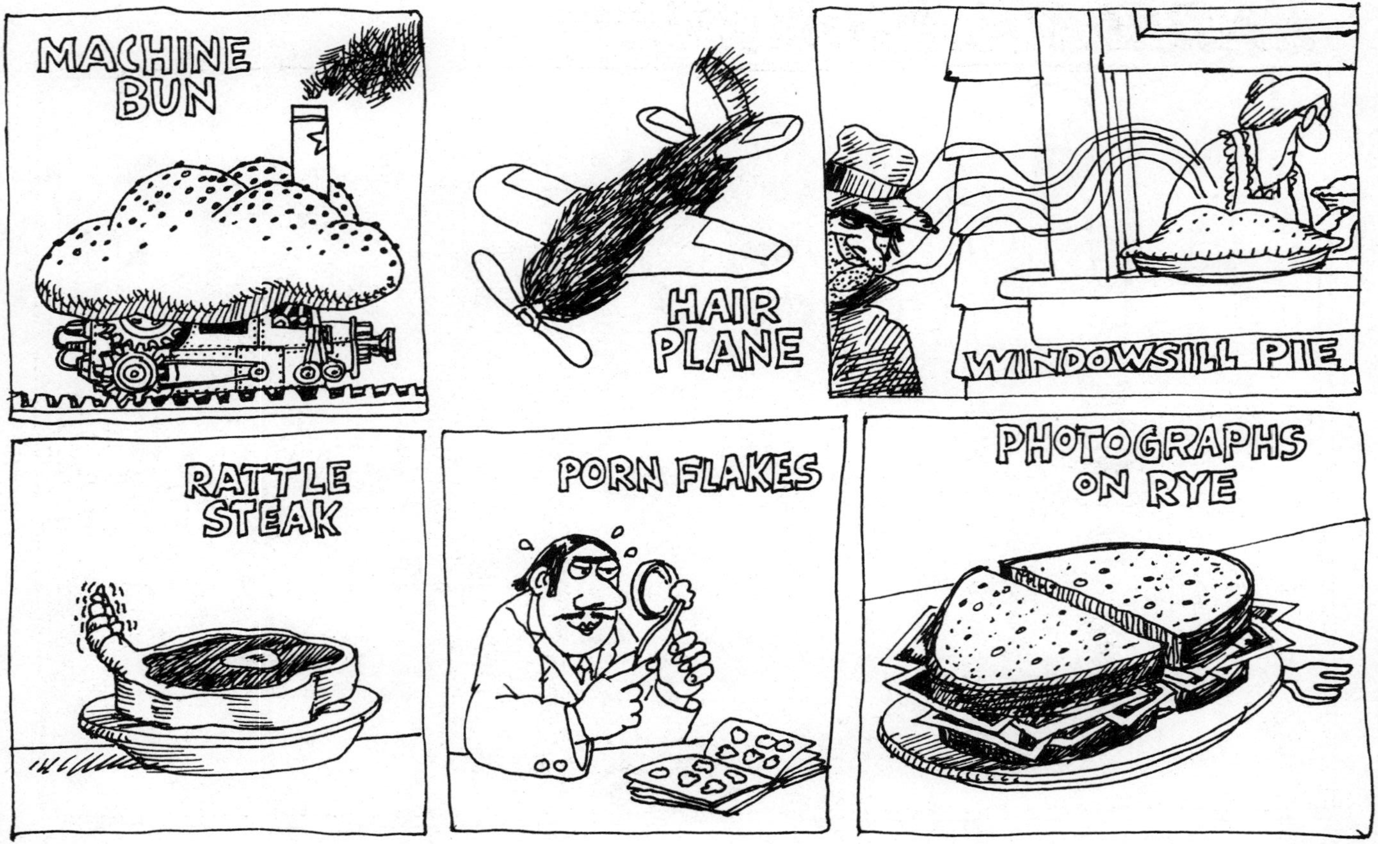
MACHINE BUN
HAIR PLANE
WINDOWSILL PIE
RATTLE STEAK
PORN FLAKES
PHOTOGRAPHS ON RYE

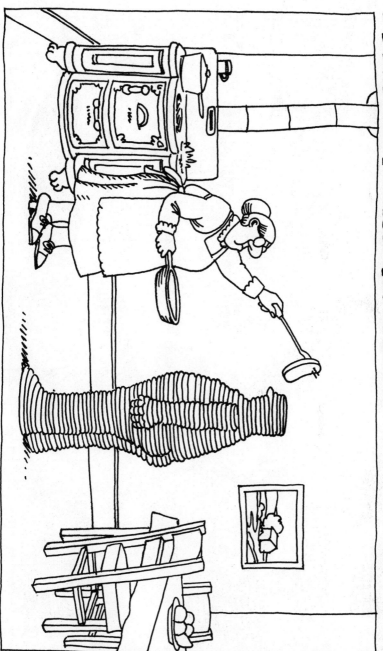

MAKING A FLAPJACK PERSON

Satisfied Hammer Owners #32

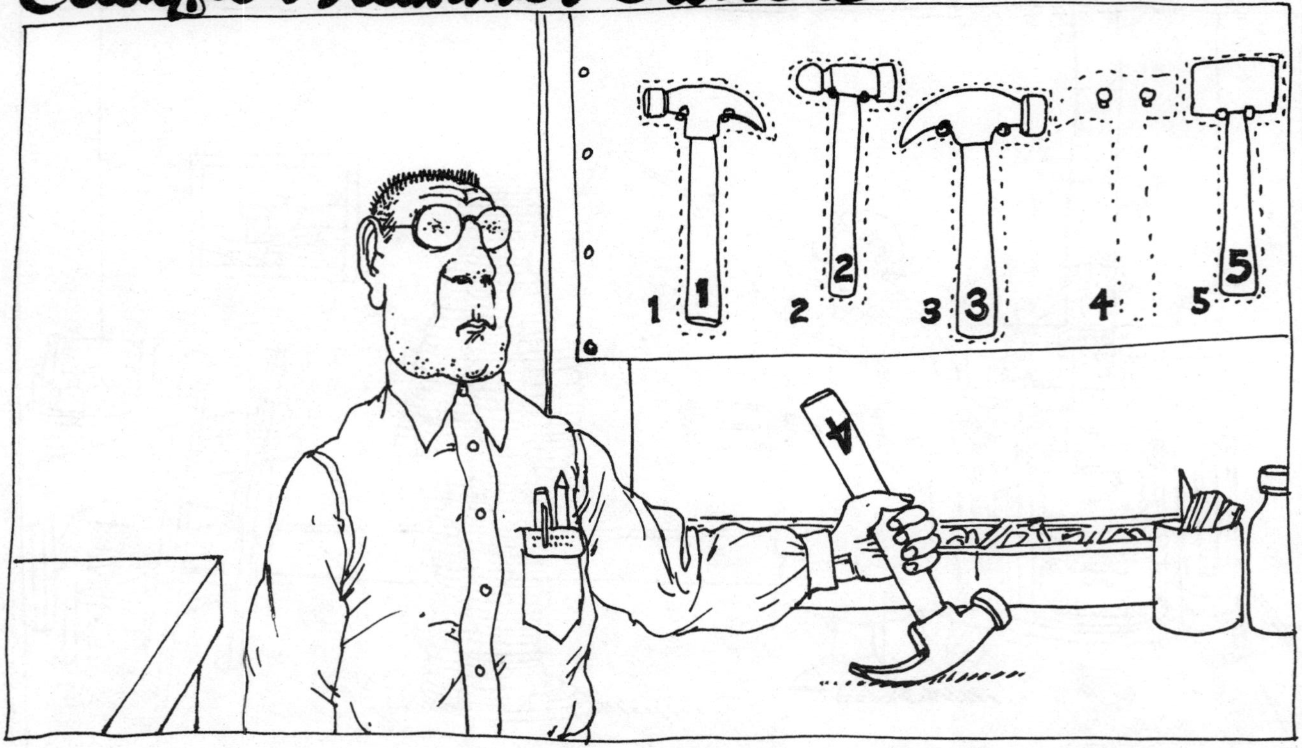

1
1
2
2
3
3
4
5
5
4

The Evolution of the Bird

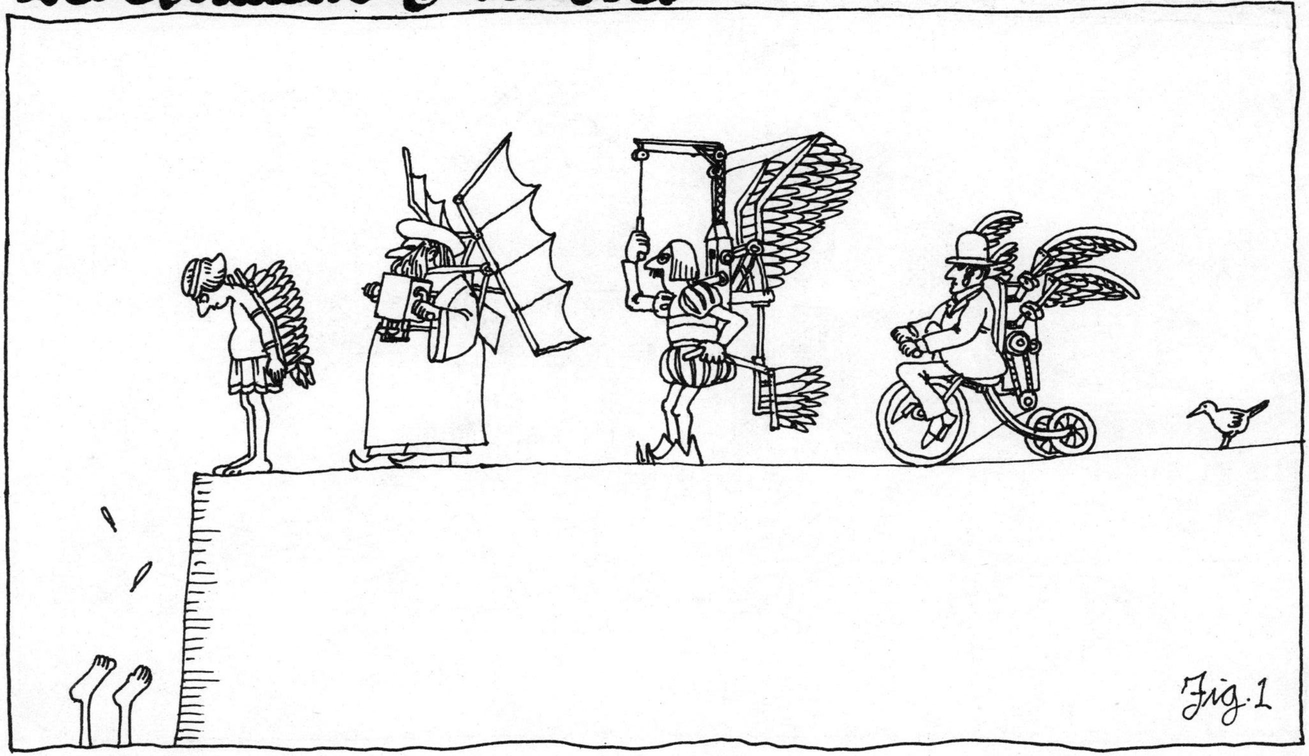
Fig. 1

Home for the Unpleasant

PORTLAND, ORE.

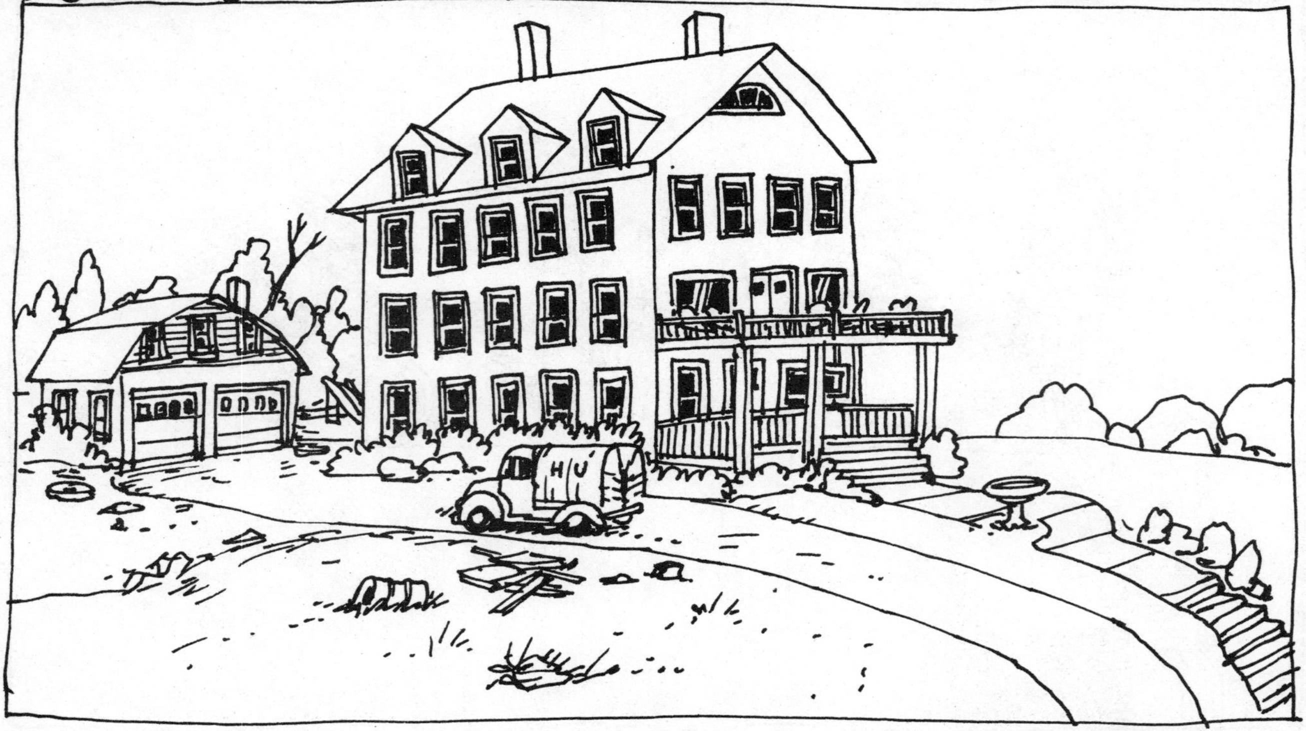
HU

Blowing the Mormon Tabernacle Choir

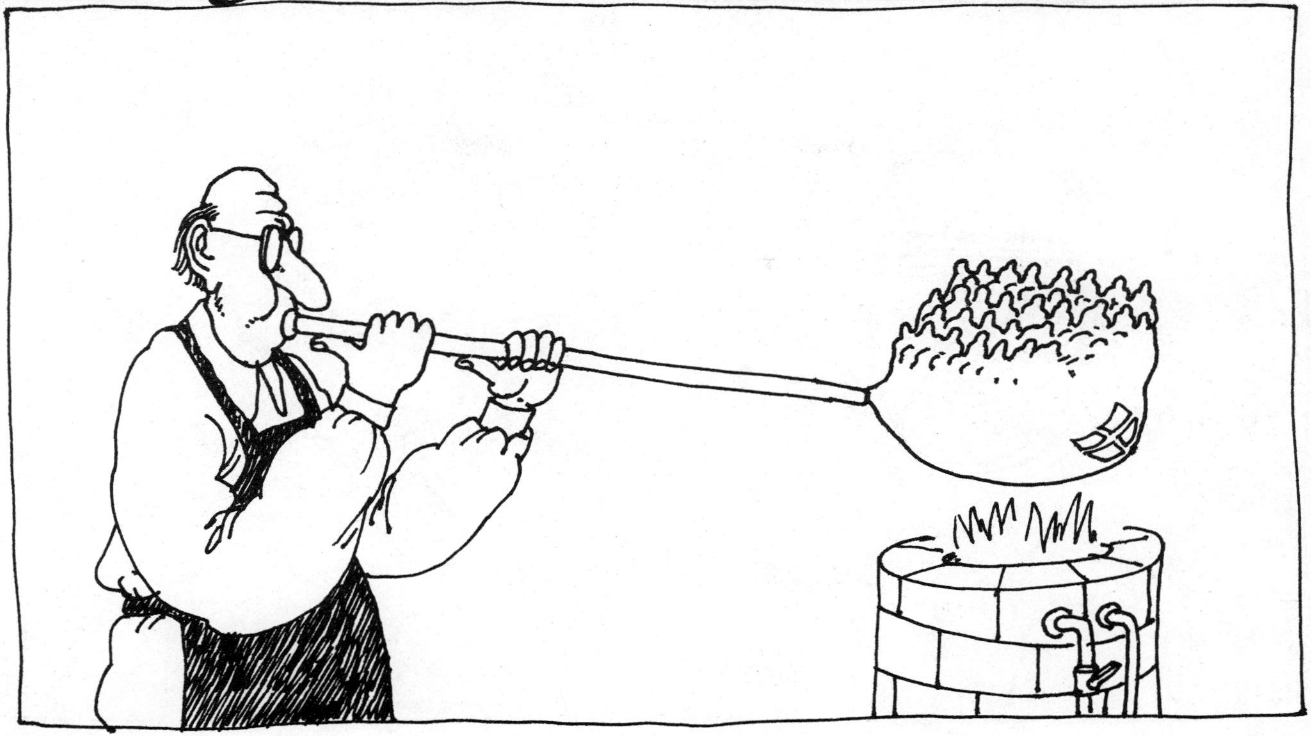

Continuous Eye Persons

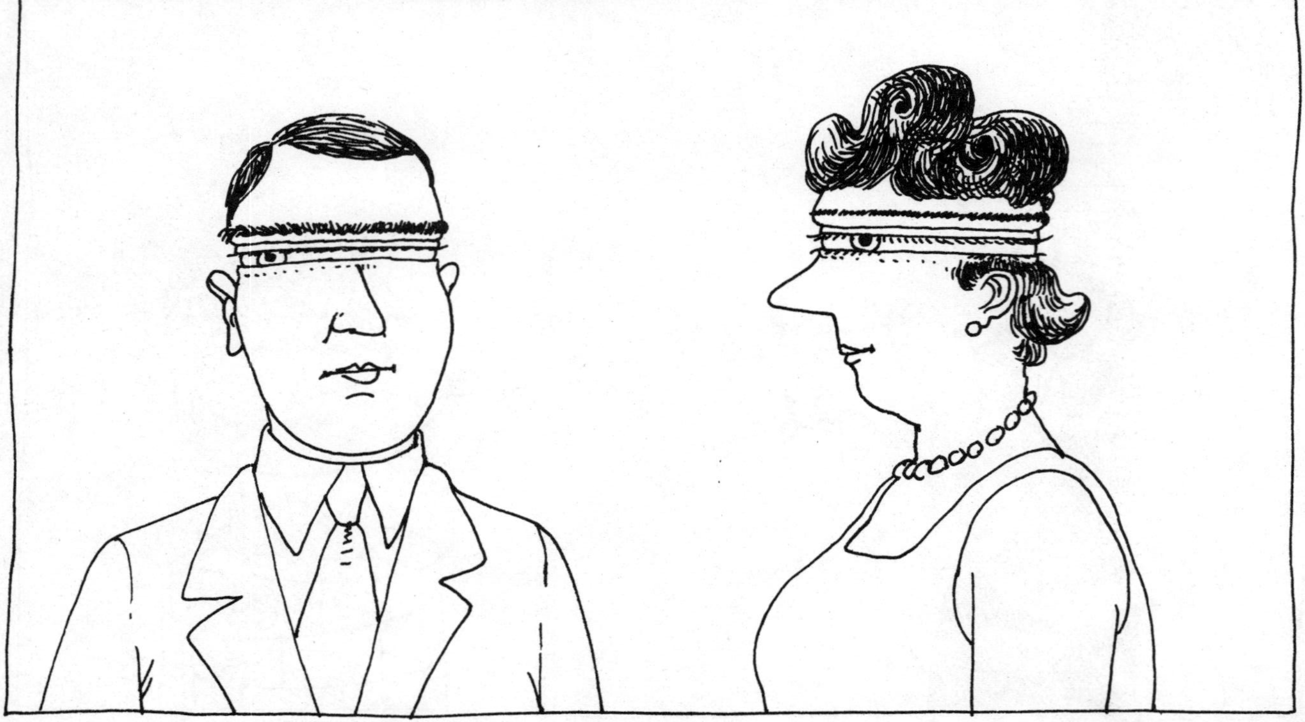

Philosophers Looting a Small Town

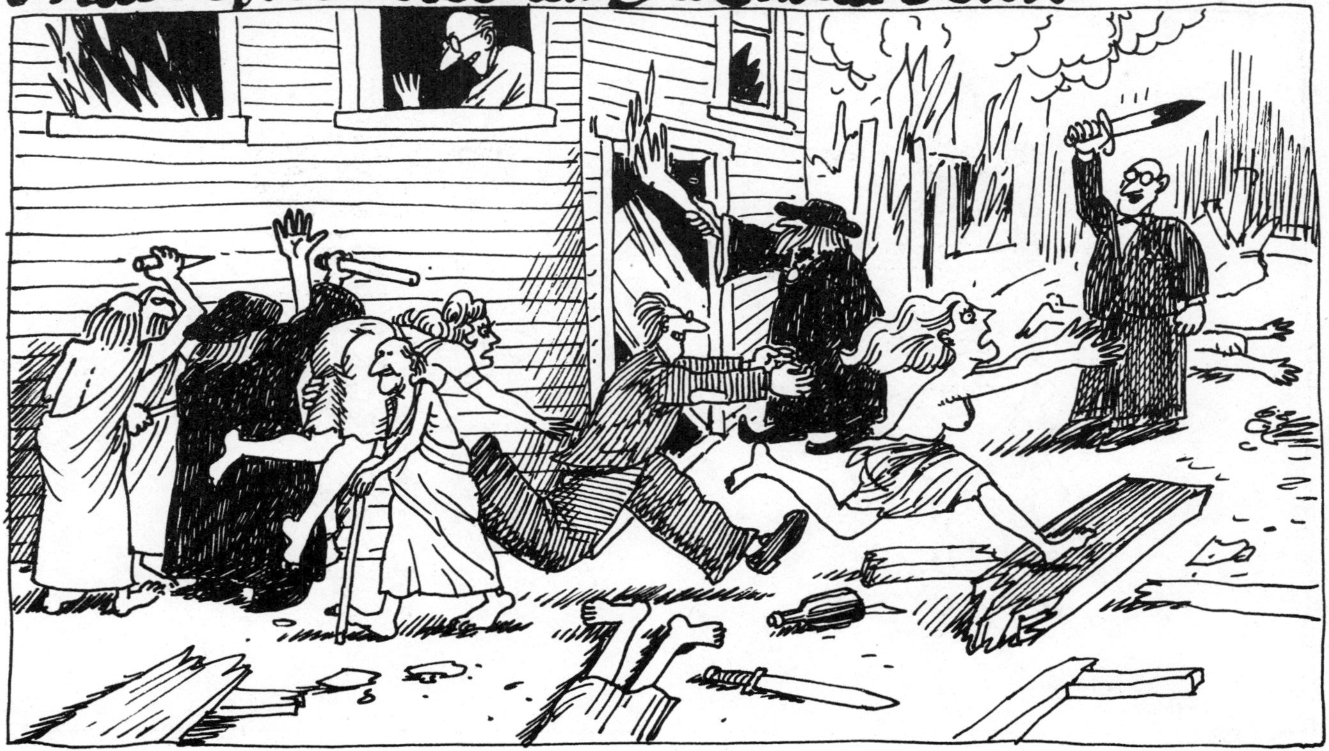

More than Coincidence?

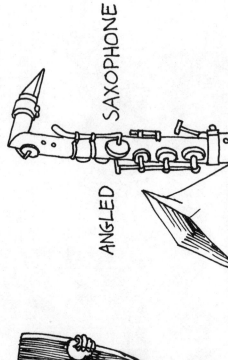

ANGLO
SAXON

Fig. 1

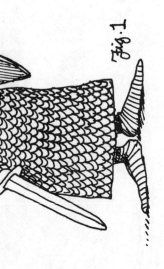

ANGLED   SAXOPHONE

Fig. 2

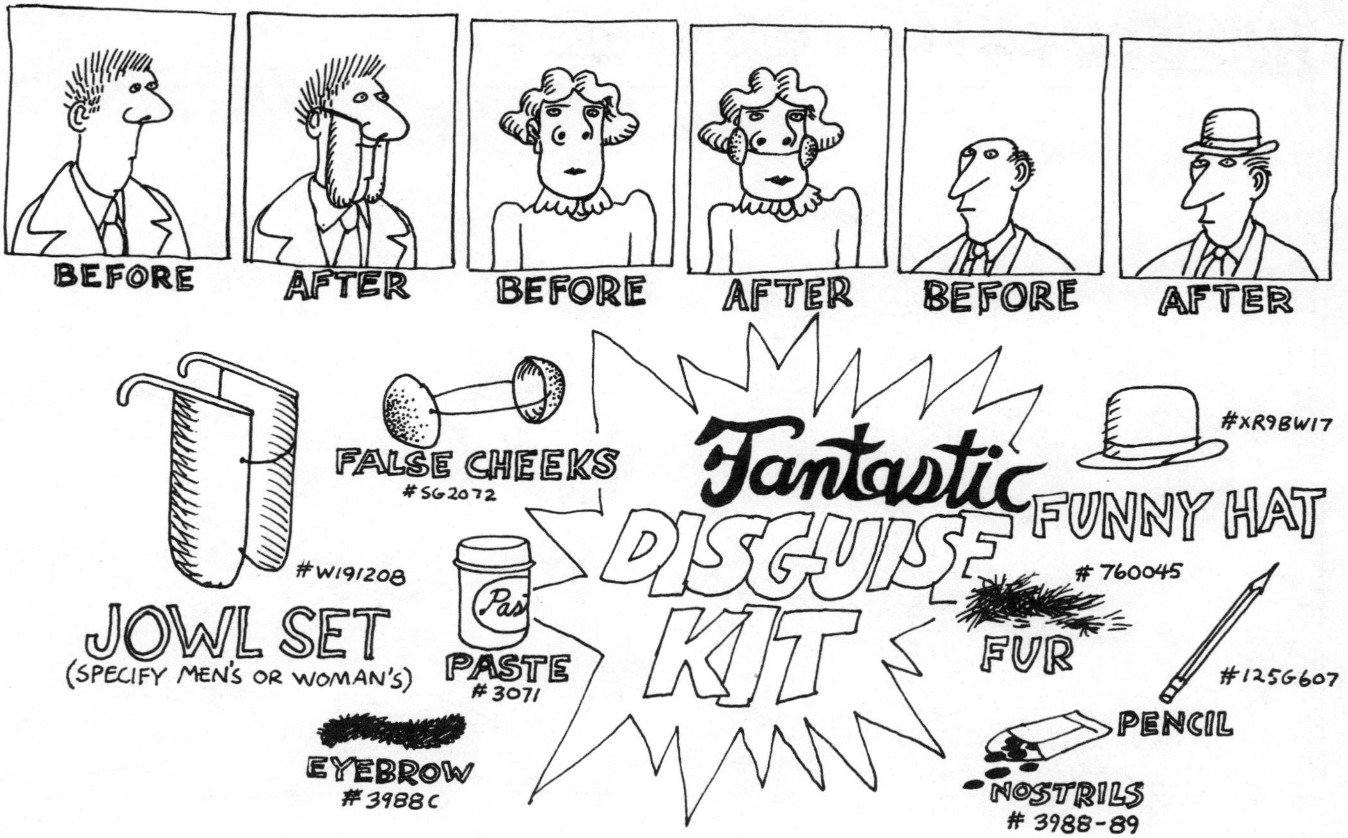
BEFORE
AFTER
BEFORE
AFTER
BEFORE
AFTER
Fantastic DISGUISE KIT
JOWL SET
(SPECIFY MEN'S OR WOMAN'S)
#W191208
FALSE CHEEKS
#SG2072
PASTE
#3071
EYEBROW
#3988C
FUNNY HAT
#XR9BW17
FUR
#760045
PENCIL
#125G607
NOSTRILS
#3988-89

Math • CONVERTING FEET TO METERS

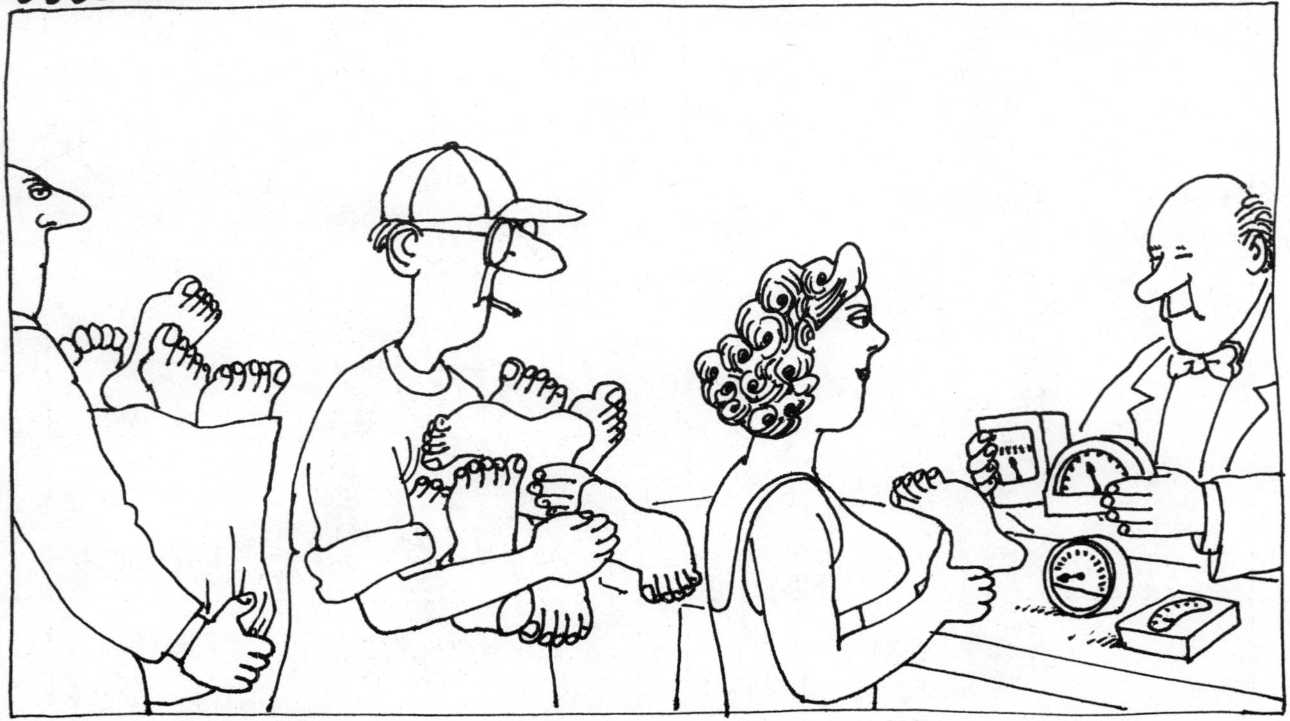

Biology - THE ANTI-JUMP MUSCLES (SHADED AREA, FIG. 1)
FLEXED
Fig. 1
74CM
RELAXED
Fig. 2

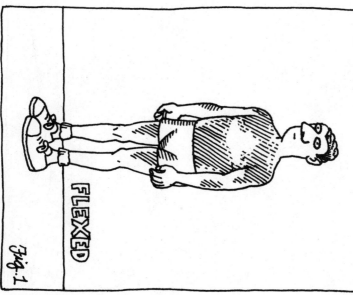

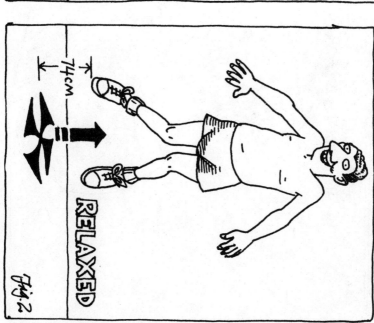

Alice

JUST GIVE ALICE SOME PENCILS AND
SHE WILL STAY BUSY FOR HOURS.

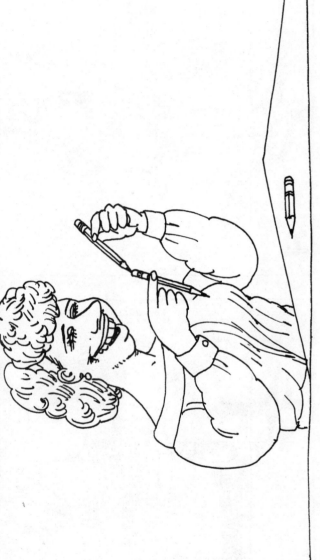

The Mini-Calculator

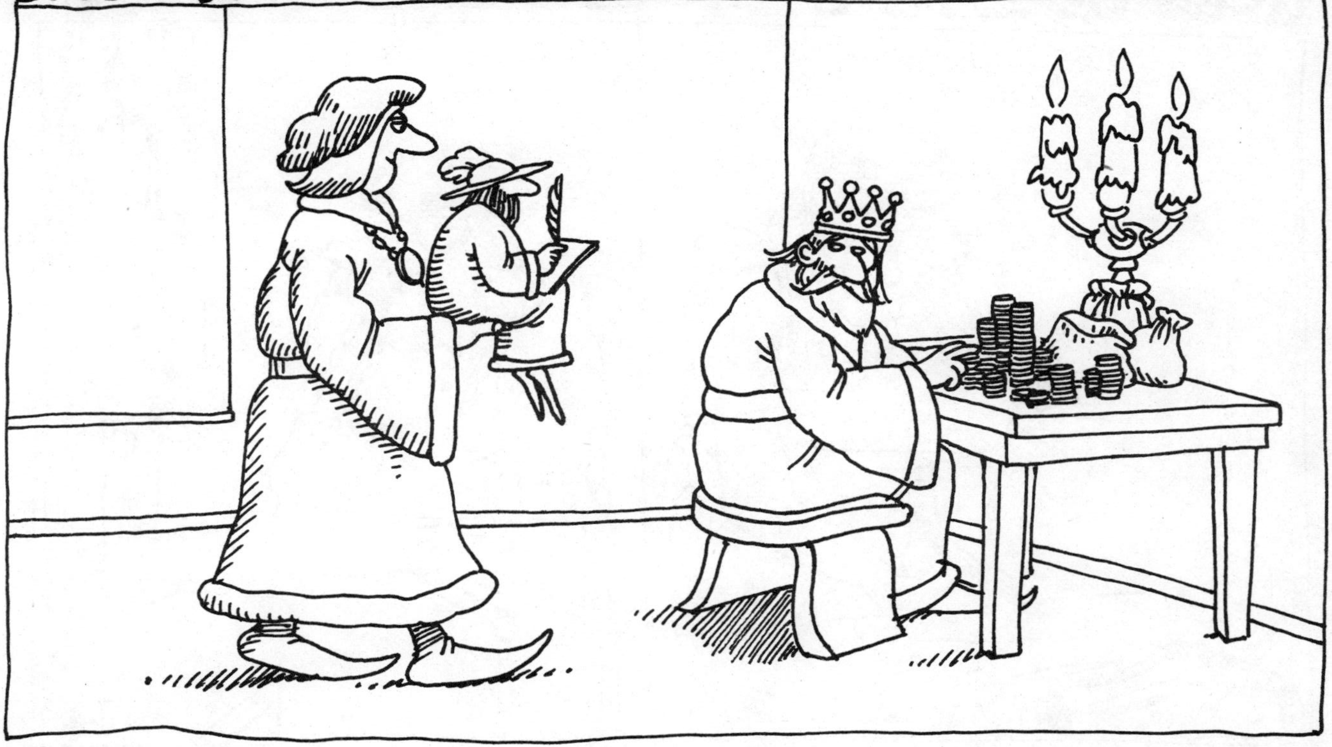

Household Hint #161

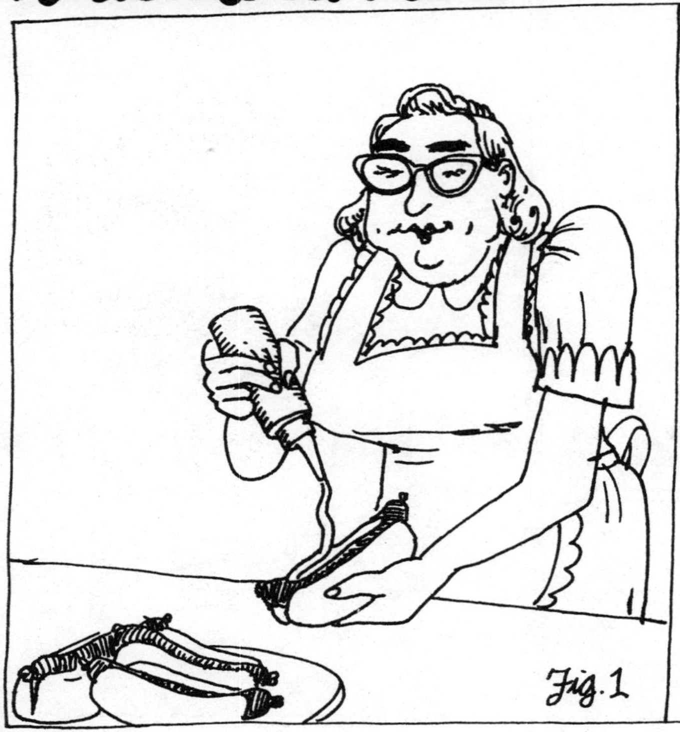
Fig. 1

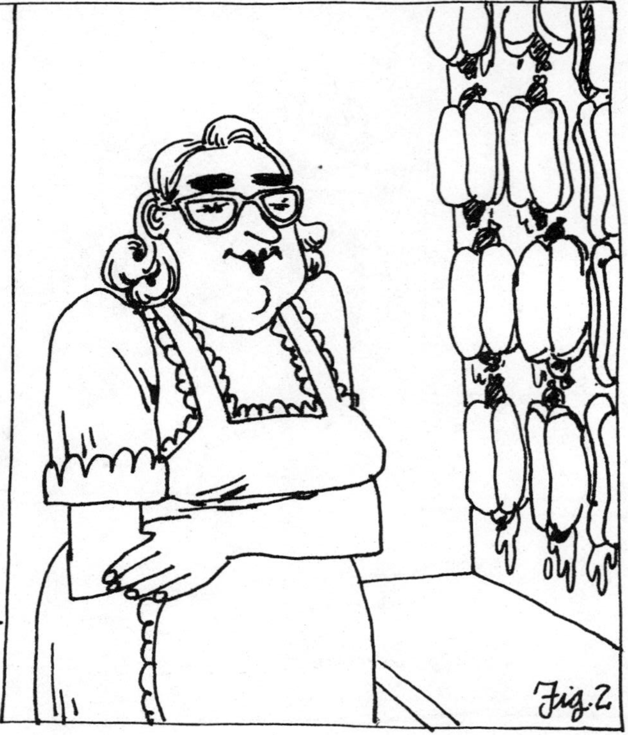
Fig. 2

People Who Don't Brush Teeth

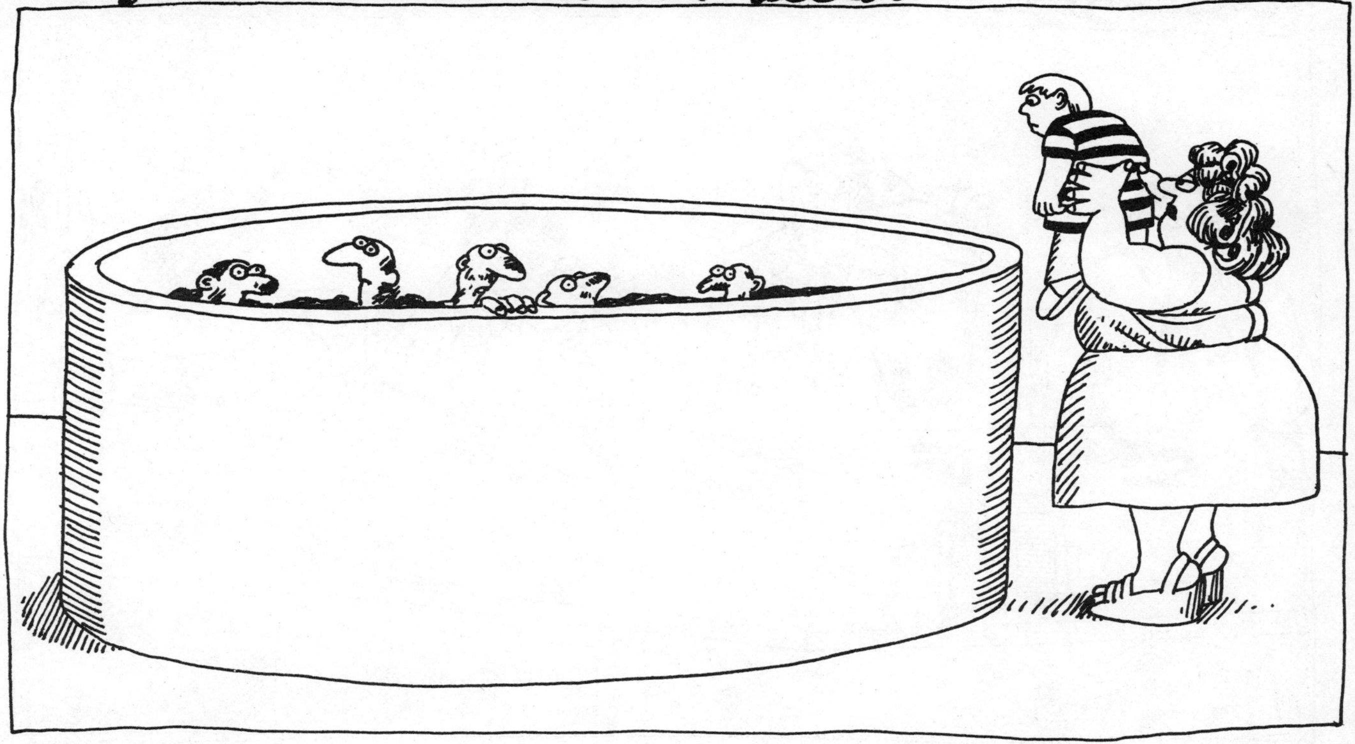

Businessman's Lunch

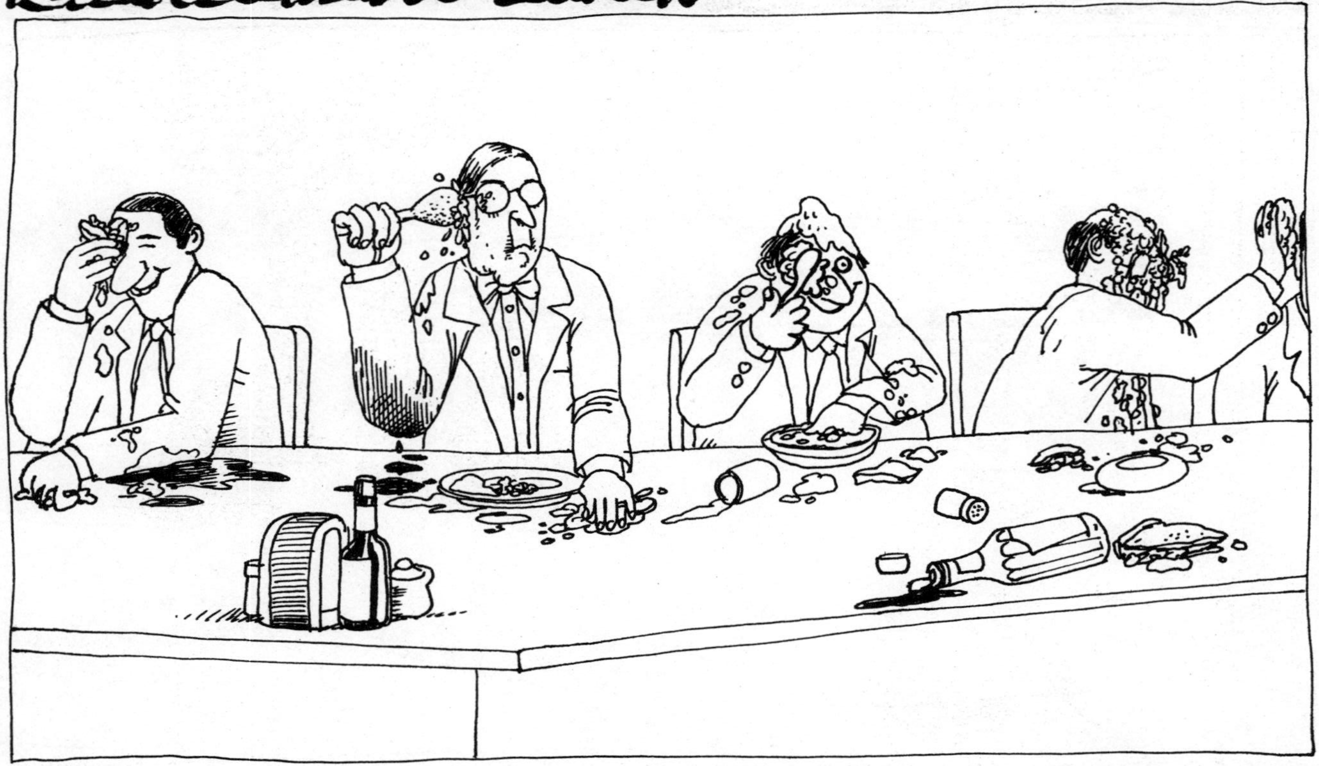

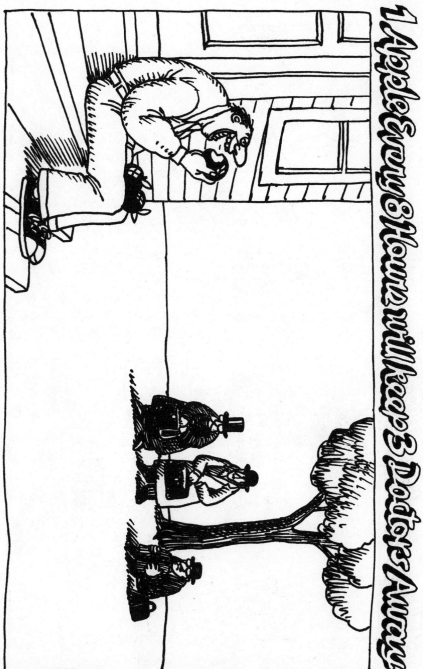

1 Apple Every 8 Hours will keep 3 Doctors Away

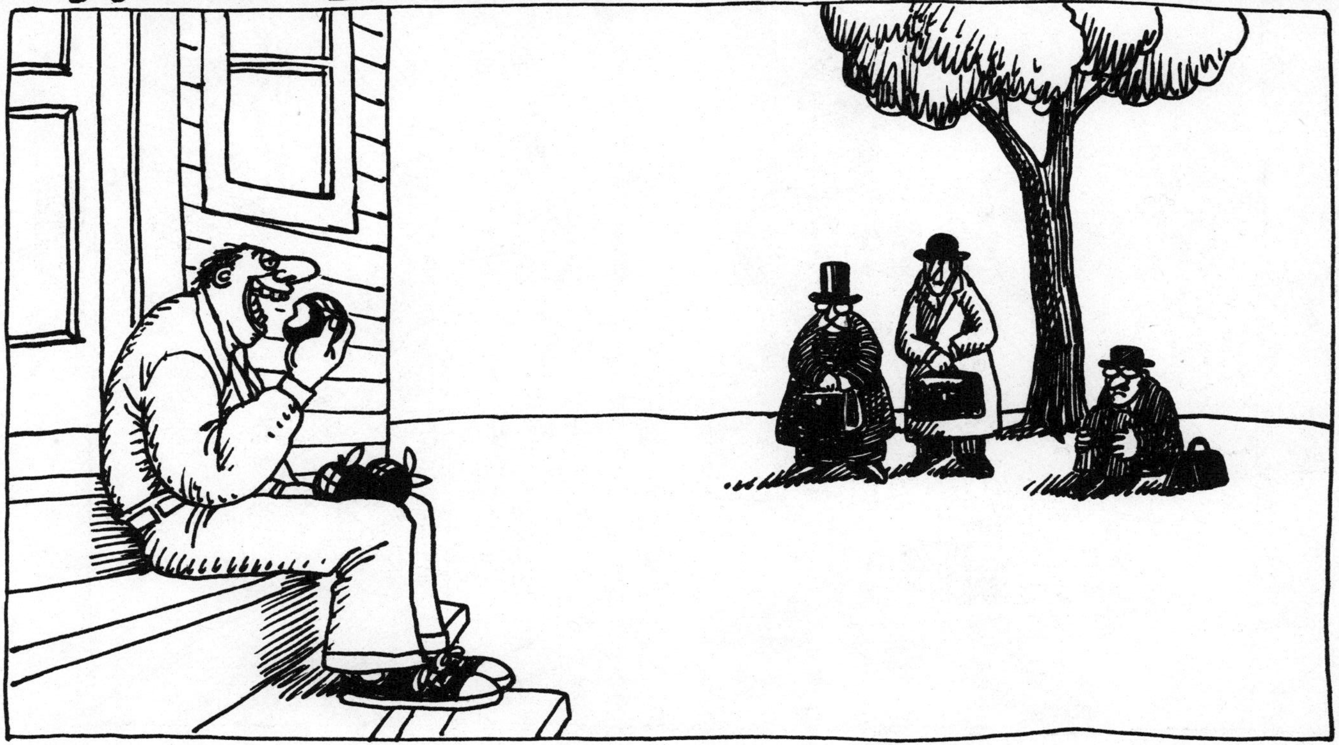

Freud's First Slip

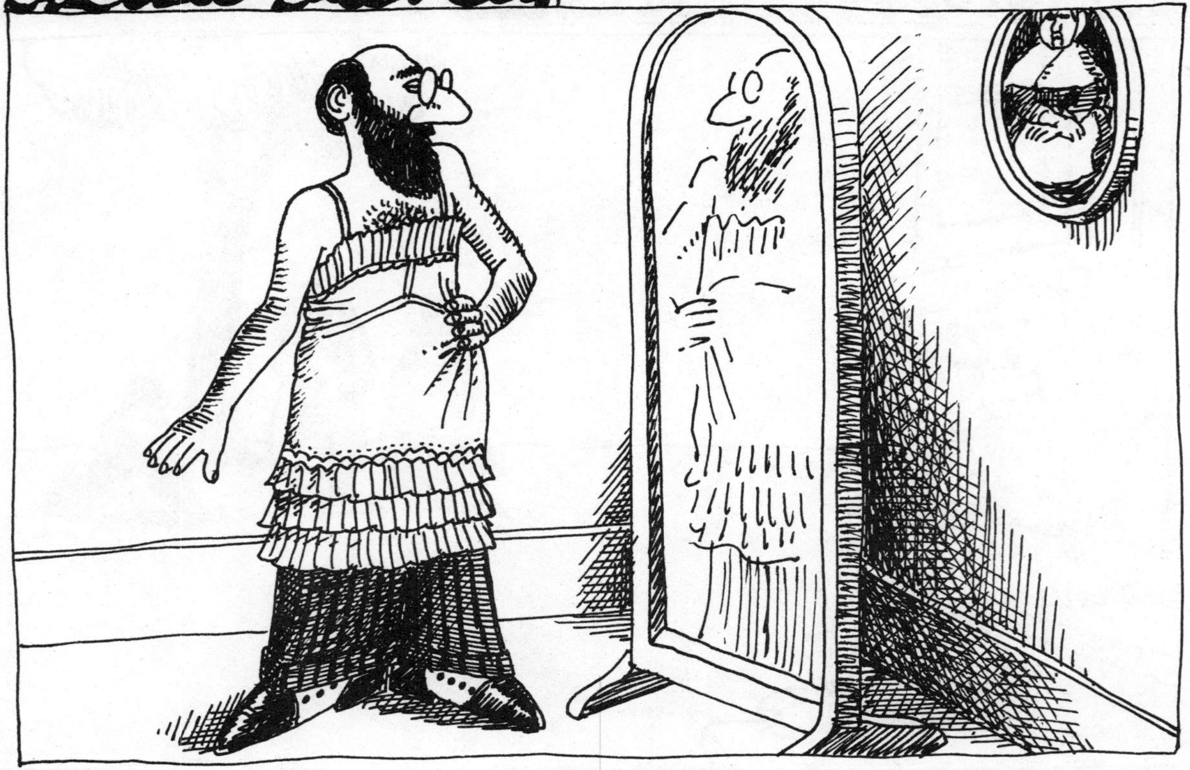

Jim of Arc

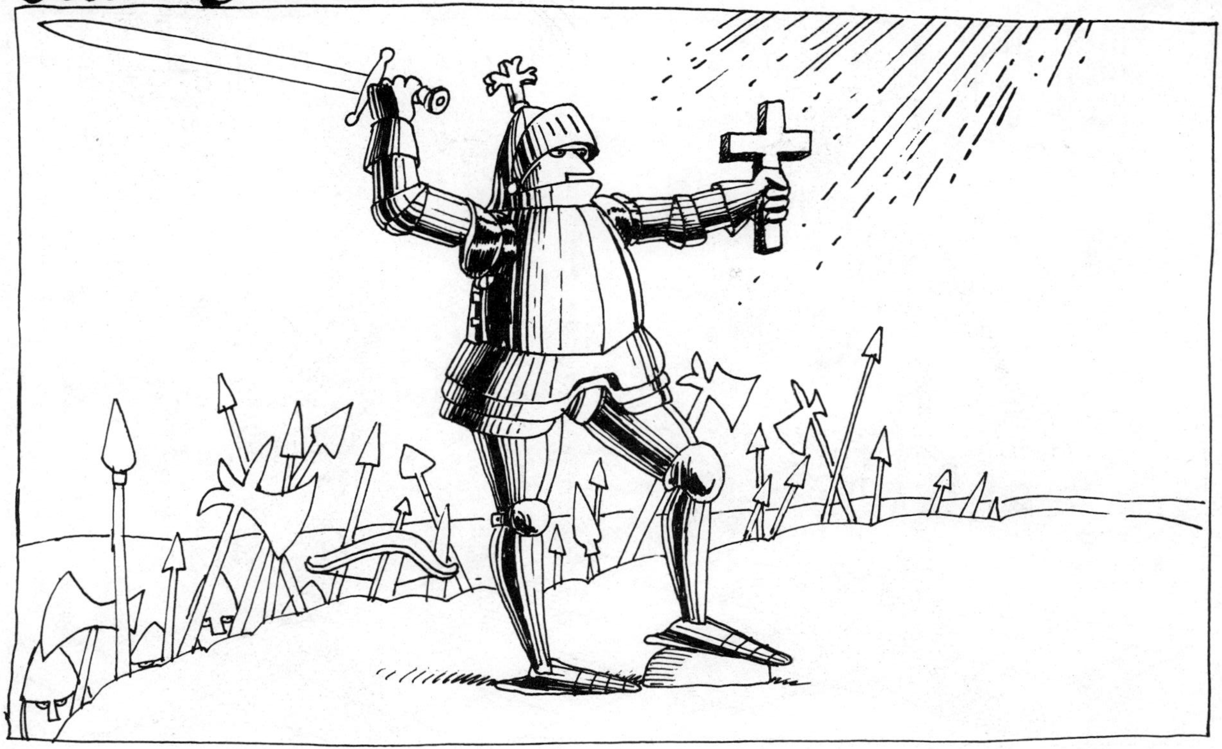

Soup to Nuts

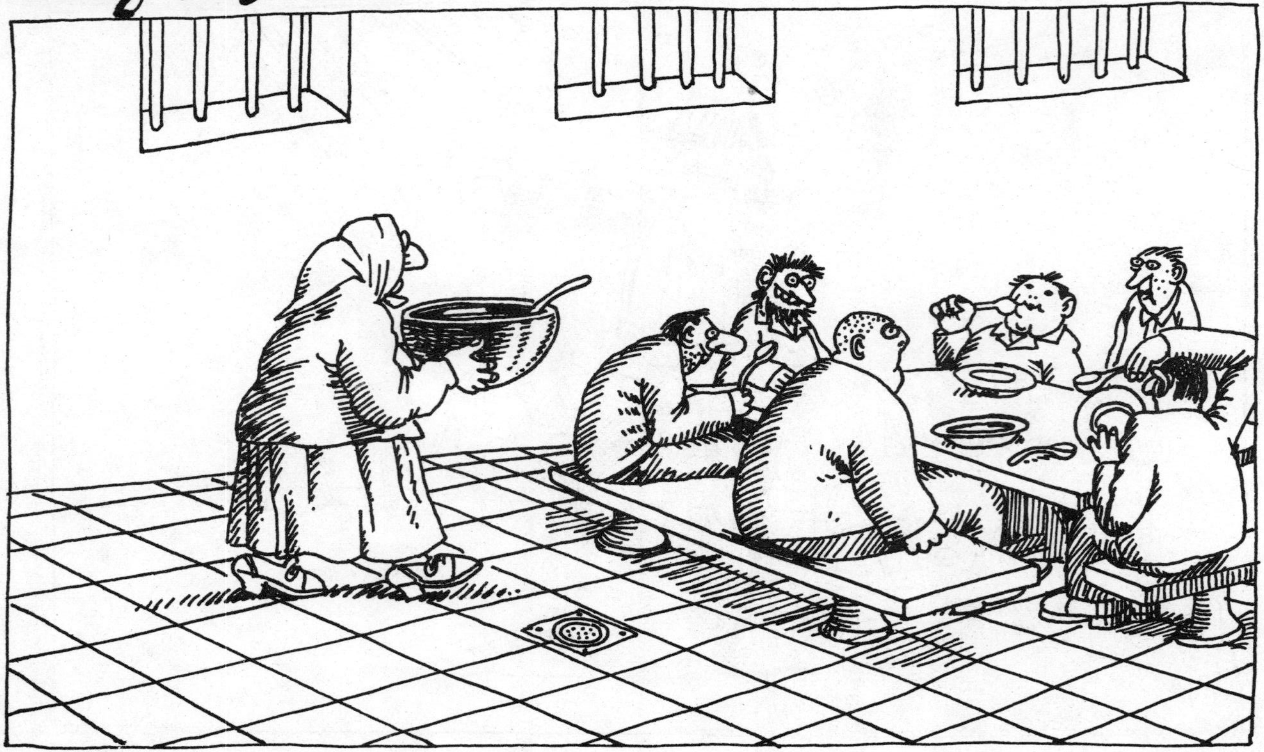

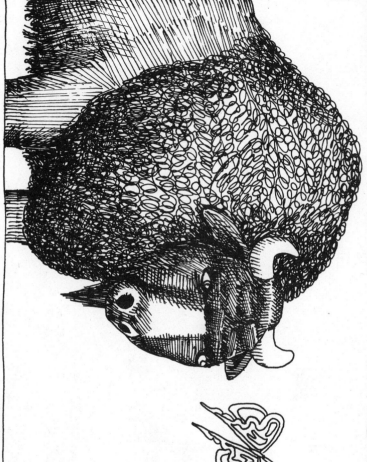

B Kliban